Curriculum, Pedagogy and Evaluation

Curriculum, Pedagogy and Evaluation

Elementary Level

Prof. H. S. Srivastava
Former Dean
National Council of Educational Research and Training
New Delhi

SHIPRA

Rs. 1500; US$ 60

ISBN: 978-93-88691-33-8

First Published in India in 2020

Curriculum, Pedagogy and Evaluation

Published by:

SHIPRA PUBLICATIONS
LG 18-19, Pankaj Central Market,
I.P. Ext., Patparganj, Delhi 110092, India
Ph.: +91 11 22235152/6152, 9650028065
Email: info@shiprapublication.com
www.shiprapublication.com

Preface

The book 'Curriculum, Pedagogy and Evaluation' while it covers the normally covered themes in the prescribed syllabi of the D.El.Ed. Examinations, deliberately moves beyond them to cover several other practical aspects of a teacher's day-to-day work. It is more than certain, therefore, that the teachers will treasure and also use it, as a ready reckoner for meeting the challenges they may face when they formally join the vocation of teaching.

The fundamental underlying philosophy of the totality of contents of the book is that

- Teaching becomes successful only when learning takes place.
- Learning takes place with the absorption of the ideas, through the senses.
- Senses react to external stimuli.
- External stimuli consist of teaching-learning-situations.
- The manipulation of the teaching-learning-situations, with a view to realizing the objectives set are (called) methods of Teaching.

Teachers choose Methods of teaching they deem most suitable for transacting the different elements of the curriculum. They are these exercises which are aimed at finally helping the learners in alround growth, in the Cognitive, Affective and Psycho-motor Domains of the development to become good human beings, good citizens of their countries, good Hindus/Muslim/ Christians/Sikhs/Buddhists/Parsi etc. and productive members of the society.

To the teachers then, the contents of the book are likely to quite naturally prove to be enabling, empowering and enriching, imparting to them motivations to learn more, inquisitiveness to know more and capacity to do more.

The Humanity House
143, Dayanand Vihar
Delhi 110092
(+91 9953532995)
25.08.2019

Prof. H.S. Srivastava
Former Dean
National Council of Educational
Research and Training
New Delhi

Contents

Section III
BASICS OF PEDAGOGY

SECTION I

Foundation of Curriculum, Pedagogy and Evaluation

1

Education for the Twenty First Century

(*UNESCO Report—Learning the Treasure Within*)

No educational document can and should in the present century start without a reference of the UNESCO report 'Learning the Treasure Within'—Education in the 21st Century. The pointers and recommendation of its different chapters are, therefore, presented as an introduction to the present book.

Introduction

The Report of the International Commission on Education for the Twenty first Century entitled "Learning – The Treasure Within" is the most exquisite document that presents the diverse facets of education in the perspective of the emerging global needs of the present century. The Commission had 15 members from different countries and was chaired by Mr. Jacques Delros. Dr. Karan Singh was the Indian representative on the Commission. The report was published by the UNESCO (to which it was submitted) in 1996.

No discussion on education in the present century can, in fact, be complete without a reference to this report, which *not only contains a robust philosophy of education but almost charts-out a road map of what education should be.*

It is not really passable to summarise the report as such. Therefore, what is proposed to be done here, is to quote some statements, adapted or as such from the report containing different ideas which are likely to be of interest and use to the Indian educationists.

From the Local Community to A World Society

Worldwide interdependence and globalisation are major forces in contemporary life. They are already at work and will leave a deep imprint on the twenty-first century. They require that overall consideration, extending well beyond the fields of education and culture, be given, as of now, to the roles and structures of international organisations.

The major danger is that of a gulf opening up between a *minority* of people who are capable of finding their way successfully about this new world that is coming into being and the *majority* who feel that they are at the mercy of events and have no say in the future of society, with the dangers that entail a setback to democracy and widespread revolt.

We must be guided by the Utopian aim of steering the world towards greater mutual understanding, a greater sense of responsibility and greater solidarity, through acceptance of our spiritual and cultural differences. Education, by providing access to knowledge for all, has precisely this universal task of helping people to understand the world and to understand others.

From Social Cohesion to Democratic Participation

Education policy must be sufficiency diversified and must be so designed as not to become another contributory cause of social exclusion.

The socialisation of individuals must not conflict with personal development. It is, therefore, necessary to work towards a system that strives to combine the virtues of integration with respect for individual rights.

Education cannot, on its own, solve the problems raised by the severance (when this happens) of social ties. It can, however, be expected to help to foster the desire to live together, which is a basic component of social cohesion and national identity.

Schools cannot succeed in this task unless they make their own contribution to the advancement and integration of minority groups by mobilising those concerned while showing due regard for their personality.

Democracy appears to be progressing taking different forms and passing through stages that fit the situation in each country. Its vitality is nevertheless constantly threatened. Education for conscious and active citizenship must begin at school.

Democratic participation is, so to say, a matter of good citizenship, but it can be encouraged or stimulated by instruction and practices adapted to a media and information society. What is needed to provide reference points and aids to interpretation, so as to strengthen the faculties of understanding and judgement.

It is the role of education to provide children and adults with the cultural background that will enable them, as far as possible, to make sense of the changes taking place. This presupposes that they are capable of sorting out the mass of information so as to interpret it more effectively and place events in a historical perspective.

From Economic Growth to Human Development

Further reflection on the theme of a new model of development, showing more respect for nature and the structuring of people's time.

A future-oriented study of the place of work in society, taking into account the effects of technical progress and change on both private and community life.

A fuller assessment of development, taking all its aspects into account, along the lines of the work done by UNDP.

The establishment of new links between educational policy and development policy, with a view to strengthening the bases of knowledge and skills in the countries concerned: encouragement of initiative, teamwork, realistic synergies taking local resources into account, self-employment and the spirit of enterprise.

The necessary improvement and general availability of basic education (importance of the Jomtien Declaration).

Four Cornerstones of Education

Education throughout life is based on four pillars: *learning to know, learning to do, learning to live together and learning to be.*

Learning to know, by combining a sufficiently broad general knowledge with the opportunity to work in depth on a small number of subjects. This also means learning to learn, so as to benefit from the opportunities education provides throughout life.

Learning to do, in order to acquire not only an occupational skill but also, more broadly, the competence to deal with many situations and work in teams. It also means learning to do in the context of young peoples various social and work experiences which may be informal, as a result of the local or national context, or formal, involving courses, alternating study and work.

Learning to live together, by developing an understanding of other people an appreciation of other people and an appreciation of interdependence—carrying out joint projects and learning to manage conflicts—in a spirit of respect for the values of pluralism, mutual understanding and peace.

Learning to be, so as to better develop one's personality and be able to act with ever greater autonomy, judgement and personal responsibility. In that connection, education must not disregard any aspect of a person's potential: memory, reasoning, aesthetic sense, physical capacities and communication skills.

Formal education systems tend to emphasise the acquisition of knowledge to the detriment of other types of learning: but it is vital now to conceive education in a more encompassing fashion. Such a vision should inform and guide future educational reforms and policy, in relation both to contents and to methods.

Life-long Education

The concept of learning throughout life is the key that gives access to the twenty-first century. It goes beyond the traditional distinction between initial and continuing education. It links up with another concept often put forward, that of the learning society, in which everything affords an opportunity of learning and fulfilling one's potential.

In its new guise, continuing education is seen as going far beyond what is already practiced, particularly in the developed countries, i.e., upgrading, with refresher training, retraining and conversion or promotion courses for adults. It should open up opportunities for learning for all, for many different purposes—offering them a second or third chance, satisfying their desire for knowledge and beauty or their desire to surpass themselves or making it possible to broaden and deepen strictly vocational forms of training, including practical training.

In short, 'learning throughout life' must take advantage of all the opportunities offered by society.

From Basic Education to University

A requirement valid for all countries, albeit in various forms and with different types of content—the strengthening of basic education: hence the emphasis on primary education and its traditional basic programmes—reading, writing, arithmetic—but also on the ability to express oneself in a language that lends itself to dialogue and understanding.

The need, which will be still greater tomorrow, for receptivity to science and the world of science, which opens the door to the twenty-first century and its scientific and technological upheavals.

The adaptation of basic education to specific contexts, the most deprived countries as well as the most deprived sections of the population, starting out with the facts of everyday life, which affords opportunities for understanding natural phenomena and for different forms of socialisation.

The pressing needs of literacy work and basic education for adults are to be kept in mind.

In all cases, emphasis is to be placed on pupil-teacher relations, since the most advanced technologies can be no more than a back-up to the relationship (transmission, dialogue and confrontation) between teacher and pupil.

Secondary education must be re-thought in this general context learning throughout life. The key principle is to arrange for a variety to individual paths through schooling, without ever closing the door on the possibility of a subsequent return to the education system.

Debates on selection and guidance would be greatly clarified if this principle were fully applied. Everyone would then feel that whatever the choices made or the courses followed in adolescence, no doors would ever be closed in the future, including the doors of the school itself. Equality of opportunity would then mean what it says.

Universities should be central to the higher level of the system, even if, as is the case in many countries, there are other, non-university establishments of higher education.

Universities would have vested in them four key functions:

1. To prepare students for research and teaching.
2. To provide highly specialised training courses adapted to the needs of economic and social life.
3. To be open to all, so as to cater for the many aspects of lifelong education in the widest sense.
4. International co-operation.

The universities should also be able to speak out on ethical and social problems as entirely independent and fully responsible institutions exercising a kind of intellectual authority that society needs to help it to reflect, understand and act.

The diversity of secondary schooling and the possibilities afforded by universities should provide a valid answer to the challenges of mass education by dispelling the obsession with a one-and-only educational 'king's highway'. Combined with more widespread application of the practice of alternating periods of education with periods of work, these approaches can provide effective tools for fighting against school failure. The extension of learning throughout life will require consideration of new procedures for certification that take account of acquired competencies.

Teachers in Search of New Perspectives

- While the psychological and material situation of teachers differ greatly from country to country, an upgrading of their status is essential if 'learning throughout life' is to fulfill the central function assigned to it by the Commission in the advancement of our societies and the strengthening of mutual understanding among peoples. Their position should be recognised by society and they should be given the necessary authority and suitable resources.
- The concept of learning throughout life leads straight on to that of a learning society, a society that offers many and varied opportunities of learning, both at school and in economic, social and cultural life, which need more collaboration and partnerships, with families, industry and business, voluntary associations, people in active cultural life, etc.
- Teachers are also concerned about the imperative requirement to update knowledge and skills. Their professional lives should be so arranged as to accommodate the opportunity, or even the obligation, for them

to become more proficient in their art and to benefit from periods of experience in various spheres of economic, social and cultural life. Such possibilities are usually provided for in the many forms of study-leave or sabbatical leave. Those formulae, suitably adapted, should be extended to all teachers.

- Even though teaching is essentially a solitary activity, in the sense that each teacher is faced with his or her own responsibilities and professional duties, teamwork is essential, particularly at the secondary level, in order to improve the quality of education and adapt it more closely to the special characteristics of classes or groups of pupils.
- The commission stresses the importance of exchanges of teachers and partnerships between institutions in different countries. As is confirmed by current activities, such exchanges and partnerships provide an essential added value not only for the quality of education but also for a greater receptivity to other cultures, civilisations and experiences.
- All these lines of emphasis should be the subject of a dialogue, or even contracts, with teacher's organisations which go beyond the purely corporatist nature of such forms of collaboration: over and above their aims of defending the moral and material interests of their members, teacher's organisations have built up a fund of experience which they are willing to make available to policy-makers.

Choices for Education: The Political Factor

Choosing a type of education means choosing a type of society. In all countries, such choices call for extensive public debate, based on an accurate evaluation of education systems. The Commission invites the political authorities to encourage such debate, in order to reach a democratic consensus, this being the best route to success for educational reform strategies.

The Commission advocates the implementation of measures for involving the different persons and institutions active in society in educational decision-making: administrative decentralisation and the autonomy of educational establishments are conducive in most cases, it believes, to the development and generation of innovation.

In view of the foregoing, the Commission wishes to re-affirm the role of the political authority, which has the duty clearly to define options and ensure overall regulation, making the required adjustment: education is a community asset which cannot be regulated by market forces alone.

The Commission nonetheless does not underrate the force of financial constraints and it advocates the bringing into operation of public/private partnership. In developing countries, the public funding of basic education remains a priority, but the choices made must not imperil the coherence of the system as a whole, nor lead to other levels of education being sacrificed.

It is essential that funding structures be reviewed in the light of the principle that learning should continue throughout individual's lives. The Commission, hence feels that the proposed study-time entitlement, as briefly outlined in the report, deserves to be discussed and explored.

The progress of the new information and communication technologies should give rise to a general deliberation on access to knowledge in the world of tomorrow. The Commission recommends:

— the diversification and improvement of distance education through the use of the new technologies;

— greater use of those technologies in adult education and especially in the in-service training of teachers;

— the strengthening of developing countries infrastructures and capabilities in this field and the dissemination of such technologies throughout society; these are in any case prerequisites to their use in formal education systems; and

— the launching of programmes for the dissemination of the new technologies under the auspices of UNESCO.

2

Advancing Horizons of Indian Education

The Change

In education no barriers have to be broken but only its advancing horizon are to be chased. In this perspective one comes across the situation where 'change' has remained the only 'constant'. But, when one thinks of the realities of this phenomenon of change one usually stops just at changes only in the fields of Science and Technology. We do not stretch our thinking and imagination to other fields to discover that even History has changed. With the recent excavations in Haryana and Kutch even our ancient civilisations have got pre-dated. Geography too has undergone a change with so many new countries having come into existence, Politics has witnessed another phenomenon of change with so many erstwhile colonies and dictatorships having become democracies. Such a dawn of democracy has also in many cases brought about corruption and criminalisation in its wake in the initial stages of their emergence in the new garb. Sociology too has undergone change with rural communities having got dismembered with onslaughts of urbanisation and migration. At the micro-level too the joint families have yielded place to nuclear families breaking away from the age-old bonds and affiliations with the cultural heritages. Economics too has changed with materialistic pragmatism replacing philosophic idealism, globalisation taking over protective consumerism, trampling the valued concept of thrift where even students have come to be treated as consumers and education a business enterprise and so on.

So, it could be safely concluded that knowledge in all fields is growing fast but to our astonishment is also becoming redundant faster. Acquisition of knowledge, therefore, has become a risky dissolvable and drainable temporary asset which cannot any more be depended upon as ones wealth. Educational ventures in this context have but to aim at not being content with just imparting '*temporary knowledge*' but work towards imbibing in the students *permanent multi-use competencies*' which are abiding assets, usable in different situations.

Changing Purposes of Education

Education for education sake, is no more an accepted proposition. It has to be purposeful and demonstrate usefulness not just to the individual and the community but to the nation and the world at large. In the context of the present situation it has to be:

- a *literacy enhancement programme* for attaining cent per cent literacy in course of time with particular reference to girls.
- a *poverty eradication programme* through the imparting vocational skills for making a living.
- an *employment creation programme* by opening up professional possibilities in unexplored fields and avenues for self-employment.
- a *wealth generation programme* which will be a natural off-shoot of the above ventures, through economic elevation of individuals and communities in both rural and urban areas.
- a *health promotion programme* through awareness about keeping healthy and thus, improving efficiency in both quantitative and qualitative terms. Reduction in child and female mortality and increasing functional longevity of all.
- a *social regeneration programme* through participative and co-operative initiatives.
- a *cultural enrichment programme* for taking advantage of our ancient wisdom and heritage.
- a *religious enlightenment programme* incorporating and advocating a concept of religion as a flowing stream and not a stagnant pool incorporating values of peaceful co-existence through tolerance and non-violence preached by all of them.
- a *human emancipation programme* heralding freedom from conservatism rigidity, and dispelling blind-faith, superstition and narrow-mindedness.
- a *visionary futuristic programme* offering opportunities for inculcation of abilities and proficiencies for meeting the challenges of the future with confidence and success. Entrepreneurship will be an essential component in this regard.

Education must aim at training individuals to be innovative, capable of evolving, adapting to the rapidly changing world and assimilating change.

Education for the future too deserves a more elaborate analysis. Future as we perceive it, is no more just *unknown* but has become *unpredictable.* Yesterday's education has no more remained relevant today and today's education will become even more irrelevant tomorrow. With reference to this phenomenon *one time education has remained completely inadequate for life-time employability.* Continuous upgradation of skills has, therefore, become imperative, further reinforcing the concept of '*life-long-education*'. Thus, the old concept of the life-cycle of individuals as consisting of 'education-work-retirement', has become redundant, having been replaced by that of education-work, education-work, education work and no retirement. *Education, thus, has to have only commas and no full-stops.*

In the words of Dr. R.H. Dave, "*Education in the life-long perspective, is a process of human transformation, human enlightenment and human empowerment for the attainment of a better and a higher quality of life.*"

Objectives, aims and goals have also to be conceived stated and defined comprehensively yet specifically in all the three domain of development. Cognitive (Intellectual), Affective (Attitudinal) and Psycho-motor (Actional). Focus of attention here, has to be not just on acquisition knowledge but application of knowledge in life situations. In addition, aesthetic sense, values and reflection about what is acquired, have also to be incorporated in the programmes of education, which would need to cover the development of total personality of the students in both scholastic and non–co-scholastic aspects for becoming enabling, empowering and enriching.

New Directions in the Content of Education

A shift of focus in regard to the content of education is also called for and this will have to imply change in spirit and not just in name like the overnight change of name of Primary Schools into Basic Education Schools, just by the change of the sign boards.

Collaboration with business and industry in the development and transaction of educational content than just lip-serviced *consultation* too is needed. This will be necessary for developing industry and business related skills and thus, strengthening the relationship of education with the clients/ consumers of our products (the educated work-force).

A shift from the concept of *Syllabus* to that of *curriculum,* is also be called for, by moving beyond course content to the enunciation of objectives, of course content, of methodology of teaching and learning, of aids to instruction and of evaluation.

Change in the enunciation of content with a *disciplinary* approach to an *integrated* one, will also have to be a part of this process.

From discipline-based *fundamentals to applications* of the basic elements of content is also needed. Thus, from the teaching of say the history of Physics (Newton did this Einstine did this) to Applications of Physics will need to be focussed upon.

A shift from only vertical treatment of subjects (like Babar, Humayun, Akbar, Jahangir…..) to both vertical and horizontal treatment of content (like who ruled France when Shajahan ruled India) will be called for. Japan it may be mentioned has introduced a new subject '*Contemporary Society*' in its new curriculum in this context.

A move from *abstract to concrete* entities and examples of realities will also be necessary for consolidating the elements of content in the minds of students.

In addition to the *immediate* use of the contents in life, to their *long range implications* is also needed to be incorporated in the courses of study for inculcating in students not just insight but also foresight in their decision-making abilities.

Besides facts, generalisations in terms of *basic understandings* would also need to be incorporated as part of content. This would imply moving beyond the statements like Aryan civilisation flourished on the banks of the rivers of the Indo-gangetic plain. Persian Civilisation on the banks of Euphrates and Tigris, Egyptian civilisation on the banks of the Nile. Basic understanding based on these facts would be "Early civilisations grew in river beds."

The fast growing changes in content would also need to be taken care of through the incorporation of the concepts of *Frontline Curriculum,* where the major part of the prescribed contents (say 90%) may be changed after four or five years, but a 10% part of it, listing new developments called the Frontline Curriculum may change say every two years.

There has to be yet another change in content. Instead of defining parameters, an attempt should be made to explain them so as to bring them within the effortless comprehension of the students. Pictorial or diagrammatic or graphical representations prove to be valuable instruments in such a consolidation of content. This not just leads to self-growth but influences the *total overall perceptions and growth* as such.

Curriculum Transaction

With different institutions following the same prescribed courses, the marked differences in the quality of education imparted by them occur mainly because of methodology of teaching and learning they advocate and practice. Transaction of curriculum thus becomes one of the key foundations of education chiefly responsible for the degree of realisation of the goals set.

The first thing that needs to be mentioned in this regard is the need for an immediate shift from the traditional *tongue and ear method* to a variety of unconventional approaches of teaching and learning. (An independent section is being devoted to these methods in the book.)

With the enormous advances in the different subjects of study the prescribed content too has swelled up. Thus an individual learner finds it difficult to cover it. *Group and participatory learning practices* have, therefore, to be encouraged and adopted. Apart from this, group and participatory learning becomes more illuminative, leading to better internalisation. It also generates team spirit which turns out to be a great asset in the live realities of professional situations.

Learning only from the *print media to internet surfacing,* CD-ROMs, etc. have also to be fully explored for enrichment of learning. Approaches to effective utilisation of these sources have also to be imparted to the students.

This will also make the teacher conversant with the new techniques and enable him to assume his real role of being a *guide rather than just a dispenser of information.* With knowledge growing fast the teacher too will need to become a *co-learner with the students* particularly so in regard to the content of the Frontline Curriculum.

Students will thus naturally become '*Subjects*' of education and not any more remain only '*objects*' of education. They will *not only learn but learn how to learn* and finally voluntarily assume the responsibility of moving ahead in their crusade through *self-directed learning* and later to the needed initiatives in this regard.

The locale of teaching and learning will, in this situation, move *beyond the classroom* to laboratories, environmental observations, different life and work settings, etc. With these situations emerging as the new locations of learning there will naturally be another great transformation. The students would thus be better prepared to meet and tackle life's *natural challenges and instead of testing imaginary concocted hypothesis (and these too) in simulated situations.* Such experimental learning will find immediate assimilation uprooting the need for memorisation.

Field Surveys and library research will also, in this context, become everyday pursuits of learning, when themes like Engel's law of consumption will not need to be memorised for reproduction at examination time, but a self-deduced conclusion which would be impossible to forget.

These new approaches will, quite naturally and not just incidentally improve the *pace* of learning, the *quality* of learning beside enhancing the *quantum of learning.*

Interactions of different kinds, with the teachers, with peers and with ones ownself, will also then take place with increased levels of motivation and concentration as one moves from one stage to another. It needs to be noted that in case of teacher-pupil interaction, the level of concentration of pupils is minimal, in situations of pupil-pupil interaction, it is higher and the concentration is at the highest level when a learner interacts with himself.

The *marriage of technology and pedagogy* will also enable transversing longer distances and digging deeper into the treasures of knowledge through all possible delivery modes, be they instructor led, or of distance learning or of on-line learning or learning through CD-ROMs.

Curriculum Transaction will also need to acquire and demonstrate flexibility for being adaptable to the needs of different times, different content, different individuals and become relevant and accountable to all settings. The *bright children* will only need to be introduced to the learning material and learning processes and they would then move on, on their own. The *mediocre children* with initial exposure will also need reinforcement. The *weaker students* would need repeated teaching, repeated clarification and repeated reinforcement for consolidation and internalisation of learning.

Learning Materials

The emergent realities will as mentioned earlier expect and require the learning materials to *move beyond the print media to technological aids.* These could be used both for teacher-directed learning as also self-learning. Both teachers and students would, therefore, need to acquire the needed proficiencies for effectively and profitably using them. In this context *they would all, not just need to be computer literate but computer savvy.* They will not learn computors as a subject of study but use technology as a means of learning different subjects.

Evaluation of Student Growth

With education as a process of human enablement, human empowerment and human enlightenment, growth among students, will also be recorded in different facets of personality. In this context evaluation would need to:

- be a process spread over the total span of education.
- consist of exercises related to an ongoing :ollection of evidences about the kind and degree of growth occurring among the students in the context of the inputs provided.
- be designed to cover all the three domains of development Cognitive, Affective and Psycho-motor—and related growth in both scholastic and non co-scholastic areas.
- press into service a variety of conventional and unconventional techniques and tools of evaluation.
- be in both qualitative and quantitative terms.
- not just assess growth but help to improve its pace and quantum.
- result in meaningful declaration of results and become useful in taking a variety of decisions about individuals and/or groups evaluated.

The above descriptive definition of evaluation assumes greater importance particularly because customarily *we teach what we test and not test what we teach.*

With shortcomings in our external/public examinations and with institution-based evaluation too becoming their replica, only academic aspects by-and-large come under the purview of our testing programmes with almost complete neglect of the non-academic areas, which are considered to be more important for success in life.

The exigencies and emergencies, the inherent defects and operational shortfalls go to greatly erode the sanctity and credibility of our external examinations. Furthermore the irreversibility of the results of such unfair examinations, do call for the emancipation of our helpless students from them.

Selective teaching and selective learning too have become common features, because of the short-falls in our traditional question papers which had few questions to be attempted out of those given and provided options.

In these traditional external/public examinations the inter-examiner variability, variations in the ranges of scores and patterns of their distribution from subject to subject, year to year and examination to examination led to the non-equivalence of a particular score in different subjects. The use of sacrosanct cut-off scores (33%, 45%, 60% and 75%) for classifying the levels of achievement of students in all subjects in all examinations and in all years thus became atrociously unscientific propositions. It has been to overcome these shortcomings that the National Policy on Education 1986/92 has suggested the use of *grades in place of marks.* When absolute grades are used, the cut-off scores for grades are *predetermined and declared subject-wise for each examination* and in Relative grading on the basis of the obtained scores of the students. The concept of Pass and Fail is also alien and not admissible when grades are awarded. The aggregation of these non-equivalent entities (marks) for obtaining an overall indicator of performance in terms of *divisions and distinctions* is *like adding temperature (in celcius), humidity (in percentage) and rainfall (in centimetres) for obtaining an index of weather.*

The prescription of year long courses in different subjects, and with all subjects required to be cleared simultaneously in a single attempt for obtaining a certificate of qualification, are provisions which have all along been the cause of undue pressure and stress on the students. It has been to eliminate this that the NPE has also recommended a change over to the *semester system,* where credits could be earned and accumulated by clearing examinations in parts, finally encashing them into certificates of qualification when the requisite number of credits have been earned.

The traditional examinations also mainly attempted to test *memorisation* and not so much other higher abilities. *Certificates of qualification* for having cleared the examination did not also effectively assess and testify to the possession of specific competencies by the students. They were, therefore, wallets without any money in them.

Yet another thing which needs a special mention is that with a perpetually used 33% score in all the prescribed subjects as the qualifying level, the all India pass percentage of class X examinations is around 50%. Such a dubbing as failure is disqualification for entering a course of higher education or a job for which these are eligibility examinations. Does that therefore mean that this half of the total number of candidates who are declared as failure are good for nothing? Even otherwise the faith in the results of external examination is continuously on the ebb with employers and institution of higher education instituting their own selection tests. The institution of external examination by itself displays a mistrust of the teacher who teaches. What is really required is the introduction of School-based Evaluation with an independent certificate issued by the school covering both scholastic and non co-scholastic aspects of pupil growth *as a supplement to the certificate of external* examinations.

Meaningful certification of abilities, proficiencies, achievements, skills, etc. is another important aspect to be realised. Thus, instead of being a certificate of having crossed the minimum required level of attainment, the examinations should certify the possession of specific competencies by the concerned students.

Globalisation of Indian Education

The educational ventures of our country in their aspiration of reaching out to the skies should not get their feet uprooted from the soil. We must appreciate that *everything that is western is not essentially modern.* Our conceptual starting point in India is *idealistic*, whereas that of the west is by and large materialistic from beginning to the end. We conceive things idealistically and practice realistically. The west aims mainly at *physical fulfilment. Spiritual fulfillment* too is one of the main targets of Indian Education beside other things.

Indians unlike the west do not discard and reject the past, they assimilate it, the west explores life the orientalists celebrate it.

These are things, which our education should also take into consideration for enabling us to live our lives nationally and think globally.

It is with the above in mind that we should proceed towards globalisation appreciating and releasing that :

- There is no escape from globalisation now.
- Globalisation has to be perceived as a holistic concept and not just a truncated one focussing on economic issues alone.
- Globalisation ventures have so far touched only macro-economics and not other facets of life and that the road map for its percolation on to the micro-level has yet to be charted.
- Globalisation has to be perceived as a reciprocative, East ⇄ West concept involving give and take and should not be taken only as a one way traffic under any conditions.
- Globalisation of Indian education presents both prospects and dangers. The pros and cons of the issues and their implications, therefore, need to be critically examined for evolving an Indian point of view.
- India should not succumb to pressures and formally guard against onslaughts on the soul of Indian culture, in the name of liberalisation and globalisation.
- Regulations for negotiating globalisation deals in education so arrived at, need to be strictly enforced for saving the country from foreign educational invasions imbued with commercialisation with a hidden agenda of economic exploitation.

Let Us Continue To Be Givers

Althrough the history of civilisations, India has been contributing to growth and progress of the world we live in. We have given to the world.

- the concept of *zero* which has revolutionised mathematics.
- the concept of *decimals* which has helped in re-inventing calculation.
- the concept of the *wheel* which became the basis of Industrial Revolution in Europe.
- the *numerals* which are the basic foundations of life and living.

Let us continue this process by further expanding such an export presently in areas like information technology and aspire to become world leaders in as many fields as possible, for which we have an inherent capacity and potential.

Our strengths and export oriented initiatives are not just ancient relies but a modern reality. We are indisputably accepted as the second largest supplier of technical manpower in the world and are also exporting it. The expertise we possess is largely an outcome of our indigenous education.

However, we have not been good salesmen because of not being outgoing. Let us now realise that *modesty is no doubt a great virtue but the introvert behaviour which often generates, invariably proves to self-defeating, as it invariably inhibits even due publicity to our strengths and achievements.*

In this context while educational philosophies and ideologies which originated in other countries, have been extensively researched upon and documented (through modern methods) those that evolved in our own country have comparatively remained less noticed by the world's community.

Let us come out of this shell with sturdier determination, even though important breakthroughs in this regard have already occurred.

Some safeguards too are necessary. We cannot afford to glorify the accomplishments made in the past and even the present, without a futuristic perspective for making further advances by empowering ourselves for successfully competing with other advanced nations in all fields, through an assimilation of international developments. This, however, should not be done without critically analysing these for their compatibility with our culture and needs.

In this context, it will also be necessary to first establish a balanced alignment between our national goals and educational aims which is being attempted hereunder in a broad manner.

National Goals

In regard to India the National Goals derived mainly from our constitution and the cultural heritage could be listed broadly as under:

- Promotion of the principles of democracy.
- Respect for the individual.
- Equality of opportunity for all regardless of race, sex, language and religion and in all other aspects.

- Respect for the Constitution and the law.
- National integrity, unity and security.
- Social and economic justice, and development.
- Preservation and promotion of the diverse cultures of the country and the world.
- International co-operation and peace on the basis of tolerance, reciprocity, mutual respect and trust.
- Support to UN and other international bodies and contribution to their activities for international understanding and peace.

Aims of Education

In the context of the above National Goals, the Aims of Indian Education could be spelt out as under :

- To develop a human person with desirable abilities, proficiencies, attitudes, values and qualities of self-confidence and creativity.
- To develop culturally conscious individuals with pride in the country and a desire to contribute to its development as good citizens of the country and the world.
- To kindle a desire for preserving and promoting democracy, secularism, unity, social justice and ethics with accountability in pursuing life situations.
- To prepare for entering the world of work easily and effectively through the development of appropriate, flexible, adaptable and multi- use competencies and a requisite mind set (This aim is best actualised by developing and transaction of courses of study not just in consultation but also involvement of business, industry and the larger job market).
- To develop sound physical health and fitness among students for undertaking physical activities, demanding dexterity, diligence and hardwork.
- To develop the innate abilities, talents and potentials to the optimum level and to further enrich the same through appropriate inputs.
- To acquire the ability of critical thinking, problem-solving, decision making and of squarely facing unforeseen situations, while pursuing education or at the workplaces.
- To develop abilities for meeting the social, cultural, economic, technological needs and aspirations of the country through an appropriate design of the curriculum and its transaction.
- To develop a sense of international brotherhood, through an understanding of contemporary society in different parts of the world and mutual gestures of goodwill.

3

Setting Educational Targets

Purpose of Objectives

Objectives are the starting points of any educational process and their understanding is a basic requirement for all educational planners, educational administrators, teacher educators, teachers and evaluators to be successful in their mission. With the goal of alround development of personality, teachers in particular ought also have an intimate acquaintance with the three domains into which the objectives stand classified viz., *Cognitive Affective and Psycho-motor*, which have been touched upon in passing earlier. They are the facts and concepts related to the objectives of the different domains which are attempted to be presented here.

Derivation of objective, the first step towards proper development and statement of educational objectives, stands to gain in several ways, by subjecting them to a proper framework of classification. It helps to view them as parts of a system rather than in isolation. It also increases their usability by providing clarity about their interconnections. A proper classification to a great extent helps avoid overlap among similar objectives in a list. They have to be properly delimited and defined. This, also helps in ascertaining as to how far the various aspects of a major objective have been covered by their specifications. A well laid out system of objectives is a must for designing an effective educational programme comprising of curriculum development, instruction and evaluation. A system of classification is also essential for the pursuit of research, particularly in the fields of instruction and evaluation. Finally, a classification is very necessary for better communication among teachers on the subject of educational objectives without which all attempts at educational improvement may go waste.

A Snag in the Classification of Objectives

Each statement of an educational objective, as we know, has two distinct components—*the modification part* and *the content part*. It is not easily possible to evolve a logical scheme of grouping objectives in a way that they cover the requirements of both these components. The subject oriented classification will tend to lean heavily on content matter, whereas the behaviour-based classification will be mainly concerned with processes, particulary the changes expected to be brought about among the educands. Besides, it is also no easy task to synthesise demands of the different, categories of sources and evolve a balanced list. Such attempts have often ended in a very complicated list without much potential for practical application. Since the main business of education is to bring about a change in terms of behavioural outcomes, the choice naturally devolves upon the behavioural classification of objectives. While many attempts have been made in this direction, much more has yet to be accomplished.

Eight-year Study Model

One of the earliest systematic works on behaviour-based classification of objectives is witnessed in the evaluation programme of an Eight-year Study under the leadership of *Ralph Taylor*. Just for historical interest, the scheme of objectives as arrived at under this experiment is given below:

1. The development of effective ways of thinking.
2. The acquisition of important information, ideas and principles.
3. The development of effective work habits and skills.
4. The development of increased sensitivity to social problems and aesthetic experience.
5. The inculcation of social rather than selfish attitude.
6. The development of appreciation of literature, art and music.
7. The development of increasing range of worthwhile interests.
8. Increased personal and social development.
9. Improved physical health.
10. The formulation and classification of a philosophy of life.

The procedure adopted for developing this ten category model of objectives was curriculum analysis and the conference method. The curricular objectives of the *thirty schools* under the study were shifted and re-grouped keeping in view their behaviour homogeneity. However, the experimenters kept an open mind and were conscious of the shortcomings of their model. They felt that "the classification of objectives would be improved as evidence accumulates regarding the social significance of different behaviour patterns and regarding the correlation and consistency among various specific reactions classified under the particular type of a behaviour". A conference of specialists, teachers and administration was finally used for vetting the list tentatively drawn up.

Sources of Educational Objectives

The philosophy of life is, in fact, the main source of all facets of all our activities including education. Educational targets too get derived from this very fundamental foundation. The main of these are :

- The *social order* and its diverse linkages with life e.g. we in India and the orient do not discard and reject the past, we assimilate it. This has important implications for life and also for education.
- The *economic structure* too, is an important determinant of educational targets which naturally differ in countries following capitalistic, and socialistic societies.
- The *political system* too exerts a powerful influence on educational targets and practices, demonstrating wide variation in democracies and dictatorships.
- The *cultural heritage* is again an undeniable factor that determines educational targets, which among other things involves pride in one's past.
- The *existing store of human knowledge* is another factor as we know many things now which we were looking for in the past. This masks a shift of ground and focus of our educational targets.
- Educational targets cannot also ignore the individuals for whom they are enunciated—their age, maturity level, previous knowledge, etc.

Levels of Educational Objectives

There is a distinct hierarchy among the educational targets consisting of :

From top to bottom it implies a journey from *whole to parts* for example there could be many *aims* in a goal, many *objectives* in an aim and many *specifications* in an objective.

It also at the same time presents a phenomenon of a movement from *general to specific*. For example, a *goal* could be 'making a good man'. Now this could have different interpretations in different situations and in different ideologies. An *Aim* in this very context could be 'making a good citizen.' Even this could mean differently in different societies. The allegiance of a good citizen in a dictatorship could be to the dictator, in a communistic state to the party, and so on. An *Objective* in the same backdrop could be making a judicious voter who will take an objective decision about whom to vote for. The next in the chain are *specifications.* They indicate the applied side of objectives giving *what a learner will be able to do to demonstrate to us that he has achieved a particular objective.*

This hierarchy can be diagrammatically presented as in Fig. 3.1.

It is at the level of objectives that targets become tangible and realisable through educational inputs and testable through evaluation for judging the quantum and quality of gain.

Specifications of different objectives in many ways are competencies which become the basic ability elements for being focussed upon for being achieved as also the basis for formulating evaluation situations and testing tools.

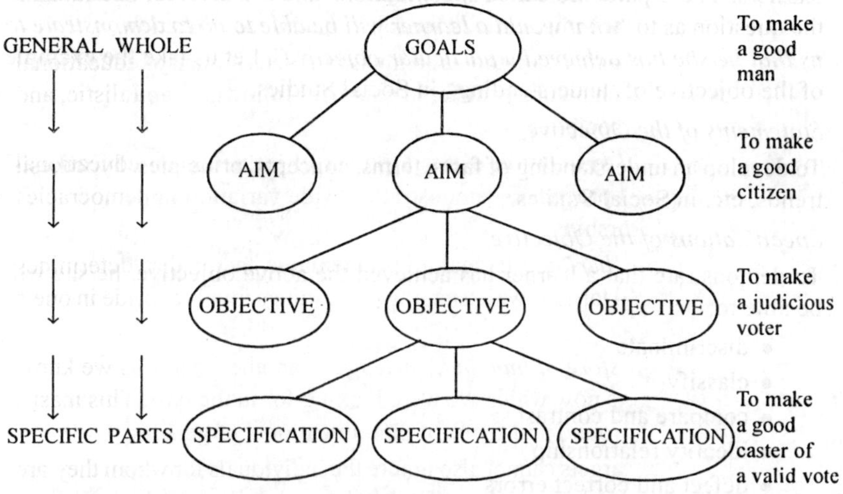

Fig. 3.1

Statements of Educational Objectives

Objectives as mentioned earlier, in fact, indicate that level of targets which are tangible for being handled in educational processes.

The statements of objectives are, therefore, governed by some characteristic conditions. These are briefly enunciated below:

- Objectives have to be stated specifically in concrete terms, without vagueness or ambiguity.
- The statement of objectives have to have both the *modification* and the *content* components i.e. the changes desired to be realised in pupil behaviour (competencies) and the *content* through which they are proposed to be realised.
- Objectives must be aligned to the subject for which they are listed.
- Objectives must correspond to the age-group and the level of abilities of the learners.
- Objectives ought to be stated in terms of pupil behaviour and not in terms of teacher behaviour ('to acquire' the ability of … and not 'to help learners acquire').
- Objectives must be achievable.
- Objectives must be evaluable.

Definition of Objectives

For purposes of being constructively utilised objectives do need to be broken down into parts. The parts ought to wear a behavioural garb in respect of the learners. These parts are called *specifications* and are derived, in answer to the question as to *'what would a learner will be able to do to demonstrate to us that he/she has achieved a particular objective'*. Let us take the example of the objective of 'understanding' in Social Studies.

Statements of the Objective

To develop an understanding of facts, terms, concepts, principles, hypothesis, trends, etc. in Social Studies.

Specifications of the Objective

To demonstrate that a learner has achieved the above objective, he/she will be able to:

- discriminate
- classify
- compare and contrast
- identity relationship
- defect and correct errors.
- give examples

These specifications as already mentioned are competencies which need to be developed and which deserve to be tested for enabling us to know about the quantum and quality of growth among learners as a result of the educational inputs selected and provided.

Taxonomies of Educational Objectives

A taxonomy is a scheme of classification followed originally in biological sciences where plants or animals are arranged in increasing degrees of specificity (diminishing degrees of generality) on the basis of certain criteria, in a way that *each succeeding class appears to be telescoping out of or into the preceding one*, depending upon the direction of views, e.g., order, family genus and species. Likewise, when applied to educational objectives, the model should yield *hierarchically arranged objectives in ascending or descending order of complexity or difficulty*.

A number of models of classification of objectives have since been developed. The most convincing of these in the recent years has been the taxonomical model of educational objectives developed by *Bloom* and his associates. It has conceived and adopted a tripartite division of competencies/ abilities corresponding to the three primary aspects of pupil growth-cognitive, affective, psycho-motor (knowing; feeling; doing).

The taxonomy of educational objectives as developed by *Bloom* and his associates, is basically a judicious combination of educational, logical and psychological classification systems. The distinction between different categories is educationally significant. The terms have been defined precisely in a manner that earlier meanings are logically consistent among themselves. Lastly, the classification is kept constant with the correct psychological findings about the mental processes. This classification employs a decimal enumeration system. This classification still awaits empirical evidence in its support although it has already been subjected to a fair degree of logical validation.

Objectives of the Cognitive Domain (Bloom's Model)

The Cognitive Domain represents the intellectual component of mental life and is certainly the most basic one, from the point of view of education. A variety of attempts have been made to classify mental processes and one may come across a variety of terms indicative of it, e.g., logical reasoning, reflective thinking, productive thinking and such others. *Guilford's three-dimensional model* (operations; contents; products) of the *Structure of Intellect* (SI model) may be of interest in this regard. It attempts to classify intellectual operations into a hierarchical order—cognitive, memory, divergent thinking and evaluation.

In Bloom's taxonomy, these operations or processes have been divided and arranged into the following six classes/categories:

1. Knowledge
    - Knowledge of Specifics
    - Knowledge of Methodology
    - Knowledge of Abstractions.
2. Comprehension
    - Translation
    - Interpretation
    - Extrapolation
3. Application
4. Analysis
    - Analysis of Elements
    - Analysis of Relationships
    - Analysis of Organisational Principles.
5. Synthesis
    - Production of a Unique Communication

- Production of a Plan
- Derivation of a Set of Abstract Relationships.

6. Evaluation
- Judging in terms of Internal Criteria
- Judging in terms of External Criteria.

The six categories of behaviours in the above schemes are obviously arranged from simple to complex. They have been further defined in terms of more specific behaviours as under:

Knowledge is taken to involve the recall of specifics, universals, methods, processes, patterns, structures, settings, generalisations, etc. The basic psychological process in use is *remembering*. This is distinguished from the remaining five which are together called intellectual abilities for the simple reason that the latter requires "organised models of operations and generalised techniques for dealing with materials and problems."

Comprehension which is next higher in the category of objectives is considered as the lowest level of 'understanding' equivalent of knowing what is being communicated and using the material or idea communicated "without necessarily relating it to other material or seeing its fullest implications."

Application is the third category which pertains to "the use of an abstract idea in a particular and concrete situation" and thereby arriving at a solution of a problem. There may be some difference of opinion about the limited scope of this objective and as such the use of the term, application for it. This may be defended on the ground that the word may be given an ad-hoc meaning by defining it adequately to connote the use of acquired knowledge in unfamiliar situations.

Analysis forms the fourth category and connotes the breaking down of a communication into its constituent elements, in a way that relationships or sequence or both of the components, of a set of ideas are made clear. Some people treat it as an equivalent of the objective of critical thinking which is only partly true. Analysis is an important component of critical thinking but the latter is something more. Analysis may lead to the identification of elements, relationships or principles.

Synthesis is the fifth category of objectives and involves the ability to put together the elements or parts in a way that a new pattern emerges therefrom. It has elements of creativeness.

Evaluation crowns all the categories and calls for the most complex mental processes necessary for judging a material, method or communication against a standard, internal or external to it.

It may be mentioned that as in a hierarchy each higher entity in a taxonomy includes the lower one. Thus, knowledge (information) is a part of 'understanding' i.e. understanding includes knowledge and similarly 'application' includes understanding, 'analysis' includes application, 'synthesis' includes analysis and 'evaluation' includes synthesis.

Some Other Taxonomies of the Cognitive Domain

Gagne's Taxonomy (Hierarchical Learning)

Reinstating
Discriminating
Identifying
Classifying
Demonstrating
Generating

Guilford's Taxonomy

(Structure of Intellect)
Cognition
Memory
Convergent Thinking
Divergent Thinking
Evaluation

Madau's Taxonomy

Knowledge
Comprehension
Application
Analysis
Synthesis
Evaluation

Decorte's Taxonomy

Perception
Recall and Reproduction of Information
Interpretation of Information
Convergent Product of Information
Divergent Product of Information
Evaluation Product of Information

Hannah's Taxonomy

Interpreting
Comparing
Classifying
Generalising
Inferring
Analysing
Synthesising

Predicting
Hypothesising
Evaluating

Objectives of the Affective Domain—Krathwohl's Model

There is often a greater lack of clarity and unanimity among educationists with regard to the statement of objectives of the *affective domain* than of the cognitive one. The terms like interests, appreciations, values, attitudes are often assigned varying shades of meaning. The term appreciation, for instance, may extend from awareness to profound aesthetic impact with a large spread in between. Apart from other factors accounting for the "erosion in respect of affective objectives in education" it is no doubt the lack of clarity about their scope and meaning which really turns out to be a very grave handicap in their proper pursuit.

The taxonomy developed by *Krathwohl* systematises these objectives into five broad categories given as under:

1. Receiving (attending)
    - Awareness
    - Willingness to receive
    - Controlled or selected response.
2. Responding
    - Acquiescence in responding
    - Willingness to respond
    - Satisfaction in response
3. Valuing
    - Acceptance of a value
    - Preference of a value
    - Commitment.
4. Organisation
    - Conceptualisation of a value
    - Organisation of a value system.
5. Characterisation of a value or value complex.
    - Generalised set
    - Characterisation.

Receiving is the lowest or rather the most rudimentary category of affective behaviour. At this level the learner shows sensitivity to certain stimuli. It is like the teacher catching the learner's attention. Awareness, willingness to receive and the selected nature of attention are its important sub-levels.

Responding which is the next category, expects greater motivation and regularity in attention. It may also for practical considerations be described as 'interest' by which we mean a tendency to respond to a particular object or stimuli. Interest in turn, is evinced at three levels: (1) compliance when expected,

(2) voluntary response, and (3) response with a clear emotional tone.

Valuing is the third category which involves increasing internalisation of the sense of worth and identification with it. It indicates the motivation of behaviour not by deliberate desire but by the individual's commitment to the underlying value guiding the behaviour." This objectives may conveniently be called "attitudes". These objectives are the "prime stuff from which the conscience of the individual is developed into control of behaviour."

Organisation forms the fourth category and connotes a system of values or attitudes. An individual's behaviour is not ordinarily motivated by a single attitude in isolation, but by an 'attitude complex'. Development of one's own code of conduct or standard of public life, may be an instance of the organisation of a value system.

Characterisation, the last of the categories, is reached when an individual is consistently found behaving in accordance with the values or attitudes he has imbibed, ultimately reaching a stage, when he has a consistent philosophy of life, of his own and an internal compulsion to pursue it.

The taxonomy of the affective domain may not appear quite hierarchical especially in as much as one order does not completely telescope into the other as a taxonomical characteristic, but surely presents an useful educational principle.

Objectives of the Psycho-motor Domain—Dave's Model

The Psycho-motor Domain concerns itself with levels of attainment in neuro-muscular coordination. As the level of coordination moves up, the action becomes more refined, speedy and automatic. In this case five broad categories have been identified by R.H. Dave as given below:

1. Imitation
    - Impulsion
    - Overt repetition
2. Manipulation
    - Following direction
    - Selection
    - Fixation
3. Precision
    - Reproduction
    - Control
4. Articulation
    - Sequence
    - Harmony
5. Naturalisation
    - Automatism
    - Internalisation

Imitation accounts for the lowest level of psycho-motor behaviour. It starts as an inner urge or push or impulse. It is represented by "Covert inner rehearsal of the muscular system" which may be taken to be more of an action at the material level. Soon it may grow into an overt act with capacity to repeat the performance with very rudimentary coordination.

Manipulation is the next higher level of psycho-motor behaviour. It involves following direction, selecting certain actions in preference to others and acting accordingly. It marks the beginning of the fixation of operation and the end of initial fumbling in the manipulative actions.

Precision is the third category and is reached when reproduction of operations is carried out with speed and refinement, giving the learner the ability to control and adjust (increase, decrease or modify) his action in response to requirements.

Articulation which is the fourth category, can be said to have been attained when the learner is able to handle a number of actions in unison, keeping in view their sequence and rhythm. It involves coordination in action, i.e., right sequence in right proportion of time or at the right moment.

Naturalisation is the final stage which is the equivalent of perfect habituation ranging from automatisation to routinlisation. At this level the performer does not expend any psychic energy in carrying out an operation. His actions are more or less automatic and mechanical and without any conscious thinking or planning, i.e., a mere reflex action.

The classification of objectives of the psycho-motor domain may not interest, the teachers of all subjects in its entirety, but in such curricular areas as writing, speech, driving, crafts, etc., it will find a very wide application. Unlike Cognitive and Affective domains the transfer value of an objective in the psycho-motor domain from one context to another may not be quite so pervasive.

Psycho-motor Skills

That can be called a skill which

- is doable
- can be physically observed in operation
- can be imitated
- involves the joint operation of the mind and the muscles
- has three basic characteristics of precaution, precision and proportion
- can be controlled at will
- can be manipulated
- in each subsequent attempt takes lesser time to do
- when repeated the quality of the outcome improves
- once learnt is learnt forever and does not need any revision or drill for retention (like swimming or cycling)

Interrelationship of Different Domains of Objectives

The tripartite division of instructional objectives into domains is not a water tight or an exclusive one. Firstly, the achievement in one domain is to a quite appreciable degree dependent on the learner's status in others. For instance, understanding (comprehension) may be a prerequisite for attaching proper value to an object or proper cognition, necessary for arousing proper interest. Similarly, interests and attitudes influence the quality of performance in both cognitive and psycho-motor domains. Comprehension again is a natural component of precision level in the psycho-motor domain and similarly interests can be traced to affective components of almost all the cognitive proficiencies. Thus, there is some degree of parallelism in terms of readiness relationship between various categories. Lower levels of each domain come relatively closer to each other, e.g., knowing, receiving and imitating are very much interdependent among themselves. In the higher categories too, there is discernible parallelism. A particular category of one domain, as already illustrated earlier, may correspond to one or more of categories of the other.

The implications of the nature of inter-connectedness are many. For example, while planning instruction for realising an objective, it may be considered as to how best the corresponding objectives of other domains can be exploited, fed or even protected. The affective domain, it could be safely mentioned, has grievously suffered on account of the over emphasis on teaching for the so-called glorious cognitive objectives as 'critical thinking' and 'problem-solving' without caring for the emotive reactions simultaneously arising out of such mental exercises. Of the dichotomy of 'mastery' and 'transfer' objectives, the effective realisation of the latter, which in fact is of real importance, will immensely be affected by the manner in which the interconnectedness among the objectives of different domains, is handled.

Pupils' growth in respect of the three domains, as a result of the learning experiences provided, is *simultaneous*. But every learning experience does not result in growth in all the domains and also in the same quantum in all the three domains. *Thus, when a learning experience is planned and provided, it emits currents of growth in different domains, which finally settles down at different levels in the different domains.* This variation in the potential of learning experiences for promoting growth leaves it to the initiative of the teachers to devise and offer an appropriate mix of learning activities for bringing about the desired behavioural changes and growth in the pupils in different domains.

It may also be mentioned that due to individual differences, the same learning experiences may result in different levels of growth in the three domains among different individuals. This highlights the need for individualised instruction.

The three taxonomies which could be called the CAP (Cognitive, Affective and Psychomotor) classification of objectives could be diagramatically presented as under in a composite model.

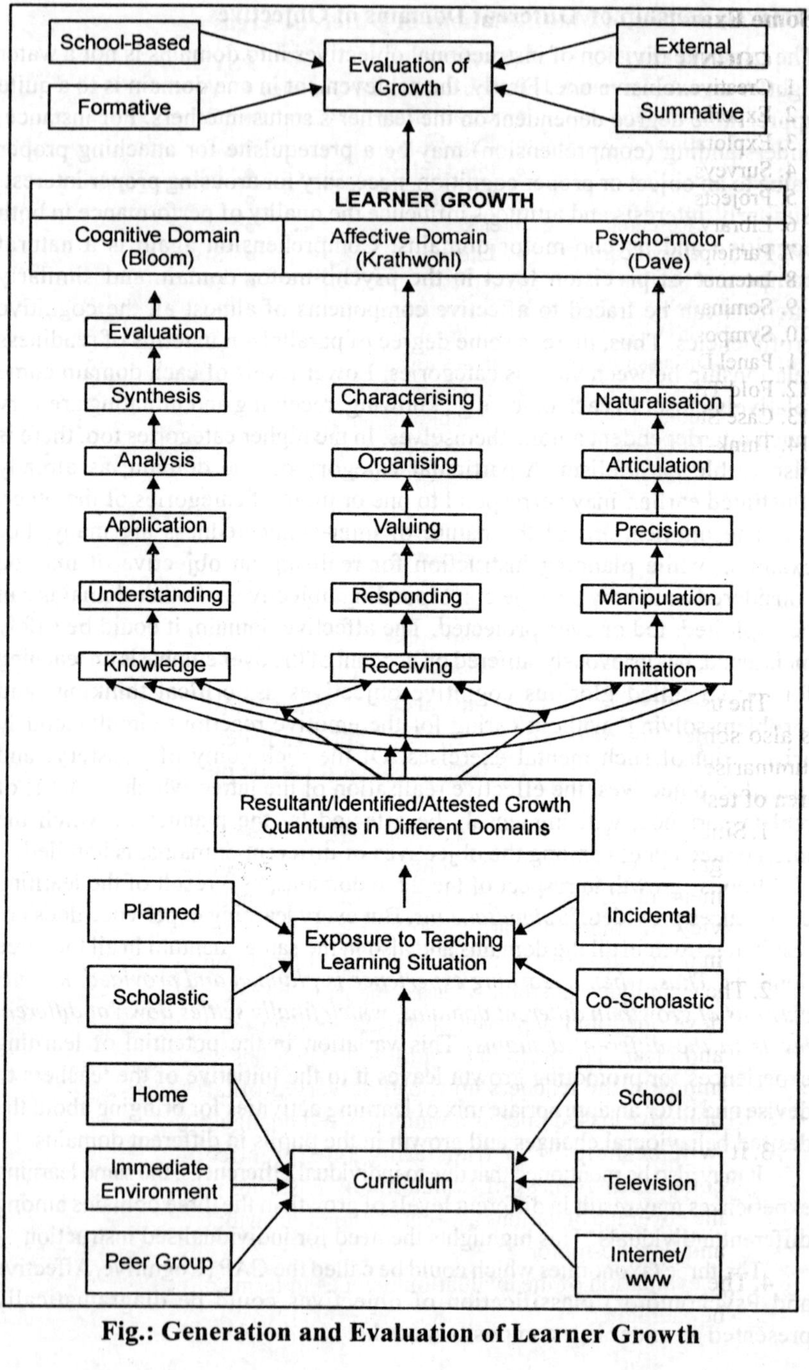

Fig.: Generation and Evaluation of Learner Growth

Some Examples of Manifestations of Different Areas of Growth

COGNITIVE

1. Creative Assignments
2. Experimentation
3. Exploration
4. Surveys
5. Projects
6. Library Research
7. Participatory Learning
8. Internet Surfing
9. Seminars
10. Symposia
11. Panel Discussions
12. Fold Trips
13. Case Studies
14. Think-Tank Sessions

AFFECTIVE

1. Personal & Social Qualities
   - Cleanliness
   - Regularity
   - Punctuality
   - Discipline
2. Interests
   - Literary
   - Artistic
   - Scientific
   - Cultural
3. Attitudes towards
   - Teachers
   - School programmes
   - School mates
   - School/Public property
4. Values
   - Dignity of Labour
   - Honesty
   - Courage
   - Courtesy
   - Team Spirit
   - Tolerance

PSYCHO-MOTOR

- Yoga
- Games and Sports
- Scouting
- First Aid
- Swimming
- Adventure activities
- SUPW
- Gardening

The usefulness of the taxonomical classification of instructional objectives is also sometimes disputed. It, therefore, appears necessary at this place to summarise below some of the uses to which it can be put particularly in the area of testing:

1. Since categories in the Taxonomy are arranged on the principle of graded complexity, the scheme is very helpful in identifying the meaningful level at which the learner is functioning, especially in view of "the upper and lower limits of the same category as well as in the context of the nature of the next higher and lower categories."
2. The techniques and tools of assessment can be relevantly decided upon, developed and deployed. Their categorisation, thus, becomes easy and clear. The form and typology, which has so much grip on the minds of the teachers now, can be very profitably replaced by the objective-based one, as a much desired change.
3. It will be helpful in translating into practice the principle of comprehensiveness of evaluation by ensuring proper realisation of the coverage of various aspects of pupils' growth: Cognitive, Affective and Psycho-motor.
4. The evaluation of the evaluation devices in terms of their validity will be facilitated.

5. Evaluation may prove very helpful in arriving at the meaningful synthesis of various dimensions of pupils growth. Identification of areas of inter-relationship among the three domains may be of particular significance in this regard.
6. The logical nature of categorisation helps in identifying and grading teaching-learning situations, which can be an important source of selecting proper testing situations and deciding their sequence too.
7. Curriculum development and preparation of instructional material should profit from such a scheme of classification in many ways. Preparation and analysis of textbooks based on well-defined objectives may prove to be a big improvement.
8. The classification through its well-defined criteria "will provide a bridge for further communication among teachers, between teachers and evaluators, curriculum and research workers, psychologists and other behavioural scientists."
9. The taxonomies have also opened new avenues for research in education. To name a few, the re-evaluation of objectives should be the immediate reaction, such as finding out the relationship between different domains, categories and sub-categories. Empirical validation of the taxonomies besides being a worthy research in its own way, will also open-up new vistas of work. The study of the problems of retentivity and recession in learning on different objectives may be an equally fruitful project. Teachers may also be motivated to undertake experimentation on objective-based teaching and testing. The scope is likely to become more wide and varied in course of time.

For the purpose of discussion that follows in this document, Bloom's taxonomy in the Cognitive Domain, Krathwohl's taxonomy in the Affective Domain and Dave's taxonomy in the Psycho-motor Domain have been taken as the basis, as they are the most widely used ones. The above mentioned taxonomies of the three domains, are, however, often, followed in the '*letter*' and not in '*spirit*'. The adaptations it may be mentioned, are an outcome of the suggestions received in the course of discussions with a very large number of learners, teachers, teacher-educators, educational psychologists and sociologists, educational administrators, educational planners in India, spread over a span of more than five decades.

The main criteria for these adaptations was their suitability to the national environment in its various facets. Attempts were, therefore, made to check that the objectives identified for classification in each of the three domains were realisable through the curriculum, textbooks, educational resources, commonly available as also the competencies of the teachers and the learners to attain them.

In regard to the objectives of the *Cognitive Domain*, they have been limited to the first three of the steps of Bloom's taxonomy, viz., knowledge, understanding and application with *analysis, synthesis and evaluation compressed and dovetailed into application*. This has been done because the average teacher is likely to find it difficult to discriminate between them and consequently to appropriately tackle them either for purposes of teaching for realising them or for evaluating them with the precision with which they have been originally enunciated by Bloom particularly so in social sciences.

The objectives of the Affective Domain again have also been condensed in the present document. They have firstly not been presented in the nomenclature proposed by Krathwohl but just limited to 'interests' and 'attitudes' and personal attributes which are commonly understood terminologies.

The objectives of the psycho-motor domain have been reduced to the muscular skills related to the subjects of study. Basically, these are, such as require the abilities of '*precision*', '*precaution*' and '*proportion*' needed in undertaking activities like experiments, drawing sketches and diagrams, pursuing performing arts.

The Author's Contribution to the Taxonomies

As we have seen, the taxonomies of the Cognitive, Affective and the Psycho-motor domains present the phenomenon of vertical growth of the individuals in the three domains individually and collectively.

In the above context the author has expounded the theory of *sequential horizontal relationship among the three domains*. When anybody acquires some acquaintance (cognitive impression) about something, it often triggers an appreciation (affective impact) of the thing, learnt. The overflow of these feelings then moves beyond emotions propelling some fulfilling (psycho-motor) action.

This sequential horizontal relationship, among the three domains can be easily and effectively explained through a commonly observed phenomenon. We observe (cognition) some likeable characteristics of a child., we come to like them (affection) and then we instinctively hug and kiss it (Psycho-motor action).

The three taxonomies can be presented through the following composite model:

Taxonomy of Instuctional objectives of language and literature—H.S. Srivastava's Model

While working on objective-based teaching and testing, the teachers of languages and literature have repeatedly complained that the Taxonomies of Educational Objectives developed by different people did not satisfy the needs of languages and literature and that a separate taxonomy for this segment of curricular content needs to be developed.

The main hurdle in undertaking such an exercise, however, came from the unique nature of content (subject matter) of language and literature which differentiates it from non-language subjects, in a marked manner. In non-language subjects, themes of content demonstrate a scene of continuity , where one theme is built upon the other, whereas in languages each one of them presents a stand alone identity.

The subject-matter of languages and literature , as we know consists of Stories, Novels, Dialogues, Dramas, Essays, Letters, Biographies, Poetry, etc. There is hardly any relationship among them, as each one of them is a unique entity by itself. At best, they can be compared or classified in a very broad manner with regard to the dates of their publication or their authorship or whether they are comedies or tragedies or whether their underlying/background settings are social or economic political or cultural or environmental and so on. These tags, however, exhale no definite clues about their content or import.

It was in the context of such an apparent non-amenability to clear-cult taxonomical paradigms of taxonomical classifications that the following list of instructional objectives applicable to language and literature was first developed:

- Knowledge of the Elements of Language
- Comprehension
  - Listening Comprehension
  - Reading Comprehension
- Expression
  - Grad Expression
  - Written Expression
- Appreciation

While this list satisfied the characteristics of objectives in terms of their alignment with the subject, matter and its achievability and testability, the list did not present a picture where the objectives were graded in terms of increasing complexity involving higher levels of mental processes. These set of objectives did not also demonstrate inclusiveness where each next objective covered the attributes of all the ones mentioned earlier.

With a view to overcoming these technical shortfalls a modified version of the objectives of language and literature, for brining the list closer to the concept of a taxonomy, was worked out as under:

- Knowledge of the Elements of Language
- Listening Comprehension
- Oral Expression
- Reading Comprehension
- Written Expression
- Appreciation

This above list proposed to be designated as the Taxonomy and Languages and Literature represents

- the natural sequence of the acquisition of the listed abilities
- a graded complexity of abilities
- the needed inclusiveness of the next stated abilities covering the lower ones.

Knowledge of the Elements of Language, however, permeates all the abilities.

It is also desirable to appreciate the coverage of the stated/listed objectives in respect of the three Domains of Development. This a presented through the following chart:

Coverage of Domains of Development through the Objectives of Language and Literature

Domains of Development / *Taxonomical Objectives of Language and Literature*	*Cognitive Domain*	*Affective Domain*	*Psychomotor Domain*
Knowledge of the Elements of Language	✓		
Listening Comprehension	✓	✓	
Oral Expression	✓		✓
Reading Comprehension	✓	✓	
Written Expression	✓	✓	✓
Appreciation		✓	

Salient Manifestations of the Objectives

- Knowledge of the Elements of Language
  - ➢ Vocabulary including basic semantics and stucture
  - ➢ Usage
  - ➢ Applied Grammar
  - ➢ Forms and formats of literature
- Listening Comprehension
  - ➢ Recognising the characteristics of speech sounds as also stress and intonation.
  - ➢ Following the sequence of the ideas listened, grasping the substance of what is listened.
- Oral Expression
  - ➢ Demonstrating correct pronunciation, stress intonation, accent and pauses

  - using appropriate words, phrases and sentences for reaching out ones ideas to others.
  - maintaining proper sequence, speed and flow in using conventional modes of address.
- Reading comprehension is envisaged to include:
  - Displaying reasonable speed in silent reading
  - Grasping the meanings of words, phrases sentences in their context
  - Locating key words phrases, sentences, important facts and ideas
  - Identifying the relationship between ideas facts, events characters, etc.
  - Interpreting, inferring and evaluating the ideas, messages, mood of the writer and feelings expressed.
- Written expression
  - Using correct and appropriate words, idioms spellings (graphics), punctuations capitalization and connectives.
  - Maintenance of logical sequence in ideas, statements and in paragraphing
  - Following apt and appropriate forms and formats of written expression
  - Writing a neat and a legible hand with normal speed
  - Appropriately introducing the topic and ending it well
  - Giving a suitable title
- Appreciation
  - Appreciation is an overwhelming experience of a sensory reaction to beauty.
  - The unique and appealing beauty of words or of sounds of music or of works of art or of the softness of touch or of the buds of taste, constitute the prime genes of appreciation. Their delicacy refinement, tenderness, sensitivity and imaginativeness often leave us pondering and speechless.

Appreciation, thus, is an amalgam of supreme understanding, elated emotions and heart penetrating sentiments.

SECTION II
Genesis of Curriculum

4

Concept and Need of Curriculum

We envisage Curriculum for School Education to be:

- an instrument of change, while at the same time catering to the changes that have already taken place.
- a hope for meeting the aspirations of a coherent Indian society, symbolising unity in diversity.
- an enabling aid providing the abilities of learning-how-to-learn and self-directed learning.
- a package encompassing advances in Science and Technology, as also in Trade and Commerce.
- a passage leading to both higher academic and professional education as also to the world of work.
- a concept incorporating the diverse dimensions of learning and teaching viz, objectives, content, teaching learning material,methodology, Instructional aids and evaluation.
- a tool for developing a wholesome personality with multi-use competencies in both scholastic and co-scholastic of personality.
- a wholistic entity embodying the elements of unity, coherence, integration and comprehensiveness.
- a ladder of learning providing for natural gradation and smooth transition from one stage to another.
- a device comfortably rotating within the groove of the time-budget.

Types of Curriculum

Somehow we have become chronically used to taking a myopic view of everything. Even in speaking and writing we invent unheard of abbreviations. Education too has been no exception to this emergent trend which has come to be considered as fashionable.

The most unsound of these in the present context is to treat SCHOOL CURRICULUM as the only prescription for erasing our ignorance and for making us knowledgeable. Furthermore, that it is something with defined perimeters. This is not true as there are a variety of Curriculum types mainly the following:

Curriculum of the **Home**
Curriculum of the **Immediate Environment**
Curriculum of the **Peer Group**
Curriculum of the **School**
Curriculum of the **Television**
Curriculum of the **Internet and the WWW**

The Curriculum of the **Home** admits no limits or boundaries. It covers life as a whole. It offers coherent and not compartmentalised education that is all inclusive. It is continuous and whole- time education without any breaks. It is both positive and negative aimed at helping us overcome our shortfalls and for inculcating in us desirable attributes. We owe our language and behaviour patterns, our manners and etiquette, our beliefs and attitudes, our social and economic mind-sets and a host of our ideologies and moral standards to this demanding school called the Home.

The Curriculum of the **Immediate Environment** differs with the location where one lives and grows. For example, this Curriculum would be different for children living in the desert areas, coastal areas, high altitudes and so on.Their life-styles, their clothing, their food habits are different. Their perception of weather too is very different. All these impacts on our thinking, willing and feeling are, in fact, the outcomes of education, one receives from the immediate environment. This education, however, is received by individuals imperceptibly without ones knowing that s/he is receiving education and that s/he is learning. Observation and experiences are the souls of this education.

The Curriculum of the **Peer Group** is transacted by those who are slightly elder or younger than ourselves. It quite often consists of quiet transmission of information which is interesting to the receiver and which the individual wants to know. Most often the kernel of the information passed on stands wrapped in secrecy. For example, sex-education is not a common subject of study and even openly talking about sex is a taboo. Therefore, information about sex is passed on through the Curriculum of the Peer Group. This information, however, is often based on hearsay and is not always authentic. The child refers to the peers to find answers to questions for which he is unable to get clear answers from parents.

The Curriculum of the **School** is something we really understand by Curriculum. It precisely presents the paradigms of education to be imparted. It is specially designed for different stages of education, for different subjects of study, for different grades/classes. It is built upon what the students have already learnt and is a stepping stone for what s/he is supposed to learn in future. It is based on the National Curriculum Framework and consists of well-defined components, viz:

Objectives
Content outline (Syllabus)
Genesis of Instructional Methodologies
Ideas about Instructional Support Material.
Evaluation Approaches for Scholastic and Co-scholastic areas of Growth

It is Syllabus with which Curriculum is normally confused, when Syllabus is taken to be a synonym of curriculum and used as its substitute. This gives a very narrow connotation to curriculum and pedagogically a very dangerous one.

The Curriculum of the **Television** is something we are all exposed to at the discretion of the Television Channels where we have no to say. We may be wanting to see something and in that quest we are compelled to see so many other things in which we may not have any interest. Some Channels are biased in favour of or against certain social, economic, political or cultural ideologies and they project them in subtle ways to inject them to convert our thinking to theirs. So far as children are concerned, *the television also often projects, enlarged images of the negative aspects of life brainwashing children to believe that they have a right to be wrong.* The Television also eulogises the gospel of consumerism and thus, diverts the attention of viewers from pursuing and practicing a higher quality of life to chasing only a better quality of life.

The Curriculum of the **Internet and the WWW** is the enrichment Curriculum. It is an enabling and an empowering curriculum bringing the unknown into the realm of the known, enhancing the circumference of the body of our knowledge. It makes us explorers, adventurers and discoverers. The outcomes of this Curriculum impart a unique sense of achievement, satisfaction and gratification to the learners.

Some of the above types of curricula or some parts of some, are controllable, others are not.It is only the Curriculum of the school that is completely in our hands.

Basic Considerations in Curriculum Construction

There are mainly three basic paradigms in curriculum construction. These are:

The Individual : Learners, their probable age group, level of mental growth, background (family & social) as well as level of knowledge possessed, aspirations, etc.

The Society : This will include the social order, national economic policies, political system, cultural heritage philosophy of life of the nation, etc.

The Human Knowledge : The existing store of human knowledge in various areas, which is fast growing and exerting an influence on our life-styles.

The above three considerations will provide the foundations of the curriculum and also be the most important of the sources of educational objectives.

Derivation and Statement of Objectives

The above basic considerations when spelt out for specific areas and subject domains are a pointer to the educational objectives. These overall objectives become the basis of deriving the objectives for different stages of education (primary, secondary, university). And finally the stage-wise objectives of education become the basis for developing instructional objectives of various grades, subject areas and courses.

These instructional objectives determine the *real operational framework of the curricula* for various courses. They will need to be conceived in all the three domains of pupil growth, viz. the Cognitive, Affective and Psycho-motor.

Curriculum Development a Collaborative Venture

After the identification of the various courses of study and their respective objectives the next step is to develop a curriculum for each of these. While developing curriculum it has to be kept in mind that *curriculum is not a one man's job and certainly not the monopoly of the subject specialists as has been the case in the past,* in several places. Curriculum Development is a process requiring inputs from several areas of specialisation. These are mainly eight specialised inputs and four environmental ones required as is shown through the Diagram 4.1.

Each one of these eight has to play a distinct role. To state briefly the *curriculum specialist* will look after the general framework of the entire endeavour. He will help establish and ensure a feasible coordination between the different experts. The *subject-matter expert,* who could be an individual drawn from higher education or University, will ensure that the content matter included is accurate and updated and that its organisation does not distort the facts. The *educational technologist* will see to it that the methodologies of instruction and modern aids to teaching (including technological ones) proposed are the most appropriate for the situations for which they are suggested. He will also be instrumental in establishing a relationship between the objectives, content and in instructional techniques. He should be an educational technologist rather than a technologist without any educational background. The *educational psychologist* will scrutinise the potential of the proposed content and methodology for achieving the targets in respect of the expected outcomes. He will look to their appropriateness from the point of view of the mental level of the learner-group and the likely adequacy of their mental preparedness for the proposed intakes. The *educational practitioner* will indeed be the practising teacher, whose job will be to see that the objectives, content and methodology are all suitable for the learners, that the

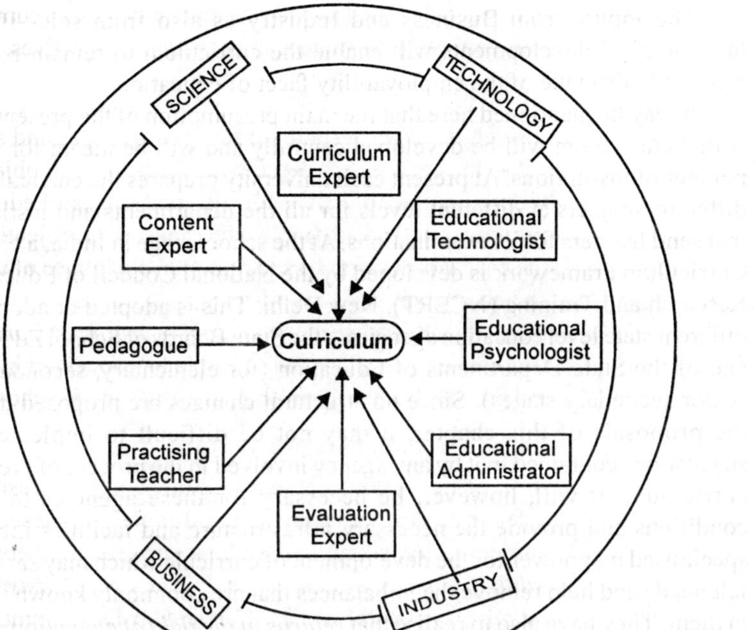

Diagram 4.1: Curriculum Development—a Collaborative Venture

objectives are neither pitched too high nor too low, that the content is graded and in line with the likely background of previous knowledge and competencies of the group and that the methodologies proposed can be employed either through the existing resources or those that can be easily manipulated or procured. He will also have to judge the implementability of the curriculum in respect of the time-budget. Above all, he will also be required to do a little introspection for finding out whether the average existing teacher can manage to impart instruction as contemplated through the proposed curriculum. The *pedagogue* will critically examine the reliability of the instructional methodologies proposed. *The evaluators* job will be to identify and select the techniques of evaluation for assessing the quantum of growth in all the three domains (cognitive, affective and psycho-motor). He will also be required, in most cases, to develop tools of evaluation of different types and forms for assessing the degree of achievement of the pre-determined objectives the mastery of content on the part of the learners. He will as well be entrusted with the task of devising formats and procedures for the recording and reporting of evaluation data and for suggesting the various uses of the results of evaluation in different situations.

The inputs from Business and Industry as also from scientific and technological developments will enable the curriculum to remain updated. They will also take of the employability facet of education.

It may be mentioned here that the main presumption of the present thesis is that curriculum will be developed centrally and will be meant for a large number of institutions. At present each university prepares the curriculum for different subjects at different levels for all the departments and institutions that send learners for its examinations. At the school stage in India, a National Curriculum Framework is developed by the National Council of Educational Research and Training (NCERT), New Delhi. This is adopted or adopted by different state level education agencies—the State Boards of School Education; and of the State Departments of Education (for elementary, secondary and senior secondary stages). Since no structural changes are proposed through the proposals of this chapter, it may not be difficult to implement the suggestions contained in it by any agency involved in the process of preparing curriculum. It will, however, be necessary for these agencies to create conditions and provide the necessary infrastructure and facilities including specialised manpower for the development of curricula which may satisfy the felt needs and help remove the imbalances that are commonly known to exist in them. They have also to realise that *returns in the field of education are not as quick as they could be in business or industry*. The benefits of what we invest now, will be reaped only by the next generation and *our interest in the future generations will be estimated with the investments in terms of time energy we make for them*.

Developing Curriculum Content and Materials

Textbooks were probably the only item in this category used in a traditional set-up. Till recently they were developed solely by private individuals and the educational agencies simply selected a few out of the many submitted to them for a particular course. These were called 'approved' or 'recommended' textbooks and were used by learners preparing for the courses concerned. However, at the school level many of them are now being developed by official agencies.

At the school stage, Teachers' Guides and Learners' Workbooks entered the educational scheme in India only in the sixties. No deliberate effort was made to develop them earlier. Those that were available had been developed in foreign countries and were unrelated to the curriculum in use in India. Furthermore, being imported they were expensive. This somehow created the wrong impression that even if they are developed in India, they would essentially be costly and out of the reach of the purchasing power of the users. This fear was a constant discouragement for initiating any project for their development. Ultimately in the sixties the *National Council of Educational*

Research and Training (N.C.E.R.T.), New Delhi, developed comprehensive curriculum projects. This was, thus, the first official agency in the country that planned and developed a wide variety of instructional materials. Besides textbooks, teachers guides, learners workbooks, handwriting books and a reading readiness kit were developed. In Social Studies, teachers guides and instructional charts were developed to go with the textbooks. In Science, teachers' guides, kits of improvised and inexpensive apparatus (for demonstration and experimentation purposes) and laboratory manuals were developed to supplement the textbooks.

The above description gives some of the main kinds of instructional materials, the development of which now needs to be explored further by the various educational agencies responsible for the different stages of education. The plea again is that the development of instructional materials of different kinds may be taken up as an integral part of the programme of curriculum development. It is not necessary for these educational agencies to create an elaborate, top-heavy infrastructure for doing this task but a core team will no doubt be necessary.

This will mean a deviation from the existing practice where the members of Boards of Studies in different subjects decide on the syllabus for courses in their respective subjects. Each Board of Studies or Committee of Courses, as it is sometimes called, works independently of the other. The situation often causes lack of coordination and often the binding thread between the various courses is found missing particularly at the school stage where integrative approach is advocated. At the university stage, however, subjects are treated as independent entities/disciplines. What is attempted to be made out here, is that curriculum construction is a highly specialised job which can best be done by an educational agency, through a centrally operated ongoing programme of curriculum development review and renewal. This could be entrusted to what may be called the Academic/Curriculum Unit set-up within the organisation. It may consist of specialists in Curriculum, Evaluation, Instructional Materials, Educational Technology besides educational psychologists and subject-matter experts, etc. This core body may co-opt. specialists from other areas, as and when necessary, for accomplishing specialised jobs. At present time, it has become more necessary than ever before, to collaborate with *business and industry. This may not just be limited to consultation but their active involvement in the development of courses and their transaction for incorporating elements relevant to the needs of the job market.* But the sole responsibility for constructing the curriculum and having curriculum and evaluation materials prepared should rest with it. It will be only then, that a coordinated curriculum development will be possible. In such a set-up the Committees of Courses or the Boards of Studies, will take the form of the curriculum development committees for various courses at the school stage for example (adapting or adopting from the National Curriculum Framework in the Indian context). With the broadening of the concept of the curriculum, the services of persons represented on these committees will need to be utilised not only for the development of instructional and evaluation materials of various types but also for a variety of other related academic endeavours. The proposal envisages that there may be two distinct divisions within the infrastructure of the educational agencies, one for the development of course content, methodology of transaction and supporting aids and the other for matters related to evaluation and certification. One of these may be incharge of curriculum specialist and the other under the charge of an evaluation expert. Both the wings will of course, need supporting staff which will have to be provided. Academic work will, thus, acquire a status that it deserves. As could be seen the academic work has very wide dimensions and hence, it does deserve better attention and position than what has so far been given to it, particularly by the examining agencies which by and large remain more than pre-occupied with the fire-fighting operations related to the conduct of examinations.

Steps of Developing Curriculum Content

- Listing of expected learning competencies in the three domains of development.
- Examining the implications of identified learning competencies in terms of the themes of content
- Identification of themes and sub-themes of content (subject matter) which can be pressed into service for realising the objectives
- Deciding about the graded complexity of the themes in the context of
  - The subject discipline in question
  - The age group of the learners
  - The preceding and the following learning
  - The environmental setting and the ethos
- Ensuring
  - Continuity
  - Gradation
  - Integration
  - Life application

Developing Evaluation Procedures and Materials

Work on the development of evaluation procedures and materials has to go on simultaneously with that of the development of instructional methodology and materials. While the purpose and function of the latter is to help the learners realise the instructional objectives, that of the former is to assess the level of achievement of the same on the part of the learners in the context of the inputs offered.

An evaluation programme to be so developed, will need to embody the following characteristics:

1. *Objective-based*—It should provide for the evaluation of all the related instructional objectives of the Cognitive, Affective and the Psycho-motor domains, in a valid and a reliable manner. It should, thus, help gauge the strengths and shortfalls in pupil growth in a precise manner, not just for assessing and certifying the attained level of competencies but for further improving them through remedial measures too.
2. *Continuous*—It should provide for a continued process of assessment built into the total teaching-learning process as an integral part instead of the usual periodical examinations which tend to test achievement only in one or two strokes. This will also help provide regular feedback to both learners and teachers for improving the level and quality of their performance.
3. *Comprehensive*—It should cover both the academic and the non/co-academic aspects of pupil growth and thereby provide a compelling motivation to the institutions in offering adequate and appropriate opportunities of the desired type, for developing the various competencies among learners, some of which could otherwise have been overlooked.
4. *Use of a variety of techniques and tools*—As the evaluation programme will be designed for covering both the scholastic and co-scholastic aspects of pupil growth, it will need to exploit various types of testing situations. They may, for example, also need to focus on observation as an important technique of evaluation and necessitate the use of variety of unconventional tools of evaluation like check-lists, inventories, rating scales, observation schedules, etc.

Curriculum Transaction/Implementation

This is a crucial step. It is here that the use of the vast inputs in curriculum construction is made. This is mainly the teacher's jurisdiction where he is the master of the situation in manipulating or providing learning experiences to the learners as envisaged by the curriculum. This is the stage of interaction between the curriculum on the one hand and the teacher and the learners on the other. The phenomenon could be diagrammatically represented through the Diagram 4.2.

Objectives are the anchor of the curriculum which in turn are the basis of the work of teachers and learners. Teachers and learners both work for the realisation of the objectives, through curriculum transaction which are ultimately evaluated through a well-defined procedure of evaluation. The

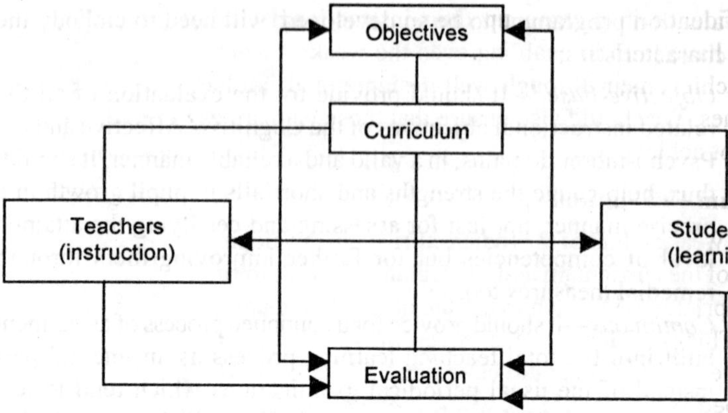

Diagram 4.2

operation of this strategy could be called curriculum implementation and its process consists of objective-based instruction and learning.

It may be mentioned here that several forces, both internal and external, influence the aforesaid process of instruction. *From the teachers point of view* they are his personal academic background and training, availability of resources and aids to instruction, his interest in and commitment for the job and the satisfaction he derives from its execution, etc. *From the learners' point of view* they are his interest in and attitude towards study, his level of achievement and growth, his previous preparation for assimilating the course, his future plans and his motivation, etc. *From the point of view of both the teacher and the learner*, it may be the ethos and the atmosphere of the school and the encouragement and motivation it provides, besides the availability of instructional materials and their use, etc.

Approach to instruction is yet another factor deserving attention in this regard. Normally while we educationalists view a teaching-learning situation, we are often guided in our thinking by the concept of the symmetrical normal probability curve and the *stanine scale* (this is being discussed in greater detail in the chapter on grading). We think that in a population only about 4% will get the top grade and another 4% will get the last one. As a nine point scale this notion has overtaken our thinking so much that we often refuse to view the situation from another angle.

In fact, a normal distribution of scores presumes chances and accidents. Indeed the distribution should not be normal, if some carefully manipulated inputs are not introduced in the process of instruction. It should then take a negatively skewed form. Thus, we have reason to argue that *the closer a distribution is to the normal one, the more ineffective has our instruction been.* This logic advocated by Dr. B.S. Bloom of the University of Chicago is bound to be of great interest to the teachers and has the potential of adding to their confidence in picking up their instructional challenges. We should, therefore, have faith in enabling even the weakest learner to attain a higher level of achievement through well-designed and implemented educational programmes. We should also ensure that those who are capable of achieving high do not achieve low.

Curriculum Evaluation

This is the weakest link of the Indian curriculum development scene. It involves the tryout of the curriculum and curriculum materials to find out their adequacy and appropriateness for achieving the objectives in advance of putting it into practice. This is seldom done and even where it is attempted, it is not done as it should be. The try out could be sequentially done *unitwise* as and when one is developed as also that of the whole *curriculum*. As a matter of fact both the above types of tryouts are necessary, when a completely new curriculum is being developed. But sometimes only a partial revision of the curriculum is desired and in this case only that part of the newly developed replacement of the curriculum may be tried out.

In all these cases, however, it is sought to find out, as to how far the various elements of the curriculum and the procedures and practices implied through it, are effective in achieving the objectives set. *More than one set of material and methods could also be tried* out in this process for identifying the most appropriate one. Questions like the following could be sought to be answered through the envisaged tryout:

- Whether the objectives of instruction set are within the competence of the learners to achieve?
- Whether one set of content matter or another is more adequate and or appropriate for enabling the learners to achieve the objectives?
- Which one of the various methodologies tried is most suitable to be adopted as compared to the others?
- What instructional materials or sets of them help the learners achieve the objectives better than others?
- Whether the scheme of evaluation is capable of providing valid and reliable results and whether the diagnosis made throught them can constructively help in the improvement of teaching and learning through the needed reinforcements etc.?

The step is mainly contemplated to put the effectiveness of the curriculum to test before putting it into practice. The step of curriculum evaluation may no doubt mean substantial investment in terms of time, effort and money but it could save educational disasters, which may mean losses multiplied several times over.

It may be mentioned that in an ideal scheme, there should be a built in system of continuous review and revision (renewal) of the curriculum.

5

Paradigms of Curriculum Development and Implementation

Overview

Curriculum is the soul of formal education. Even though in India, the schools by themselves have no hand in its development but only to abide by its dictates it is desirable that its operational genesis is familiar to the teachers who also ought to ideally participate in its development. This is being attempted here without going into any technicalities. In fact, the presentation of the concept has been presented in only bullet points.

Purposes of Curriculum

- an adaptable Teaching-learning road-map for reaching educational targets
- an instrument for optimum physical, intellectual, social and spiritual growth of the educands.
- a hope capsule for realizing individual and collective aspirations.

Components of Curriculum

- Objectives/Expected Learning Competencies
- Contents/Subject-matter
- Teaching Aids/ Instructional Support Materials
- Curriculum Transaction (Methodology)
- Evaluation of Students' learning and the Curriculum

Collaborators in Curriculum Development

Educational Collaborators

- Curriculum Expert
- Evaluation Expert
- Educational Psychologist
- Pedagogue
- Practising Teacher
- Content Specialist

- Educational Technologist
- Educational Adminstrator

External Collaborators from the areas of

- Science
- Technology
- Business
- Industry

Instructional Objectives and the Curriculum

- Coverage of all the three domains for pupil development
  - Cognitive Domain
  - Affective Domain
  - Psychomotor Domain
- Alignment of the targeted competencies with the subject, the age group and the environmental setting.
- Integration with other themes of the subject, with themes of other subjects and with life situations.

Steps of Curriculum Evolution

- Planning of paradigms
- Development
- Try-out
- Finalisation
- Implementation
- Monitoring
- Review
- Renewal

Uses of Curriculum

- A guide for teachers
- A ready-reckoner for heads of schools
- A road-map for students
- A path-finder for educational administrators

Developing Curriculum Content

- Listing of expected learning competencies
- Examining the implications of identified learning competencies in terms of the themes of content
- Identification of theme and sub-theme of content(subject-matter)
- Deciding about the graded complexity of the themes in the context of
  - The subject discipline in question
  - The age group of the pupils

  - The preceding and the following learning
  - The environmental setting and the ethos
- Ensuring
  - Continuity
  - Gradation
  - Integration
  - Life Applications

Characteristics of Curriculum Transaction

- Interest evoking, interest capturing and interest retaining activities
- Sequential treatment of content displaying a logical relationship with preceding and following learning
- Compatibility with the maturity level of students
- Demonstrating the relationship of the identified themes in a subject with other themes of the same subjects, with themes of other subjects and with life situations
- Fuller utilisation of 'specific' methods, in addition to the 'standard' methods
- Focus on practical work in subjects for illuminating the theoretical concepts and constructs
- Offering opportunities for abiding self-deduced inferences
- Imbued with motivations for learning-how-to-learn, finally culminating into self-directed learning
- Containing potential for empowering students for tackling other problems in unfamiliar situations
- Diagnosis of strengths and weaknesses, for developing and providing remedial or enrichment exercises, built into the process as integral parts of the educational process, for further improving the level and quality of learning
- A road-map for abiding learning and its use

Evaluation of Learner Attainments

- is a continuous and a comprehensive process of making judgements about educational strengths and weaknesses of individuals
- is aimed at not just assessing but improving the level of achievement and proficiency of pupils
- uses a variety of techniques and tools for covering the evaluation of both the scholastic and non-scholastic aspects of growth
- attempts to ensure accuracy, dependability and justice for maintaining credibility of the process.

Note: Because of its importance 'Evaluation of Pupil Growth' is being dealt with separately in detail.

6

Role of Curriculum and Curriculum Material in the Teaching-Learning Process

Curriculum defines the parameters of the total teaching-learning process in all its components, viz:

- Objectives
- Subject-matter (syllabus)
- Curriculum material
- Support material and aids
- Evaluation

The role of the curriculum already stands enumerated in the earlier chapter, the current one proposes to deliberate on **Curriculum Material** which mainly includes:

- Text-books
- Supplementary books
- Student workbooks
- Techer's guides
- Teaching Aids and other support materials

Textbooks faithfully reflect the proposed subject matter in totality. They are used both by the teachers and the students for their personal guidance about what to learn for the pupils and what to teach for the teachers.

Texts books present the subject-matter in a cogent and a coherent manner in the correct sequence and appropriate gradation.

The contents of the textbooks are built upon what the students have learnt earlier for taking the students easily to what they are expected to study in the future. They present facts, terms, concepts, principles, etc. related to the concerned themes in logical sequences and give them examples, pictures, diagrams, etc. to enable the students to effortlessly learn them.

The textbooks also give recapitulatory exercises for consolidation of learning. In addition they also give lists of assignments, surveys, projects, etc. from which the teacher could choose for giving to the students.

References about further reading particularly in higher classes and for surfing the internet are also sometimes given for enrichment.

Supplementary books are not supposed to be studied in great depth like the textbooks. They are books to be read cursorily for catching the ideas contained. The purpose of recommending these is to enable the pupils appreciate the morals they exhale, the sentiments their stories convey and so on.

The questions asked on the supplementary books are generally related to the crucial twists and turns in the story, the uniqueness of some characters. Sometimes a question is given about one or two likely events after the story of the book end.

Learning of some new vocabulary is often an incidental gain form the study of the book.

Student Work-Books: The exercises in the student work-books normally follow the sequence of the Textbook chapters. The purpose of these exercises is:

- drill for practice
- revision of content
- application of content in life
- consolidation of learning

Student workbooks save the time and labour of the teacher in designing after-lesson exercises for his classes and gets quality exercised developed by experts.

The workbooks also cover the hard spots in learning by way of suitable drill and enable better learning.

Teachers' Guidebooks provide concrete guidance for the teacher in transacting his/her *duties of teaching and testing*. In regard to teaching they give suggestions about chapter/theme wise:

- instructional methodologies, both conventional and unconventional
- ideas about explorations, experimentation, excursions, etc.
- cautions and precautions about handing of instructional aids
- possible group and individual activities
- suggested outlines of pupil reports, about projects, surveys explorations, etc.

About testing the teachers guides normally give ideas about the junctures of testing and the possible techniques and tools of testing possible to be pressed into service along with some samples of tests. A full end of the topic test with all ingredients (Designs/Blueprint/Tests/Marking Scheme/Question-wise analyses) is very helpful as a model for the teacher to follow.

Teaching Aids take the form of apparatus for experimentation charts, models, tables, etc. In some cases, Teaching Aids, enrich the teaching-learning process and in some others they are essential foundations of teaching. *Working models* lead to understanding of processes, which no oral description can possibly provide. Pictures enable children to know about places they cannot possibly visit. Working of certain factories like sugar mills, enable an understanding of the total process of the production of items of our daily use.

Role and Importance of Textbooks and Supplementary Books

Textbooks are the most important of the tools of curriculum implementation. They constitute the foundational instructional material. They cover the total course of the concerned subject. The total content of a course is analysed and divided into major themes and a chapter is devoted to each major theme. The chapter theme is again sub-divided into topics and sub-topics for purposes of paragraphing and for giving titles and sub-titles to them. Some important points in the paragraphs are also highlighted by printing them bold or in italics. Some textbooks also give pithy sentences on the margins. The titles, sub-titles, highlighted statements and the marginal notes all help learners in revision.

Some textbooks also have a CD giving motion pictures of working models, or of establishments which learners cannot visit, or of rare phenomena of nature not commonly seen and so on. This is enrichment material.

The end of the chapter items are of no less importance. The main of these are:

- Re-capitulatory Questions
- List of assignments (individual and group)
- List of possible surveys
- List of theme related possible explorations
- List of possible projects
- Themes of possible library /internet research, etc.
- All these possess the potential of providing learning experiences, many times more valuable than memorising the contents of the textbooks.

Sometimes one of the end-of-the-chapter items, is also an-end-of-the-topic scientifically prepared complete test comprising of a Design, a Blueprint based on the Design, the test , a Marking Scheme, the Question-wise Analysis. This test should be possible to be administered within a class period .The teacher should feel free to make any changes he may deem desirable in the test. While making these modifications, the basic principles of preparing balanced tests, should stand well-guarded.

While the textbooks have to be read from cover-to-cover, with full attention and a tireless striving for grasping, understanding and digesting each word and phrase for instant recall at a future time, we read the

SUPPLEMENTARY BOOKS in a cursory manner. We have only to broadly capture, the central idea, the plot of the story, the main players, the messages, etc. We read them a little more carefully than a novel and less carefully than a textbook. The example of 'Tales from Shakespeare ' could be cited as a commonly prescribed supplementary book in English. Supplementary books help in improving ones vocabulary, in imparting a reading habit, in enlarging ones mental horizon, in offering to the learners a pleasant diversion from compulsive reading to voluntary, self-willed reading of ones interest, as also in taking learners away from the often painful reading for examinations to reading for pleasure. Testing in regard to Supplementary Books too is simple.

The questions in examinations asked on supplementary Books do not entertain high expectations from the answers. The questions are straight requiring simple factual answers. There could, however, be questions on sequence of events or those that require the description of events themselves or sequences of events, characters in the story, the twists and turns in the story, the morals exhaled by the particular stories, etc.

Role of Text-books and Supplementary books

Curriculum is the anchor of the teaching-learning process. It defines the perimeters of 'Why', 'What', 'How', 'Where' and 'When' of educational programmes. It is the instrument for setting standards. It is a roadmap for learner activities both inside and outside the classroom/school. Its undisputed aim is to reinforce and consolidate learning in a coherent manner. While the Curriculum as such provides broad indications, the actual details in terms of learner activities stand incorporated in the instructional material viz. the textbooks, laboratory manuals, student work-books, teachers' guides, etc.

The bare content outline of the curriculum becomes the basis of the Syllabus, which is a detailed document containing, among other things, major themes and topics. Each one of these themes and topics admits some activities in terms of assignments, surveys, projects, explorations, library research, internet surfing, experimentation, etc. The autonomy in functioning on these activities and the assumption of related responsibilities, pull out a host of hidden abilities, imparts confidence and a sense of achievement.

The variety of activities required to be pursued by the learners conveys a very valuable message to the learners that schooling and learning are not just passive listening but more so 'active doing'. It is not always being dependent on the teacher but also becoming autonomous. The generation of such a mind-set is likely to prove to be a great enabler in facing life situation with confidence and success.

In identifying and using Methodologies of teaching, we have to take into account the content area to be taught .They may not always be the conventional methods that may be found to be appropriate and we may decide to press into service, unconventional ones. We may even use a combination of methodologies. Here again, each methodology would have its own set of activities, each imparting to us its own lessons.

While preparing 'Time-budgets' for conducting the courses we may even in the beginning itself allocate specific time-spans for different activities in view of the methodologies we might be planning to use. This will presume a through grounding of the teacher in not only in the methologies but also the principles of pedagogy with an insight into it.

In more concrete terms, Curriculum, Text Books and Supplementary Books play definite roles in the teaching-learning process.

As we know teaching-learning process is governed by:

- The objectives to be realised
- The content identified for enabling the achievement of the objects
- The suitability of the methodology used for achieving the objective
- The aptness, appropriateness and adequacy of the supporting material
- The comprehensiveness of the evaluation for discovering shortfalls in learning to be addressed

The curriculum lists the objectives in terms of outcomes, in respect of the abilities and proficiencies desired and expected to be acquired by the learners, through the diverse educational inputs invested.

The curriculum also identifies the content/subject-matter likely to be helpful in helping realise the educational targets set. This step is imbued with "gradation" being based on the previous knowledge of the learners and with the potential of leading the learners to the next higher levels of learning.

In addition, the curriculum also lists the possible methodologies, out of which the teacher has to use his discretion in selecting for being pressed into service in his/her specific situation related to the ability of group of learners.

Similarly, the teacher will stand benefitted by the availability of a list of support material to choose from, for enriching the teaching-learning process. However, there no doubt is a baffling block, related to the often non-availability of the required aids obliging the teacher to choose and use the second or the third or the fourth best in most situations. Teachers have to be mentally ready for the facing such frequently occurring situations.

It is possible for the curriculum to provide concrete guidelines about tools and techniques as also procedures and practices to be pressed into service. The teacher, however, will need to have a background of the fundamentals of evaluation for adepting the principles to his specific situation in preparing tools, administering them, identifying and addressing individual shortfalls.

Textbooks are an enlarged mirror image of the curriculum. They are teaching aids used both by teachers and learners. They:

- provide elaborations to the briefly stated postulates by the curriculum
- present examples for enabling a better understanding of the subject
- give diagrams, pictures for helping learners in internalising learning
- have developmental exercises for enabling smooth learning
- provide references for further study and investigation
- give a list of possible projects, surveys assignments and encourage learning, learning to learn and self-directed learning

Supplementary books, do not directly reflect the curriculum, but indirectly support it by providing a generalised background to the specified content. Unlike textbooks, the supplementary books do not give conclusions which the learners themselves have to draw by themselves. This creative and insightful activity is enriching and empowering.

7

National Curriculum Frameworks and Their Conceptual Evolution

Historical Overview

Until the middle of the Twentieth Century there was almost negligible uniformity in education in India. Its constitutional status as a State Subject further promoted the idea of autonomy which was forcefully exerted by the Universities and the School Examination Boards.

It was the Mudaliar Commission (1952) that proposed a uniform structure of education and offered suggestions about its content and process. This Secondary Education Commission was also the only one for implementing the recommendations of which, a special autonomous organisation called the All India Council for Secondary Education (AICSE) was created. As the recommendations of the Commission were many, the AICSE identified, through a nation-wide Survey, the following three priority areas to start work on:

Science. Education
Examination Reform and
In-service Teacher Education

While the AICSE, then on focussed attention on the above three areas, it continued working in other important areas of school education as well. As a part of this activity, the AICSE, with the help of teachers, pedagogues subject-matter specialists from different parts of the country, prepared a Syllabus for the Secondary Stage. This was circulated to the State Governments and the School Examination Boards. The initiative was highly appreciated and coupled with wide-ranging intensive field-work, the activities of the AICSE helped the Central Government in establishing a foot-hold in the States, in the field of education. The glowing reputation of the AICSE became so impressive that the Government of India, decided to make it a Governmental organisation on April 1, 1959, when it was also renamed as Directorate of Extension Programmes for Secondary Education (DEPSE). It is worth mentioning that it was DEPSE where the National Council of Educational Research and Training (NCERT) was conceived and planned. DEPSE was also one of the organisations that merged to constitute NCERT, when it came into being on September 1, 1961.

It was with the establishment of the NCERT that ideas at bringing about uniformity in education at the national level crystallised through the following formal sequential steps:

- Preparation of National Policies of Education
- Development of National Curriculum Frameworks
- Production of Instructional Material

The National Policies of Education are based on wide ranging research into realities from a close range, for the purposes of having our feet on the ground while trying to reach the skies. The items that capture our attention in this regard are :

- The Environmental Settings
- The Inputs
- The Processes
- The Immediate Outcomes
- The Long Range Impact

All these will relate to the content and process of the projects and programmes of education, we design and implement in regard to the curricula of the school.

After such extensive and intensive research exercises, the outcomes of these tireless strivings are discussed in meticulous detail at the Local, Regional and National levels, to evolve the fundamental foundations of education for the country. In this process, the earlier ventures and adventures in this regard, are also subjected to critical scrutiny for justifying to ourselves the departures we may have in mind to make. This is because, unlike the West, India does not discard and reject the past but assimilates it.

We, thus, arrive at the broad perimeters for our education. They are these that find their way into the National Curriculum Frameworks. While documenting these we do ensure their alignment with:

- Our Social Order
- Our Economic Structure
- Our Political Ideology
- Our Cultural Heritage
- The Maturity Level of the Learner
- The Existing Store of Human Knowledge and above all
- The Tenets of the Constitution of India.

As the National Curriculum Frameworks are over-view documents, they have but to be general and not specific, containing principles rather than practices, titles rather than texts.

The National Curriculum Frameworks normally focus on certain well-defined stages of education as a whole like "National Curriculum Framework for School Education". They are holistic in composition and attempt to cover all relevant technical facets of that particular stage, setting targets and preparing road-maps.

Two of the latest Indian Curriculum Frameworks for School Education do deserve to be referred to at this place.

It is desirable to present a summary of both the 2000 and 2005 National Curriculum Frameworks for School Education of India because both to have different philosophical approaches. The strategies of developing the two Frameworks too were different.

National Curriculum Framework for School Education 2000: Salient Features

The National Council of Educational Research and Training has to advise and assist the Government of India in formulating and implementing policies and programmes in the field of education, particularly school education. To that end, it has been preparing, after the interval of roughly every decade, a National Curriculum Framework for School Education and giving broad guidelines about how to address the major concerns and issues before the nation. The states have been, subsequently, adopting or adapting these curricular guidelines to develop their own detailed curricula, syllabi and curricular materials.

The 2000 Curriculum Framework encompasses all the stages of school education from the pre-primary to the higher secondary. It is a product an open democratic national level discussions and deliberations generated through a Discussion Document produced by the NCERT after extensive and intensive multi-level consultations and debates. Almost all the sections of the Indian society directly or indirectly contribute to the development of the Curriculum Framework. These include noted educationists, experts, teachers and teacher educators, parents, representatives of voluntary organisations, Boards of School Education, State governments and community in general.

While the framework responds to many new societal and pedagogical changes, it remains well within the broad parameters of the National Policy on Education framed in 1986 as revised in 1992. Some of the salient concerns that lay the foundation of the new framework are:

- Building a cohesive society based on pillars of relevance, equity and excellence.
- Integrating indigenous knowledge and recognising India's contribution to the world civilisations.

- Inculcating and nurturing a sense of pride in being an Indian, patriotism and nationalism tempered with the spirit of *Vasudhaiva Kutumbakam.*
- Universalising elementary education and linking education with life-skills.
- Value development at all stages of school education.
- Meeting the challenges of information and communication technology and globalisation.
- Reducing the curriculum load.
- Using culture specific pedagogy.
- Viewing the child as a constructor of knowledge.
- Recognising the interface between cognition, emotion and action.
- Empowering teachers for curriculum development and implementation.
- Coordinated decentralisation of the process of curriculum development.

Some of the major recommendations made for the qualitative improvement at the different stages of school education are as follows:

- Ensuring availability of pre-school education to all children in the country and prohibiting formal teaching and testing of different subjects at this level.
- Integration of environmental education with languages, mathematics and other activities in the first two years of the primary stage.
- Integration of art education, health and physical education and work education into the 'Art of Healthy and Productive Living' at the primary stage.
- Education about religions and inherent values of all religions to be imparted at all the stages of school education.
- Integration of science and technology upto the secondary stage.
- Bringing mathematics closer to life and setting up of mathematics corner in the existing science laboratory for practical mathematics upto the secondary stage.
- Integrated, thematic approach to the teaching of social sciences upto the secondary stage.
- Sticking to the basic policy of three language formula and emphasising the teaching of Hindi as the official language of India and Sanskrit as the language of traditional wisdom and culture of the country.
- Emphasising the implementation of semesterisation at the secondary and higher secondary stages.
- Provision for wide flexibility and freedom in the choice of subjects among the courses to he offered at the higher secondary stage.
- Providing a strong vocational stream for enhancing employability and entrepreneurship at the higher secondary stage.
- Provision for a general academic and specialised elective language course at the higher secondary stage.

- Evolving a humane, learner friendly, error free, responsive and transparent evaluation system.
- Reducing the predominance of external examinations and removal of the concept of pass and fail categories upto Class X.
- Use of different methods of grading scholastic and co-scholastic areas of learning.
- Use of alternative evaluation procedures for learners with special needs.

Towards the effective implementation of the framework the following specific recommendations have been made:

- Adoption of suitable implementation strategies for the orientation, participation and accountability of teachers, parents, community and the managers of the system.
- Suggestions for specific implementation strategies for promoting values, ensuring the inclusion of learners with various challenges in the mainstream, and mobilising the requisite resources for achieving the educational goals of the country.

National Curriculum Framework for School Education 2005: Salient Features

The National Policy on Education (NPE, 1986) proposed the National Curriculum Famework as a means of evolving a national system of education, recommending a core component derived from the vision of national development enshrined in the Constitution. The Programme of Action (POA, 1992) elaborated this focus by emphasising relevance, flexibility and quality.

Seeking guidance from the Constitutional vision of India as a secular, egalitarian and pluralistic society, founded on the values of social justice and equality, certain broad aims of education have been identified in this document. These include independence of thought and action, sensitivity to others' well-being and feelings, learning to respond to new situations in a flexible and creative manner, pre-disposition towards participation in democratic processes, and the ability to work towards and contribute to economic processes and social change. For teaching to serve as a means of strengthening our democratic way of life, it must respond to the presence of first generation school-goers, whose retention is imperative owing to the Constitutional amendment that has made elementary education a fundamental right of every child. Ensuring health, nutrition and an inclusive school environment empowering all children in their learning, across differences of caste, religion, gender, disability, is enjoined upon as by the Constitutional amendment. The fact that learning has become a source of burden and stress on children and their parents is an evidence of a deep distortion in educational aims and quality. To correct this distortion, the present NCF proposes five guiding principles for curriculum development *(i)* connecting knowledge to life outside the school; *(ii)* ensuring that learning shifts away from rote methods; *(iii)* enriching the curriculum so that it goes beyond textbooks; (iv) making examinations more flexible and integrating them with classroom life; and (v) nurturing an overriding identity informed by caring concerns within the democratic polity of the country.

All our pedagogic efforts during the primary classes greatly depend on professional planning and the significant expansion of Early Childhood Care and Education (ECCE). Indeed, the revision of primary school syllabi and textbooks needs to be undertaken in the light of the well-known principles ECCE. The nature of knowledge and children's own strategies of learning are discussed in Chapter 2, which formulates a theoretical basis for the recommendations made in Chapter 3 in the different curricular area. The fact that knowledge is constructed by the child implies that curricula, syllabi and textbooks should enable the teacher in organising classroom experiences in consonance with the child's nature and environment, and thus, providing opportunities for all children. Teaching should aim at enhancing children's natural desire and strategies to learn. Knowledge needs to be distinguished from information, and teaching needs to be seen as a professional activity, not as coaching for memorisation or as transmission of facts. Activity is the heart of the child's attempt to make sense of the world around him/her. Therefore, every resource must be deployed to enable children to express themselves, handle objects, explore their natural and social milieu, and to grow up healthy. If children's classroom experiences are to be organised in a manner that permit them to construct knowledge, then our school system requires substantial systemic reforms (Chapter 5) and re-conceptualisation of curricular areas or school subject (Chapter 3) and resources to improve the quality of the school ethos (Chapter 4).

In all the four familiar areas of the school curriculum, *i.e.,* language, mathematics, science and social sciences, significant changes are recommended with a view to making education more relevant to the present day and future needs, and in order to alleviate the stress with which children are coping today. This NCF recommends the softening of subject boundaries that children are coping today. This NCF recommends the softening of subject boundaries so that children can get a taste of integrated knowledge and the joy of understanding. In addition, plurality of textbooks and other material, which could incorporate local knowledge and traditional skills, and a stimulating school environment that responds to the child's home and community environment, are also suggested. In language, a renewed attempt to implement the three-language formula is suggested, along with an emphasis on the recognition of children's mother tongues, including tribal languages, as the best medium of education. The multilingual character of Indian society should be seen as a resource to promote multilingual proficiency in every child, which includes proficiency in English. This is possible only if learning builds on a sound language pedagogy in the mother tongue. Reading and writing, listening and speech, contribute to the child's progress in all curricular areas and must be the basis for curriculum planning. Emphasis on reading throughout the primary classes is necessary to give every child a solid foundation for school learning.

The teaching of mathematics should enhance the child's resources to think and reason to visualise and handle abstractions, to formulate and solve problems. This broad spectrum of aims can be covered by teaching relevant and important mathematics embedded the child's experience. Succeeding in mathematics should be seen as the right of every child. For this, widening its scope and relating it to other subjects is essential. The infrastructural challenge involved in making available computer hardware, and software and connectivity to every school should be pursued.

The teaching of science should be recast so that it enables children to examine and analyse everyday experiences. Concerns and issues pertaining to the environment should be emphasised in every subject and through a wide range of activities involving outdoor project work. Some of the information and understanding flowing from such projects could contribute to the elaboration of a publicly accessible, transparent database on India's environment, which would in turn become a most valuable educational resource. If well planned, many of these student projects could lead to knowledge generation. A social movement along the lines of *Children's Science Congress* should be visualised in order to promote discovery learning across the nation, and eventually throughout South Asia.

In the social sciences, the approach proposed in the NCF recognises disciplinary market while emphasising integration on significant themes, such as water. A paradigm shift is recommended, proposing the study of the social sciences from the perspective of marginalised groups. Gender justice and a sensitivity towards issues related to SC and ST communities and minority sensibilities must inform all sectors of the social sciences. Civics should be recast as political science, and the significance of history as a shaping influence on the child's conception of the past and civic identity should be recognised.

This NCF draws attention to four other curricular area: work, the art and heritage crafts, health and physical education, and peace. In the context of work, certain radical steps to link learning with work from the primary stage upwards are suggested on the ground that work transforms knowledge into experience and generates important personal and social values, such as self-reliance, creativity and co-operation. It also inspires new forms of knowledge an creativity. At the senior level, a strategy to formally recognise out-of-school resources for work is recommended to benefit children who opt for livelihood-related education. Such out-of-school agencies need accreditation so that they can provide 'work benches' where children can work with tools and other resources. Craft mapping is recommended to identify zones where vocational training in craft forms involving local craft persons can be made available to children.

Art as a subject at all stages is recommended, covering all four major spheres, *i.e.* music, dance, visual arts and theatre. The emphasis should be on interactive approaches, not instruction, because the goal of art education is to promote aesthetic and personal awareness and the ability to express oneself in different forms. The importance of India's heritage crafts, both in terms of their economic and aesthetic values, should be recognised as being relevant to school education.

The child's success at school depends on nutrition and well-planned physical activity programmes, hence resources and school time must be deployed for the strengthening of the mid-day meal programme. Special efforts are needed to ensure that girls receive as much attention in health and physical education programmes as boys from the pre-school stage upwards.

Peace as a pre-condition for national development and as a social temper is proposed as a comprehensive value framework that has immense relevance today in view of the growing tendency across the world towards intolerance and violence as a way of resolving conflicts. The potential of peace education for socialising children into a democratic and just culture can be actualised through appropriate activities and a judicious choice of topics in all subjects and at all stages. Peace education as an area of study is recommended for inclusion in the curriculum for teacher education.

The school ethos is discussed as a dimension of the curriculum as it pre-disposes the child towards the aims of education and strategies of learning necessary for success at school. As a resource, school time needs to be planned in a flexible manner. Locally planned and flexible school calendars and time-tables which permit time slots of different lengths required for different kinds of activities, such as project work and outdoor excursions to natural and heritage sites, are recommended. Efforts are required for preparing more learning resources for children, especially books and reference material in regional languages, for school and teacher reference libraries, and for access to interactive rather than disseminative technologies. The NCF emphasises the importance of multiplicity and fluidity of options at the senior secondary level, discouraging the entrenched tendency to place children in fixed streams, and limiting opportunities of children, especially from the rural areas.

In the context of systemic reforms, this document emphasises strengthening *Panchayati Raj* institutions by the adoption of a more streamlined approach to encourage community participation as a means of enhancing quality and accountability. A variety of school-based projects pertaining to the environment could help create the knowledge base for the *Panchayati Raj* institutions to better manage and regenerate local environmental resources. Academic planning and leadership at the school level is essential for improving quality and strategic differentiation of roles is necessary at block and cluster levels. In teacher education, radical steps are required to reverse the recent trend towards the dilution of professional norms as recommended by the Chattopadhyaya Commission (1984). Pre-service training programmes need to be more comprehensive and lengthy, incorporating sufficient opportunities for observation of children and integration of pedagogic theory with practice through school internship.

Examination reforms constitute the most important systemic measure to be taken for curricular renewal and to find a remedy for the growing problem of psychological pressure that children and their parents feel, especially in Classes X and XII. Specific measures include changing the typology of the question paper so that reasoning and creative abilities replace memorisation as the basis of evaluation, and integration of examinations with classroom life by encouraging transparency and internal assessment. The stress on pre-board examinations must be reversed, and strategies enabling children to opt for different levels of attainment should be encouraged to overcome the present system of generalised classification into 'pass' and 'fail' categories.

Finally, the document recommends partnerships between the school system and other civil society groups, including non-governmental organisations and teacher organisations. The innovative experiences already available should be mainstreamed, and awareness of the challenges implied in the Universalisation of Elementary Education (UEE) should become a subject of wide-ranging cooperation between the state and all agencies concerned about children.

8

Highlights of Right to Education Act, 2009

Salient Provisions Right of Children to Free and Compulsory Education Act, 2009 (No. 35 of 2009 – 26th August, 2009)

1. A child has a right to education until the completion of elementary education.
2. A child will be admitted to a class on the basis of age.
3. The government or the local authority to establish schools in the neighbourhood for catering to this need.
4. The central and the state governments to share expenditure in this regard.
5. All parents will have an obligation to send their children to school.
6. Schools may not charge any capitation fee.
7. Teachers to possess minimum prescribed qualifications (that is academic and professional qualifications and would have qualified at the Teachers Eligibility Test).
8. Each school may have a Management Committee.
9. Schools may maintain the prescribed teacher-pupil ratio.
10. Services of teachers may not be used for non-educational work.
11. Teachers may not engage in private tuitions.
12. Schools may follow the Curriculum Content and Evaluation practices as prescribed by the designated Academic Authority i.e. NCERT. State governments may notify these.
13. Every student may be given a certificate on the completion of Elementary Education.
14. Child Rights as enunciated by the National Advisory Council may be protected. The Central government may constitute a National Advisory Council and the States will constitute State Advisory Councils for ensuring this.
15. The Central government shall have the power to make rules and issue directions for carrying out the provisions of the Act.
16. There will be no prosecution for offences without the approval of the appropriate government.
17. The Norms prescribed by the Act are:

Number of Teachers

Class I-V

Students Strength	*No. of Teachers*
Up to 60 children	– Two Teachers
61-90	– Three Teachers
91-120	– Four Teachers
120-200	– Five Teachers

Above 200 Teacher-Pupil Ratio of 1:40 to be maintained

Class VI-VIII

At least one teacher for Science and Mathematics

At least one teacher for Social Studies

A full time Head Teacher

Part time instructors for

- Art Education
- Health and Physical Education

Buildings

- One classroom per teacher
- Office room, Store, Head Teachers' Room
- Separate Toilets for Boys and Girls
- Safe Drinking Water
- Kitchen (for mid-day meals)
- Playground

Working Days and Teachers Work

- Classes I-V: 200 working days with 800 instructional hours
- Class VI-VIII: 220 working days with 1000 instructional hours
- 45 Teaching and Preparation Hours per teacher per week

The RTE-2009 among other things provides that:

- Education is compulsory for every child upto the age of 14 Years.
- Every child has a right to free education upto 14 Years of age.
- Every child can seek admission to any class upto class 8, only on the basis of age.
- No child shall be detained in any class upto class 8.
- Every school will admit 20 % students from the deprived sections of the society.

Doubtlessly the provisions of the RTE 2009 were made with good intentions but its implementation in letter and not in spirit raised many eye-brows and even created problems.

The schools declined to admit students to classes I to VIII, only the basis of age, on some pretext or the other. Wherever this was done, these children invariably were much older than their peers which created problems of social adjustment. The problems got compounded when they could not by law be detained. When these children reached the secondary classes and where detention was not prohibited, they could not move with the class and clear class IX. At this they and their parents raised a hue and cry for undeservingly claiming a pass.

The RTE 2009 also provided for the admission of 20% students in class I belonging to the reserved categories in all schools including the private schools without paying any fees. A large proportion of these students were often first generation learners. Their parents had migrated from villages to towns in search of work. They had no value for education, and thought that only going to school means getting educated without effort. They also had poor standards of health and hygiene. The children, therefore, often got unwell and had to remain absent from classes. Furthermore, the arrival of a guest in the house too was good enough reason to remain absent from school without any remorse.

For such children the RTE 2009 did not provide for any remedial classes. In fact every teacher should have had a Teaching work load, a part of which should have been reserved for teaching such remedial classes.

In fact special learning material and aids should have been developed and regular compulsory remedial classes organized as a part of the school time tables.

The schools too took these non-fee paying children as a drain in their incomes and were indifferent to their special needs.

As an off-shoot of the provisions of the RTE, the teachers to be recruited or confirmed in their positions for teaching classes I-VIII had to qualify at a Teacher Eligibility Test (TET) in addition to the normal prescribed qualifications. But there were a large number of unqualified guest teachers appointed on contract bases on fixed salaries, who claimed to be confirmed as regular teachers. This also ignited agitations and generated court cases. These teachers could be given a two year time to acquire the needed qualifications.

SECTION III
Basics of Pedagogy

9

Phenomena of Learning

A Macro Overview

Teaching becomes successful only when learning takes place. It is, therefore, necessary for teachers to be conversant with the manner in which learning comes to occur.

As learning is the undisputed goal of teaching, it is desirable to understand the phenomenon of learning—the factors that accelerate it and those that retard it, the conditions which make it easy and those that prove to be road blocks, in its way, the situations which promote its success and those that don't.

Education is supposed to create:

— enablement
— empowerment and
— enrichment

and learning for inculcation of competencies is the most important means for attaining these goals through the abilities it creates in the individuals, which result in enhancement of his capacities as reflected through his behaviour.

Three main types of interactions take place in schools as a part of the teaching-learning process.

Teacher-Learner Interaction where the teacher normally plays a dominant role and the student usually a passive one. In these situations *the concentration level of students is minimal.*

Learner – Learner Interaction, where the students work in situations of participatory learning or group work or project work. In these situations *the level of concentration rises/increases.*

Self-Self interaction or self-learning or auto-instruction which marks the beginning of self-directed learning, where the challenges increase and *the level of concentration is the highest.*

It, therefore, becomes an important function or responsibility of the teachers to make the students independent of him by making them the '*subjects*' rather than '*objects*' of education.

Technology too has now come to play an important role in the teaching-learning process. Technological aids, working models, video films are now being increasingly used, not just for augmenting knowledge but more so for providing insight into varied facts and phenomenon of the environment. *The television has added a new curriculum, on the educational scene, as an important supplement to the curriculum of the home, of the immediate environment, of the peer group and that of the school. The internet is the new source of enrichment curriculum.* It has, however, to be simultaneously appreciated that *technology can only at best be an enabler and not the answer.* It can never replace the teacher though it can surely provide valuable reinforcements to his plans and designed programmes of instruction. Technology has surely to be adjusted and adapted to the maturity level of the students and the curriculum they are learning from. The technological resources have also to take care of the pre-requisites *of availability* and *accessibility.* Technological aids because of their versatile and universal applications have but to admit adaptation, as they can be used at any time, at any place and by any individual. These aids to instruction, therefore, have to be relevant, efficient and utilised with accountability.

The delivery modes in education too have of late undergone a dramatic change and these changes have but to be taken cognisance of, for being relevant to the environmental transformations and transactions. The methodologies pressed into service, therefore, have to cater to these demands and be open to other changes that may get ushered in, in course of time. The main of these according to present day demands are:

- Instructor-led learning
- Distance learning
- Learning through technological aids
- On-line self-learning

The extensions and diversifications of techniques have not just become desirable but necessary, as education cannot survive in its present form and *students have to take over the responsibility of learning from the teachers.* In this context it will be *undesirable to take students as customers and consumers of education by converting the philanthropic activity that education should be into commercial and a business enterprise.* The concept of 'Education for All' has, therefore, to receive our focussed attention.

There has also to be a *marriage of technology and pedagogy* for self-growth for influencing the process of growth in its wider context.

Irrespective of the variations in the methods of teaching, some of the common purposes to be served and challenges to be met by them are those of:

- Modernisation
- Globalisation

- Liberalisation
- Technologisation
- Professionalisation and
- Indianisation

The last of these, is the most important because education cannot succeed, if it is alien to the social and cultural ethos as also the heritage.

The salient aspects of theory and practice of learning have been vary explicity and yet briefly enunciated by *Rajamal P. Devadas* in her book Methods of Teaching Home Science which is given below:

"How does Learning take place? What are the conditions which favour learning? Learning is change or modification that occurs in performance as a result of training and experience, (*McConnell*). Learning in school means, modifying or changing the behaviour of the pupils, in terms of achieving the goals. It is the process by which the pupil profits from past experience. According to *Skinner* "learning is a process of progressive behaviour adaptation." When learning takes place, new technique or ability, based on past experience, develops.

Learning leads to establishing relationships between the stimuli and the responses, through a mental connection. Learning, thus, implies connecting ideas, events phenomenon and so on. Man is the greatest of all learners, because he is capable of forming many connections. Good teaching based on the psychology of learning and adequate preparation, leads to numerous connections born out of effective thinking, planning and execution. Understanding the factors involved in the learning process is, therefore, important for the teacher. Pupils respond to knowledge in different ways. When the teacher recognises the factors which favour learning, she will make the teaching-learning process efficient accelarated and economical leading to deeper learning, by discarding the wrong steps and establishing the correct connections.

Principles of Learning

Hullfish and Smith have expounded five principles of learning. According to these authors, learning is:

1. Motivated when the learner has some stake in the activity.
2. Geared to the learner's level and compatible with his physical and intellectual ability.
3. Patterned when the learner can see meaningful relationships between the activity and the goal.
4. Evaluated when the learner has some way of knowing the progress he is making, and
5. Integrated with personal and social development, when the learner experiences satisfactory growth and adjustments.

Motivation in Learning

Motivation is the most powerful director of learning. In learning and living motivation is indispensable for success. Achievement in learning depends largely on how much the pupil really wants to study and succeed and how far he is willing to put forth the cost in terms of time human effort and energy to reach the goal.

Teachers use many approaches for motivating children to learn. *Compulsion, coercion, tempting with reward or praise and rousing their interest and eagerness to acquire knowledge are some of the common methods used.* Wherever all-round development of character and personality through voluntary self-activities, self-direction and self-expression are emphasised, coercion and tempting will have no place. Pupils learn and develop best when they exert their utmost, when they energise their responses and behaviour and when they have dynamic relationship with their environment.

Teachers must learn the *art of stimulating and sustaining pupils' interest in learning*. A high degree of motivation helps in impelling pupils into action and ensures their active participation in learning activities. Mere repetition does not lead to learning. The repetition must be purposive and active; it must enlist the involvement of the pupil. The teacher needs to direct the learning process through such a positive motivation.

Richardson has formulated the following principles linking teaching and learning.

Learning

1. results from the active involvement of the learner,
2. begins with the learner's present achievement,
3. increases its effectiveness with motivation,
4. occurs through various channels,
5. bases meanings of words and other symbols on experience,
6. takes place in the total organism in response to the total situation, and
7. varies with individual differences in respect of needs and abilities.

In *Thorndike's* view, the laws which operate in the learning process are those of *readiness, effect and exercise including frequency and recency*. If the pupil has been prepared to learn through meaningful suggestions, he is ready to learn. The *law of readiness* then operates. If an effort brings success, reward or satisfaction, it is likely to be repeated. If the size of the incentive or reward increases, the efficiency of learning may also increase, provided the motivation continues. This illustrates the *law of effect*. The speed of performance depends on the satisfaction-value of the reward. 'Adaptation', 'adjustment', 'regulative change' and similar terms describe successful learning, indicating effect. Repeated effort gathers strength making repetition easier. This is the *law of frequency*. The act that has been performed recently has an advantage of being easy to repeat. This is the *law of recency*. The laws of frequency and recency together constitute the *law of exercise*. However, as learning ability depends upon the stages of growth reached by the nervous and muscular systems, mere exercise or drill alone cannot effect learning.

Maturation and Learning

Maturity has an important bearing on the learning process, particularly the maturity reached by the central nervous system and the muscular system. As the organism matures, the innate potentialities unfold themselves. In the development and functioning of brain, adequate nutrition during pregnancy and early childhood plays a dominant role. The degree of maturation necessary for a particular training to be effective, is usually called '*learning readiness*'.

Thyne points out four features of learning in terms of behavioural outcomes:

(1) In each learning situation the learner learns to do something. This is the feature of behaviour;
(2) Also previously he did something differently—hence, there is change of behaviour;
(3) The change of behaviour occurs in a particular kind of situation and
(4) Finally the old and new behaviour do not merely happen in the situation—each is occasioned by, or is a response to it. To learn is to adopt a new response to a situation.

There are four requirements for learning to take place; cue, force, promptness and reinforcement. Cue means, "In any instance of learning, there must be a series of situations showing the 'cue' of that instance. The teacher has to ensure a series of situations containing the cue. For example giving the page numbers in the references assigned to the pupil. Behaviour has two aspects: form and time of beginning. The learner must make his response in terms of these two which constitute the situation, which must have '*force*' for learning to take place. The situation must make the learner react and elicit a response." In any instance of learning, the 'cue' must have 'force'. '*Promptness*' ensures that the response which the cue evokes has the specified form. In any instance of learning, a 'prompt' must appear in one or more of the successive situations. In the school, the 'prompt' is usually in the form of instruction form the teacher. '*Reinforcement*' implies that the specified form of 'response' must be tied to the 'cue'. Learning will occur only when all these four functions are fulfilled.

Conditioned Learning

Conditioning is a form of learning in which the capacity to elicit a response is transferred from one stimulus to another. Conditioning means the establishment of a connection between a response and a stimulus which may not have a known natural connection with it. Conditioning represents learning at a simple level. The principles of conditioning in learning were first established by *Pavlov*. He was conducing some experiments on dogs. Food is a natural stimulus to the salivary reflex. Pavlov demonstrated that the dog can be made to salivate to any stimulus associated with food, such as resonating a tuning fork. Since the secretion of saliva, which is a reflex action, resulted from the dog's response to the stimulus of the tuning fork, Pavlov designated such reflexes as 'Conditioned reflexes'.

Trial and Error

Clayton describes that as early as 1898, *Thorndike* published a theory of learning, based primarily upon animal experiments, such as the cat in a box. Later, he expanded and developed this approach with applications to school situations. The unit of demonstrated or displayed behaviour was a relationship, an association or connection between sense impressions and impulses to action. Faced with a situation, the learner will engage in a number of responses eventuating in the one that 'solves' the problem. In repetitions of the situation, the incorrect responses will diminish and the correct response will become fixed. Learning, therefore, is a trial and error process. In the initial trials, there are a large number of errors, but as trials are repeated, there is no error and the result is success.

Insightful Learning

Kohler put a chimpanzee in a cage and suspended a banana from the roof outside the cage. Two sticks were placed inside the cage. Neither of the two was long enough to reach the banana. After some unsuccessful attempts, the monkey incidentally found that one stick fitted into the hole of the other, but not properly. This gave the animal a bright idea. It joined the two sticks firmly together and got the banana. This was not an exploratory type of learning involving conditioning or trial and error, but a sudden flash, leading to insight. 'Insightful learning' is common among human beings.

Learning by Imitation

Learning by imitation, happens by observing others doing things which one finds difficult to do himself and imitating them. Imitation helps to curtail errors, supplying cues for the learner. Speaking, writing, playing and numerous other skills are learned by observing others and repeating what they do. The pupil imitates the person he admires, one whom he would like to resemble. He identifies himself with the role model in the sense that he wants to be like him. According no *Nunn*, "Imitation is but the first stage in the creation of individuality, and the richer the scope for imitation, the richer the developed individuality will be." Imitation is never a complete reproduction. There is always variation indicating choice, preference for details and creativity.

Remembering and Forgetting

There are several factors and practices which influence remembering and forgetting. Remembering is an active process. Remembering is important for the pupil because by remembering what he has learnt, he can recall and learn more. Studying a material at a stretch is known as *massed learning*. When the material is learnt with intervals of rest, the method is called *distributed learning or spaced learning*. It has not been established that distributed learning is better than massed learning since unspread learning often leads to confusion.

Learning should proceed from the *simple to the complex*, from *whole to parts*, from general to specific, from concrete to abstract. Learning a lesson as one whole unit is known as '*whole learning*'. Dividing the lesson and learning the smaller units is termed *part learning*. Whole learning is more advantageous to the pupil, since he can comprehend the whole. However, if a passage is too long, dividing it into meaningful subgroups (paragraphs) will facilitate learning.

The more often a learned material is repeated, the better is the retention. The pupil must be encouraged either to recite or review often, the lessons learnt.

The meaningfulness of a lesson to be learned is the most important feature affecting the rate of learning and the amount of retention. *Guilford* demonstrated that *the more meaningful the material is to the pupils*, *the greater is its retention*. Retention over various intervals of time is greater for substance learning than for rote learning. Factual information is forgotten faster than the ability to explain, interpret and apply general principles. Therefore, *Guilford* has stressed the use of concrete rather than abstract materials and direct experience rather than second or third hand experience, particularly with young children.

All lessons should be made as meaningful as possible. It is purposeless to ask children to spell words, which have no purposeful meaning for them. Scientific facts are rapidly forgotten, unless reinforced by relevant experience. Dates and names are valueless as isolated facts. They must be incorporated into units which have significance for pupils. *Meaningful organisation of material* can be developed by attention to similarities and differences and by emphasis on the who, what, when, where and why of relationships.

Curves of forgetting generally show greater forgetting of verbal lessons as compared to those of motor skills. *Ebbinghaus's* pioneer work on learning and forgetting with the nonsense syllables, which he invented in order to have learning tasks free of previous experience, showed a rapid initial drop followed by a gradual slide to nearly complete forgetting. The curve of forgetting varies considerably depending upon the extent to which school work has meaning, relatedness and organisation. There are also situations when overlearning or occasional recall occur.

Transfer of Training (Learning)

Mastery of one skill may facilitate the learning of another skill. This is known as *transfer of training (learning). Thorndike's* experiments and experiences have proved that transfer of learning is not a universal occurrence.

The distinction between retention and transfer, rests upon the similarity or difference between the test situation and the learning situation. *When the situation in which learning is being tested replicates the situation in which it was learned, retention can be measured, but when the situation differs, transfer of training is being measured.*

The following factors appear to influence learning and its transfer:

1. The perceptual clarity of the task, in points of relevant cues and appropriate responses.
2. The meaningfulness of the material and the understanding obtained.
3. The context in which the skill or knowledge is acquired.
4. Conditions contributing to, or reducing the interference between tasks, such as similarity of stimuli or responses, and degree of overlearning.

Ultimately, each aspect of the school curriculum must be seen as part of the total curriculum—the situations which provide learning experiences including those outside the school and its prescribed courses used for teaching and testing situations. They also include those that cater to individual differences, motivations, interests, attitudes, achievements and development.

Optimising Learning

Lacey's guidelines based on the principles of learning, emphasise that pupils learn most effectively when:

1. teaching is within the context of their previous experience.
2. an emotionally and intellectually stimulating environment is present.
3. they feel secure with the learning situation and have respect for the teacher.
4. multiple, concrete and first hand experiences are available as bases for concept formation.
5. they see the whole situation as well as the various parts in relation to the whole.
6. they are engaged in activities calling for critical thinking and problem-solving.
7. they participate and share actively in selecting problems and goals which have meaning for them.
8. learning experiences are planned in a meaningful, sequential pattern, in which every learning activity has a definite objective.

9. there is provision for differences in meeting the individual abilities, interests and needs.
10. meaningful practice reinforces sensory experiences.
11. the teacher plans learning experiences as carefully for attitudes and appreciations as for knowledge and skills.
12. learning gained in the classroom leads to purposeful action related to it and transfers readily to out-of-school situations, and
13. they participate in the evaluation of their learning experiences and receive emotional and intellectual satisfaction and a sense of achievement.

Since learning cannot be separated from teaching, good guidance and effective procedures are required of the teacher. She needs to apply knowledge of the principles of both teaching and learning, in planning the educational activities and more particularly for relating them to life experiences with a view to making the pursuits concrete and meaningful to the children.

10

Process, Principles and Maxims of Teaching and Learning

Emergence of Concept of the Pedagogy

Pedagogy was originally conceived.as the art of teaching, particularly because of the limitless flexibility it was imbued with and the freedom that the teacher enjoyed in giving direction to it. With almost no documentation, the teacher used to be the source of all the tenets of pedagogy and the students were known as the disciples of such and such a teacher whose stamp and legacy they carried. Education then was individualised and multi-faceted. In those times 'Tomorrow' was not very different from 'Yesterday', therefore, teachers tailored their educational programmes accordingly to prepare their students for effectively discharging their future responsibilities. Towards this end they continuously kept on changing the content and process of their educational programmes.

The pressure of growing numbers, then led to the emergence of small educational units. These were housed in places of worship and scriptures were among the textbooks. The pedagogy was oral one way traffic and memorisation the methodology of learning. There was no standardisation among these institutions.

The Universities were no doubt great seats of learning and Centres of Excellence. Education in India became organised and systematised under the influence of Western Education from the second half of the nineteenth century. .The establishment of the first three Universities at the Presidencies of Calcutta, Bombay and Madras after the Wood's Despatch (1854) and of the School Examination Boards the first of which was established in UP in 1921 marked the formal beginning of this systemisation.

Pedagogy originally used to be considered as something concerned only with the theory and practice of teaching and as an 'Art'. However subsequently when the phenomena of teaching was analysed and dissected, it came to be realised that teaching becomes successful only when learning takes place. The formal acceptance of this experiential inference, amalgamated teaching and learning and pedagogy and is now referred to as 'Art and Science' of pedagogy, covering operations of the teaching-learning process as a whole. On the side of teaching, it deals with the conventional and unconventional methodologies of instruction and on the side of learning with the principles of learning.

> Learning, is the core determinant of growth and the sole path of progress. Our main effort, therefore, ought to be to make it *enabling empowering and enriching.*

Fundamental Foundations

As already mentioned in passing earlier, objectives are the anchor points of both learning experiences and evaluation. As the teacher must be thoroughly acquainted about 'both these' they are being briefly discussed in this context below:

The most important understanding, which the theoretician and practitioner of education ought to develop, is the intrinsic two-way relationship between the instructional objectives, learning experiences and evaluation techniques. Teaching is planned so as to achieve the objectives set in advance and evaluation techniques help us know the extent to which the inputs provided have been effective in helping pupils realise attain the desired objectives.

Objective-based instruction and objective-based evaluation, thus, ought to form the crux of all educational programmes and practices of educational institutions. The relationship has been presented through the following well-known diagram by Rolf Taylor :

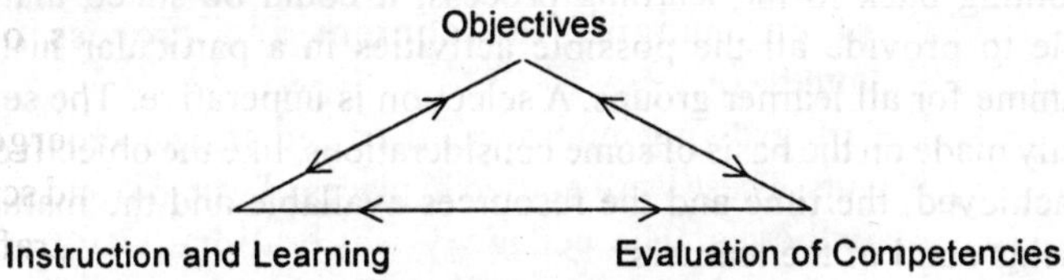

Diagram 10.1

First of all, let us examine the mental processes involved in the achievement of instructional objectives. The whole process of instruction indeed ought to be geared to this end. Tracing the steps of the process, we can say that *teaching* becomes successful only when learning takes place. *Learning* takes place through experiences. *Experiences* consist of the absorption of ideas through different senses. *Senses* react to external situations (*stimuli*) for absorbing ideas. These situations are made up of learners' activities which are, thus, the starting points for the attainment of objectives The manipulation of teaching learning activities with a view to realising the desired objectives are 'Methods of Teaching'.

Based on the gains of participation, in the teaching-learning activities and processes, the evaluation instruments are designed for assessing the degree of the realisation of the expected goals. The analysis of performance reveals the shortfalls in performance or hard spots in learning, if any. The process is then reversed and the learning experiences are examined, revised and re-provided for the effective realisation of the goals. If it is considered necessary even objectives are modified, to make them realistic—both achievable and evaluable.

Objectives, have two specifications the *'competency'* specification and the *'content'* specification. Both these specifications converge on to a central point which we call *teaching-learning situations*. These situations as the synthesis of the two aforesaid specifications of objectives, become the basis for designing instructional programmes and evaluation strategies in respect of both the content and competency specifications of the objectives.

The extension of the model also shows the relationship between evaluation and learning. This process can be expressed as under :

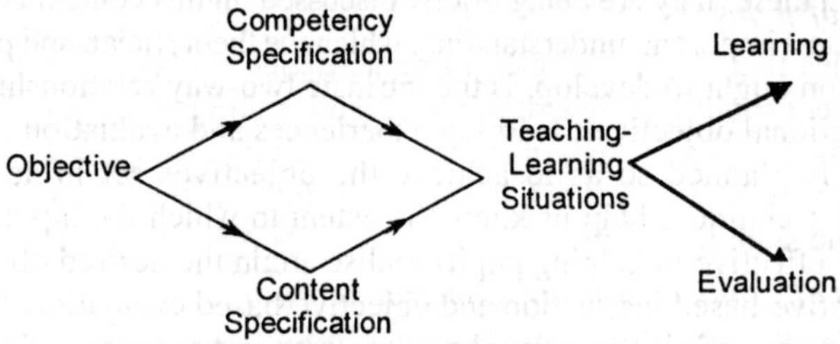

Diagram 10.2

Coming back to the learning process, it could be stated that it is not possible to provide all the possible activities in a particular instructional programme for all learner groups. A selection is imperative. The selection is primarily made on the basis of some considerations, like the objectives desired to be achieved, the time and the resources available and the maturity level and background of the learners.

In order to clearly visualise, the relationship between objectives and learner's activities, let us for a while study the following table, giving the activities and the corresponding objectives that each can help achieve and try to draw some conclusions from it:

Pupil Activities	*Objectives*
Execution of Practical Work	Understanding, Skill
Organising an Exhibition	Interest, Appreciation, Application, Skill
Excursions /Field Trips	Knowledge, Understanding
Discussions	Understanding, Critical thinking
Lectures	Knowledge, Understanding
Dramatisation	Comprehension, Interest

The generalisations which can be easily drawn from the above table are as under :

- Different activities lead to the realisation of different objectives or conversely it is not possible to realise all the objectives through a single activity.
- For the achievement of any one objective, it may be necessary to employ one or more activities or conversely one activity may, at the same time, lead to the achievement of more than one objective.

Principles of Objective-Based Instruction

These generalisations lead us to some of the following important principles of objective-based instruction:

Principle of Relevance

This implies that the teaching-learning activities chosen for being pressed into service, should be relevant to the objective and possess the potentiality of achieving it. As it is not possible for all the activities to help in the realisation of all the objectives, they will have to be carefully selected to conform to the needs of the situations.

Principles of Concomitant or Collateral Learning

This implies that activities when undertaken by learners, do not help in the realisation of only a single objective. Indeed, they act in varied directions and while deliberately attempting to develop a particular objective, they may also help achieve some other objectives as well simultaneously, in an incidental manner.

Principle of Adequacy

This implies that the activities selected should be adequate for achieving the desired objectives of instruction, comprehensively. This adequacy in respect of activities is achieved through the selection of relevant activities in adequately sufficient number, the frequency of their repetition and the spacing of offering these learning experiences.

Principle of Variety

As a corollary of the above three principles, it could be said that for accomplishing the desired objectives, it is necessary to choose and use a variety of activities.

Instructional Approaches

The above principles lead us, almost naturally to a discussion on teaching methods for curriculum transaction, which could be defined as *the systematic organisation of activities that result in learning and thus, in the achievement of the desired objectives of instruction.*

Teaching methods can be sub-divided into two categories :

(a) *The Standard Methods of Teaching*, and

(b) *The Specific Methods of Instruction* designed for achieving certain emergent purposes.

The Standard Methods of Instruction are quite well known. The activities to be pressed into service in the process of instruction, through them are also almost fixed. These designated activities are followed sequentially almost in a ritualistic manner. The objectives that are possible to be achieved through such methods are also commonly known.

The Specific Methods of Instruction on the other hand, are a product of teachers' ingenuity for achieving the specific purposes which may emerge in the course of teaching or those that the teacher may deem necessary. These are original in their nature and involve a unique organisation of activities with a view to achieving specific goals desired to be realised by the teacher in the process of instruction. They do not admit any rigidity either in the sequence of the steps or in the number or kind of the activities to be used.

Objective-based instruction would mainly follow the latter of the two methods, though efforts can be made to incorporate some of the features of the formal methods of instruction as well.

Planning Enriched Objective-Based Instruction

Objective-based instruction can be divided into the following main operational steps:

- Statement of instructional objectives.
- The preparation and use of objective-based instructional material.
- Planning instruction in keeping with the objectives.

  This planning may consist of the preparation of:

  (a) a year's plan

  (b) a term's plan

  (c) a unit plan

  (d) a class period plan

In advance planning for objective-based instruction, the preparation of an yearly plan is very important. It is the first step for *preparing a time-budget* for covering the course, as a teacher is allotted only a given number of class periods for covering the given specific quantum of the subject matter. As an initial step of planning, the whole content area is divided into different sub-units and allotted class periods in terms of a *time-budget* in the instructional programme. Here the measure of emphasis will be determined by the degree of difficulty of the theme, proportion of resources, energy, time, etc. proposed to be pressed into service for achieving the objectives. This plan can be *hypothetically presented* through a table (Diagram 10.3) based on the supposition that there are six major units of content to be covered and that eighty class periods are available for accomplishing the task.

The next step in the planning of instruction is the preparation of teaching units. These units are to be generally prepared by experts with the help of

Domains of Development →	*Cognitive Areas*			*Affective Areas*		*Psycho-motor Areas*	*Number of Class Periods*
Objectives → ↓ *Units of Content*	*Knowledge*	*Under-standing*	*Application*	*Interests*	*Attitudes*	*Skills*	
U_1	✓				✓		15
U_2		✓		✓			10
U_3	✓		✓			✓	25
U_4		✓			✓		15
U_5	✓		✓				10
U_6	✓	✓		✓		✓	5
Total number of available class periods							80

Digram 10.3

teachers, and are supplied to teachers. Teachers, however, should always remain the masters of the teaching operations and must never become slaves of the teaching units handed down to them. Teachers are supposed to make use of these units according to their specific needs and requirements. Resourceful teachers can also prepare their own teaching units, if they have time and facilities. The preparation of lesson-plans is the subsequent step. From a teaching unit a teacher can prepare lesson-plans for each class period according to need and convenience to fit into the overall time budget.

It will not be out of place to re-emphasise here that *educational objectives as mentioned earlier are derived from several primary sources, chief of which, are the level of psychological development of the child, the social order, the economic environment, the political system, the cultural heritage and the existing store of human knowledge in the society in question.* From the overall educational objectives, are derived the *stage-wise objectives* which become the basis for curriculum development of the different stages of education. From the stage-wise objectives, in turn, are derived the *subject-wise objectives* of teaching which become the basis of the development of the curriculum plans of particular subjects for a particular stage. These subsequently help and guide the preparation of unit-plans and lesson-plans. Taking the processes in the opposite direction, it could be said that the achievement of the different lesson-wise objectives leads to the achievement of unit-wise objectives, the achievement of different unit-wise objectives leads to the achievement of different subject-wise objectives, the achievement of the subject-wise objectives leads to the realisation of stage-wise objectives and these finally lead to the achievement of overall objectives of education.

The above discussion leads us to conclude that there is a parallelism between testing and teaching-learning which can be diagramatically represented as under :

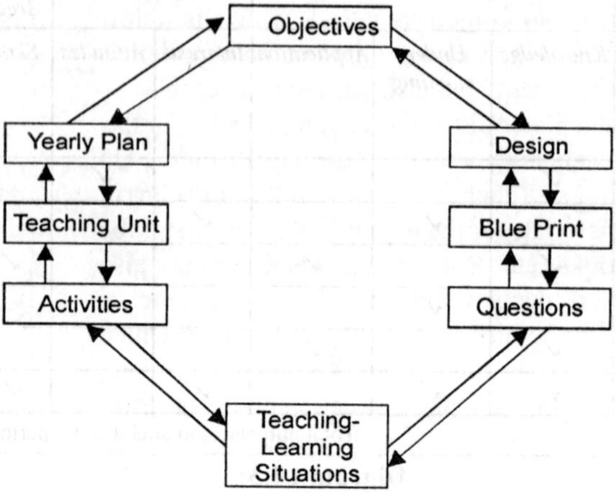

Digram 10.4

Nature and Purpose of Instructional Material

Suitable instructional material is an essential prerequisite for ensuring enriched instruction. There has, of late, been a phenomenal explosion of knowledge. In a good many cases different subjects and topics have assumed new dimensions and meanings. In many places, however, there is a paucity of aids and materials having relevance to related classroom instruction. Syllabi in different subjects are also often very sketchy and generalised in nature. They do not indicate the exact scope of subject-matter desired to be taught and tested. Until 1961, when NCERT came into being curriculum and textbooks also used to be very deficient in many respects.

New types of instructional materials and ways of structuring the content of different subjects and topics of study, leave nothing which is not teachable. Methods of instruction, however, well-conceived will also remain ineffective without a solid grounding in the subject-matter, which is basically offered by instructional materials. Instead of giving only some recapitulatory questions at the end of the chapters, possible projects, surveys, library research, and references about possible websites ought also be given and related exercises built into the content of the related chapters. The books should also give teacher guided and computer assisted curriculum transaction.

Furthermore, evaluation also will fail to appropriately test the objectives, unless the objectives like understanding of major ideas, skills and attitudes are drawn from the solid base of the subject-matter. Activities too in order to be purposeful must fit into the context of what is to be taught. These activities will lose their significance unless teachers have a complete perspective of all the dimensions of the subject-matter.

The main available source of subject-matter to both teachers and learners is instructional material. Instructional material to be effective has but to incorporate enriched content material, which is helpful to the teacher in curriculum transaction. It also ought to contain guidelines for the teacher not only on 'What to teach?' but also on 'How to teach?'

Instructional materials can be developed both for the teachers and for the learners. For teachers they take the form of Resource Units, Teaching Units, Reference Books, Teacher's Handbooks and Curriculum Guides, etc. Instructional materials for the learners comprise of textbooks, supplementary books, workbooks, etc. Both teachers and learners also make use of some common material like textbooks, atlases, internet, etc.

At this place the difference between Teaching Units and Resource Units also needs to be clearly appreciated. Resource units contain basic information from which a teacher can make a selection on the basis of his need. A teaching unit on the other hand lays down specific guidelines about the content and process of education related to the unit of teaching in question which is a part of the curriculum. The teaching units have a direct relevance to the syllabus prescribed as also to the periods of instruction allotted to the particular teaching units and to the classes to be taught. The preparation of teaching units is a crucial exercise and needs both the mastery of the subject-matter as well as the skills related to instructional methodology. Teaching units should neither duplicate the content of textbooks nor should they be a mere compilations of materials culled from advanced books. They have indeed to be specially tailored to specific needs.

The syllabus of the entire year is first to be split into a number of viable units. Each one ought to be autonomous in some ways—in respect of subject-matter, a sequence and relationship with what has gone before and what is to follow in the scheme of instruction should not be overlooked. One teaching unit may be further split into more than one teaching lessons or class periods.

This assumes particular importance in professional courses where there is almost exclusive focus on the development of competencies related to application of knowledge in life/work situations.

The contents of teaching units are merely suggestive. The teachers may use them flexibly according to the needs and exigencies of actual classroom situations. Length of descriptive statements is not a guiding criterion of a good teaching unit. Its usability and the support it offers to the teachers which are the real yardsticks for judging its utility.

Such freedom and flexibility is required because of variations in the students'

• Needs • Abilities • Work-Style • Inter-personal Skills • Exposure

A Suggestive Format of an Instructional Unit

The format of the teaching unit is not rigid. It also need not be uniform in all the subjects and at all levels. However, a broad outline is suggested below.

Introduction

The introduction of the teaching unit should bring out the significance of the topic, its conspicuous character or novelty, its implications and relevance in life. It is to be based on what the learners have studied before and also becomes the basis of the content of the following units.

Specific Objectives

A teaching unit must indicate specific objectives of the topic to be taught. These will comprise the understanding of major ideas, application of related knowledge, in unfamiliar situation development of skills, the development of desired interests and attitudes as expected outcomes of the learning of the unit in question. The formulation of specific objectives is based on the general objectives envisaged in the study of the particular subject.

The formulation of objectives has to be precise, clear and their wording ought to indicate what is significant for learning in respect of the content unit in question. Formulation of objectives is also very crucial, because they give a sense of direction and a perspective to our entire approach of presentation of content, incorporation of activities and evaluation. They should indeed be stated in terms of 'specifications' of the objectives, as to what a learner will be able to do, to demonstrate that s/he has realised the objective in question.

Content Analysis

The content analysis given in a teaching unit as mentioned earlier should not merely reproduce the content given in the textbooks. It should unfold details more vividly and in the correct perspective, which will make teaching graphic and powerful. It may contain extracts from original sources or enriched materials which may not be within the easy reach of the teacher. The content may even contain materials not necessarily falling within the precise purview of specific major ideas, but which may provide appropriate links to forge continuity of its sequence or in supporting it.

Major ideas, which are, in a way, basic concepts, come to be the basic learning points, which are supposed to be internalised by the learners while some peripheral things could be permitted to be forgotton. Some examples of 'Major Ideas' in social sciences are given here under:

- Ashoka's administration symbolised a centralised monarchy.
- Raja Rammohan Roy brought modernity to Indian education.
- A citizen has both rights and duties.
- Industrialisation has brought problems in its wake.
- Early civilisations grew in river beds.
- Scientific developments have not always been for the good of mankind.

The content should also be regularly reviewed and revised to be authentic and up-to-date. If it deals with controversial issues, it should present the different conflicting viewpoints objectively. If it has a generalisation, it should be fully substantiated with supporting data. The content ought to err on the side of comprehensiveness rather than on that of too much simplification or generalised form of global presentation.

Teaching Hints and Activities

Instruction in order to be effective must be objective-based and revolve round *activities.* These activities should be purposeful. They should flow out of the content aimed at the realisation of objectives. Suggestions in this regard must be specific and in the context of the subject-matter. They should necessarily outline the process of instruction, the teacher's role as also the learner's activities and the approaches to their execution. If discussion is suggested, the stages of its actual conduct and various possible questions and issues to be deliberated upon, ought to be broadly indicated. The hints to teachers should be specific. Assignments, projects, surveys whenever suggested, need also to be broadly outlined. They should be creative and not routine and repetitive.

Evaluation of Competencies

Evaluation is an integral part of instruction. It has to be continuous and built into the total teaching-learning process. It ought to be objective-based and comprehensive covering both scholastic and co-scholastic aspects of learners growth. It should also be valid (accurate), reliable (dependable), objective (just), and practicable (feasible). The questions should not merely test memory. Teacher's mastery of the subject-matter and about the rules for framing different forms of question and other tools of evaluation, however, is essential for framing questions properly. In evaluation various procedures and tools of evaluation should be utilised in a bid to fully realise the instructional objectives, in the *Cognitive, Affective* and *Psycho-motor domains.*

Reference Material

This section of a teaching unit should indicate the reference material including books and other support material which the teachers/learners may consult on the topic. The list should not be unduly ambitious. It should be complete—containing full specifications of authorship and publishers, year of publication, edition, relevant chapters, pages, etc. for being easy to be accessed.

Conclusion

To conclude, it may be said that enrichment of instruction for improved learning will remain a vague slogan until we impart to our teachers greater competence and mastery in the use of instructional materials through *pre-service and in-service teacher-education programmes.* Development and supply of skilfully prepared teaching units is an important step in this direction.

Objective-based evaluation and objective-based instruction are the two sides of the same coin. Preparation of good teaching units needs the co-operation of the teacher, the pedagogue, the subject expert and the evaluator and this ought to be solicited in letter and spirit.

A diagramatic representation of objective-based instruction is given in Diagram 10.5.

Objective-based Instruction: A Diagramatic Representation

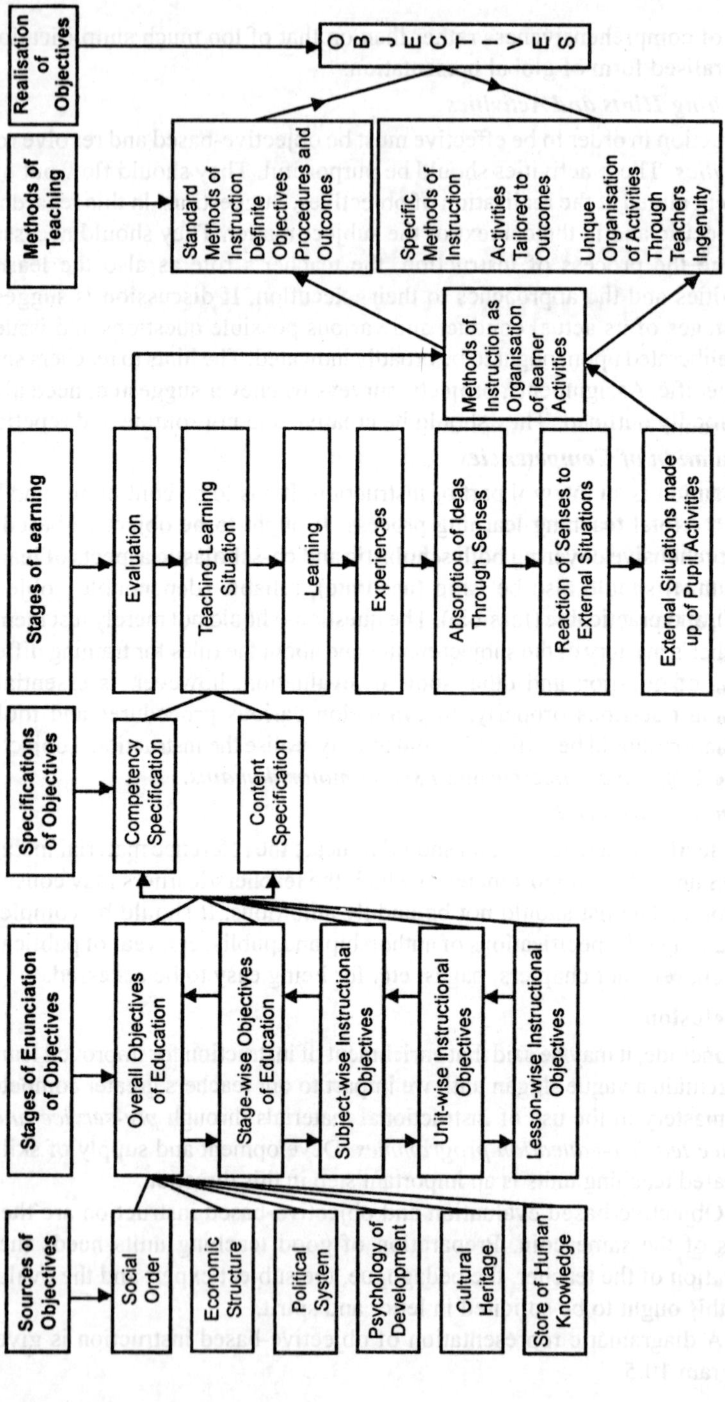

Diagram 10.5

11

Correlation between Teaching and Learning in the Classroom

Classroom is the most important of the locations where a learner is exposed to planned learning experiences aimed at imparting education based on the prescribed curriculum. The focal single-minded target of the teacher and the learner is to enable the learner to acquire desired subject-matter and abilities as enunciated by the curriculum. Towards this end the teacher normally adopts an interactive process of continuous dialogue with the students, consisting of ongoing recapitulation, ensuring consolidation of pupil learning. He uses:

- The word of mouth for communicating basic information,
- Examples for better understanding,
- Discussions for clarifying ideas,
- Charts, Diagrams for creating insight,
- Working models for clearing cobwebs,
- Elicitation for judging the degree of assimilation.

He also as a follow-up of classroom activities assigns empowering and enriching individual or group exercises by way of:

- Assignments,
- Library Research,
- Projects,
- Surveys.

The discussions on the outcomes of these activities prove to be very powerful learning experiences with an abiding educational impact.

While learning takes place incidentally and informally as well, the learning in the classroom presumes

- a teacher
- a group of students
- a particular location for learning (classroom in a school)
- a definite curriculum to abide by
- a time budget for completing the course

In this context

- teaching becomes successful only when learning takes place.
- learning takes place through the absorption of ideas by the senses.
- senses react to external stimuli.
- external stimuli consists of the planned and provided teaching learning situations and
- the manipulations of the teaching-learning situations, with a view to achieving the objectives are called methods of teaching.

There is, therefore, a close and a permanent relationship between teaching and learning. The methodology could and should vary from situation to situation and the quantum of learning by each individual also differs both in degree and in kind inspite of the educational inputs and manner of their transaction being the same.

The teacher, however, has to ensure that every learner has acquired the basic minimum level of learning about what has been taught. This has to be accomplished through developmental questions in the course of the lessons and re-capitulatory questions when the teaching on that topic is over.

This by itself is not all, as the teacher must also ensure the consolidation and internalisation of learning through remedial measures based on diagnostic tests. These tests cover each and every facet of the topic for discovering the shortfalls in learning of individual learners leading the teacher to address them for further improving the level of performance of the learners. Even in large classes, the computer makes it a practicable proposition. Such individual feedbacks in different subjects prove to be a powerful aid for self-realisation about attained levels of achievement and proficiency, motivating individual learners for self-learning for making up deficiencies.

For the bright students of the class, the teacher is expected to suggest references for extra study, extra explorations, extra experimentation, and internet surfing for gaining better insight into the subject. These exercise will also prove to be enabling, empowering and enriching to the learner. The intellectual gains so made will also facilitate the learner to establish a relationship of classroom learning with facts and phenomenon of life.

Some Conventional Methods of Teaching and Learning

Introduction

A teaching technique, method or approach connotes the manner of curriculum transaction. There are many of these and such a one should be selected for a particular teaching situation which:

- is aligned to the concerned age-group,
- is found to be of interest by the learners,
- is based on the previous knowledge and experience of the learners,
- is within the ability of the learners to pursue,
- can motivate children for further learning on their own,
- enhances pupils' competencies by imparting enablement, empowerment and enrichment to the learners,
- encourages learning initiatives of self-directed learning among learners, and
- helps in the realisation of instructional objectives.

Thus, not all methods are suitable for all situations. The choice of a method will have to depend among other things on the learners being addressed, the teachers own abilities, the facilities available.

Some of the main of the commonly used of these are described below alongwith their diverse manifestations and the approaches of their effective use.

12

The Lecture Method

This '*Tongue and the Ear Method*' is by and large the most widely used method of teaching and learning and consists of dispensing of information by the teacher to the learners. The teacher is *active* and the learner is *passive*. The method conceives that the completion of the prescribed course content by the teacher, in this fashion, is the main purpose of education. The teachers proficiency is judged by the quantum of information transmitted and not by its assimilation by the learners. *Teaching, thus, becomes both the means* and *the end and learning not conceived as the core concern.*

The lecture method is the most economical method. More information can be transferred to a large number of learners in a given period of time than by any other method. To be fruitful the lectures must be supplemented by some other methods or activities. Active participation of the learners, in the process of learning helps in augmentation, acceleration and internalisation of learning.

Socrates distrusted the lecture method on the ground that the lecturer puts ready-made ideas into the minds of pupils without giving them a chance to explore and experiment for drawing their own conclusions and thereby discover their own potentials. In fact, we want and expect the learners to become *adventurers, explorers and discoverers*. To *Socrates* questions are a powerful means for triggering thinking besides being powerful instruments of evaluation. The Socratic method aims at leading pupils (through self-evaluation) from '*unconscious ignorance to conscious ignorance*' through an ironic or destructive stage of questioning and then on to 'truth' through a constructive stage of further questioning.

There are two essential steps involved in the lecture method:

- Lecture Preparation
- Lecture Presentation

Lecture Preparation

Preparations for using the lecture method of teaching are not easy by any chance. It means the collection and compilation of information from different sources. Systematic organisation and sequencing is an important subsequent part of this exercise.

The prescribed course content and the maturity level of the learners is the basic foundation of this endeavour. *What has gone before and what is to follow determine the direction and dimensions of preparation.*

Time Budgeting is yet another basic necessity because the course has to be completed within the time available. The number of lectures that can be delivered is, thus, determined on the basis of the total time available. This in turn becomes the basis of the decision about how much of the content can be contained in a lecture.

The teacher has also to identify *the hard spots in learning*, in the subject-matter, covered through a lecture and be amply prepared for clarifying the related ideas and material for overcoming them.

The teacher has also to collect the latest references, statistics, information about latest developments beyond the text books for enriching the process of his teaching to enable learners to overcome the related hurdles.

Lecture Presentation/Delivery

To make an impact, the presentation has but to be effective. And to be effective it has to have some *distinct characteristics*. Some main of these are described below:

- A lecture though called a lecture, should not just be a one way traffic but *an amplified dialogue with learner participation*. Studding and punctuating the ideas with examples and augmenting them with new ideas can save them from being reduced to monotonous monologues as they often become.
- An *attention capturing introduction* can also prove helpful in retaining pupils' attention and this has to be very carefully prepared.
- Couching the lecture in appropriate words and catching phrases are useful fodders for whetting the cutting edge for the learners.
- *Speech and delivery* are other criteria for success and this implies clarity of thought, simplicity of words, as also good pronunciation, intonation, articulation and above all fluency.
- *Graded sequence* of presentation which may carry learners from known to the unknown, from concrete to abstract, from general to specific, are well tried prescriptions for effective teaching.
- *Emphasis on anchor points* and definitions even at the cost of repetition become important measures for assimilation of knowledge. This is also of great help to the learners jotting down points to remember.
- Proceeding to the *next point* after making sure that the *previous one* has been well understood is a confirmatory test of teaching. This

could be ensured by recapitulating what is taught through pointed questions and cross questions. In fact, the learners too ought to be encouraged to ask questions to clarify any misgivings they may have. The clarifications given are, in fact, a better methodology than just lecturing and the teacher should welcome interruptions by learners in this regard.

- Alertness of learners has but to be ensured in the course of lectures and one of the easiest methods is to ask questions in the course of the lectures and these questions should be so distributed over the class as to keep learner attention althrough, with a constant apprehension that the next question may be asked of any of them.
- A *congenial* is conducive to learning. It should always be a friendly atmosphere that should permeate the learning environment. It is desirable in this context to address learners by name.

There are also some ***don'ts*** in this regard. The teacher should never try to show off by mentioning facts and terminology which the learners cannot understand. He should address learners in their face, watching their eyes and their forehead wrinkles which are great indicators of their having understood or having not understood the ideas communicated. The teacher should neither chew nor swallow words. He should also not speak to himself but to the class. The lectures from a pulpit or a public dais are to be differentiated from those in the classroom. A clergy-man or a political leader can call it quits after a lecture which a teacher cannot, as the lecture is a means to the end of learning and not an end in itself. A teacher has but to ensure that he has communicated what was necessary and that it has also gone down the throats of the learners. Even enabling learners to learn and understand is not enough, they should also be empowered to use that knowledge gained in unfamiliar situations. The teacher, therefore, has to work with that ultimate goal in mind.

13

The Discussion Method

There are issues where there is a likelihood of differences of opinion or problems admitting different solutions or some conceptual confusions needing clarifications where some consensus is required to be obtained. These are to be put up for discussions.

Purposes Served by Discussions

- permit learners to freely express their viewpoints
- stimulate group thinking
- enable learners to agree to differ from other co-learners.
- promote public speaking.

Teacher's/Leader's Role

Discussions must always have a leader, a role which the teacher could assume himself or he may delegate that position to some learner.

In case it is necessary or is considered desirable, a class may be divided into groups for discussion on the theme as a whole or on sub-themes and each may have its own leader.

The leader in such situations would need to execute the following responsibilities:

- ensure that everybody gets an opportunity to speak and to be brief
- honour the time-limit
- pacify heat in contradictions.

Process of Discussions

A discussion starts with an introduction by the leader, who must make a thorough advance preparation not just for presenting the theme, but more so for the needed unforeseen interventions and for making the concluding remarks. The theme should be presented comprehensively, highlighting the differing viewpoints.

In the course of discussions, it is always the leader who is addressed and not another member of the group as a part of the *discussion decorum and etiquette*. Speakers should be given a clear idea of the time constraint and be tactfully reminded/interrupted, whenever necessary.

The leader should also not allow the discussion to get derailed. Deviations from the focus of the discussion needs to be promptly checked.

The leader should not necessarily intervene after each observation unless absolutely unavoidable. The learners should take their turns one by one. The leader should resist the temptation for repeated intervention and go on jotting points. He may make his balancing concluding observations at the end to save himself from imposing his views on the group. A black-board or white board summary, in telegraphic language, is always helpful for highlighting the conclusions or focal points. This is helpful in consolidating and internalising learning.

No learner should ever be snubbed but listened to with respect. Freedom of speech and an informal ethos, are guarantees for the success of discussions. Humour always eases tense moments and deserves to be inducted like 'commas'. In the event of confusions the black-board or white board should come to help.

Pre-requisites for Effective Discussions

With the goals clearly defined and the road-map drawn, the discussion should at its close impart to every participant a feeling:

- of having contributed to the joint effort.
- of taking the conclusions convincingly as his own.
- of having gained a clearer picture of the situation than before.
- of realising that there are also points of view other than his own.

Discussions imply both listening and speaking. Listening has to be patient and speaking relevant. Being attentive to whatever any member of the group speaks and to understand what is meant to be conveyed by the speaker, enables a pin pointed and meaningful response, which is always appreciated by everybody.

Logical presentations and responses always need the marshalling of ones own arguments. Ones own classify about the term of discussion is very necessary and for this some self study is always called for. In fact a habit of general reading, always comes to the aid of everybody and this ought to be constantly pursued.

14

Demonstration

Introduction

Demonstration as a method of teaching is used in practical subjects like Physics, Chemistry, Biology, Mathematics, Geography, Home Science, etc. It is used by itself or as part of a lecture.

Demonstration by the teacher or a professional or a learner demonstrates to the learners the steps of the *process* in executing a task for ensuring the quality of the outcome or *product*. Experimentation on ones own is the follow up of demonstrations.

Demonstration is able to explain the do's and the don'ts of the process of performance or a practical task, more convincingly than any oral description, because *demonstration is an action picture*. An old *Chinese proverb says that one picture is worth a thousand words* and demonstration, therefore, is much more than that.

Demonstration as a Teaching Device

Demonstration as such is a valuable teaching device and as an action-cum-demonstration lecture, it brings to the fore the precise relationships between theoretical foundation on one hand apparatus, materials, articles, machinery and appliances and the methods of handling them. On the other hand *Necessary precautions in avoiding damage and accidents, of avoiding wastage, of the meticulous maintenance of equipment, of their orderly placement for ensuring ease in locating them when required also get automatically highlighted during demonstrations.*

Demonstrations serve as models of laboratory work by the learners independently. They bridge the gap between theory and practice, stimulate thinking and motivate further learning through exploration and experimentation on the part of the learners.

Demonstrations require special seating arrangements for the learners so that everybody can see the process of operations. Specially designed class-rooms with rows in stair-steps, semi-circular in shape are considered appropriate as in an amphitheater.

Preparation for Demonstration

In preparing for demonstration, the demonstrator must brush-up his theoretical knowledge about the theme and its relationship with other themes going before and coming after it, to be able to answer questions learners may ask. This will also give him the confidence in performing the experiments for the demonstration. He should also be relaxed and friendly in the course of the demonstrations and should also display an infectious vitality and enthusiasm.

An *inventory* of the equipment required for the experiments must be made and a *checklist* for checking not just the availability but also their workability should be ensured while it is often proposed that the best of equipment should be used for demonstrations it is desirable to use, the like of the same which the learners would be using in real situations. This will impart greater confidence to the learners when they perform the experiments and practical exercises on their own.

Pre-requisites for Demonstration

The most appropriate height of a demonstration table is supposed to be 75 cms or 30 inches. The length and width of the demonstration table would depend on the kind of demonstration. Usually the traditional demonstration halls mentioned earlier have large-sized fixed tables with taps and sinks and drawers. Appropriate lighting and seating arrangement will need to be ensured for adequate visibility of the micro-level details of the micro-level details of the demonstration. A rehearsal of the total operation about how to begin, how to proceed and how to conclude is a valuable preparatory step. This practice about what to say and what to do, will lead the teacher to better success.

The main steps of preparation in this regard will, therefore, be:

- preparation for the presentation (oral).
- arrangement of the apparatus/equipment to ensure easy accessibility.
- checking seating, lighting and other arrangements.
- rehearsal of the total operation.
- the wordings of the questions.
- the stepwise development of summary in bullet points.
- the special points of significance and relationships to be highlighted.

In case it is possible for the learners also to do some experiments/or parts of experiments simultaneously, it can be a useful teaching method.

The demonstrator should also simultaneously clarify all misgivings of learners, for a clearer understanding and for avoiding any subsequent confusions.

Limitations of the Demonstration Method

Demonstration as a method of instruction, also has some limitations. It proves to be an expensive proposition financially. It also takes quite a lot of time. Furthermore, it presumes that all learners learn at the same speed. It is, therefore, that it is proposed that demonstrations and practical work by students should go on simultaneously. But advantages outweigh the shortcomings as experimentation and demonstrations consolidate learning.

15

Observation

Observation is basic to learning, enquiry and discovery. It is the process through which pupils can be stimulated to think and learn.

Observation helps:

- to develop the ability to see phenomenon and processes as they exist and operate and to note important details, which otherwise might be overlooked.
- to develop an objective approach and to participate efficiently in individual or group work.
- not just to 'see' but also to critically perceive and realise what they see. This augments what they learn from the book.

Directed observation can be carried out by an individual learner or by small or larger groups. Individual observation offers broader experience as a learning technique, than group observation, since greater amount of competency, independence and responsibility, get engineered among learners through a critical observation. Participation in activities such as field trips, video films, exhibitions, promote group observation.

Preparation for Making Observations

The pupils ought to be given an orientation about the situation in which observation has to be made and a list of what exactly they have to observe. In fact, giving them a list of things to be observed is very helpful.

Some situations in which observation has to be made may be natural and others contrived or simulated. Specific activities facilitate learning through observation. Sometimes for consolidation of learning, drill by way of repetition of activities may be necessary. Repetition may also be needed for arriving at self-validated or self-confirmed generalisations which finally culminate in abiding learning.

Process of Observation

All observations must be recorded without lapse of time immediately and accurately. Observation sheets/schedules prove helpful in this regard, as the fact/phenomenon observed can be entered easily and quickly in the relevant column, which may even save future labour of classifying information.

Attention is the key to accurate observation, which leads to learning. Children should not talk among themselves during the process of observation. Learners should also be asked not to maintain a casual detached attitude while observing. No questions may be asked by the observers or the teacher or the other learners in the course of observation as the *phenomenon observed are mostly fleeting*. All question, doubts, apprehensions may be jotted down to be presented during the discussion time allocated for discussing the observations.

Observations made should be discussed after the process is over. In this session all the things observed by all the learners may be listed and their similarity on a particular issue, may then be summarised and conclusions drawn to reinforce the understanding of learners about the observations made by them. When their observations are confirmed, by others too, that will not only give them confidence about the accuracy of their observations as also in their ability to draw conclusions on their own in subsequent situations.

Observation of Individuals

They are not just the facts and phenomenon that are to be observed but also the behaviour of the learners themselves. In fact, many aspects of personality, need only observation so as to be evaluated. The areas of personality attributes, *attitudes and values*, etc. can only be observed, in different situations. These situation have, therefore, but to be provided by the institutions in a systematic manner. These situation should not look like external unrelated interventions but built into the entire teaching learning process as an integral part.

The areas of physical competencies in outdoor co-curricular co-scholastic activities too require only observation for being judged. In fact, the ways in a learner behaves in different situations unmistakably reveals many traits and attributes of the individual besides the level of proficiencies attained in them.

The insight that observations provide are authentic evidence for being used for different purposes.

As a subject for evaluation, they also require different types of assessment tools like *rating scales* and the collection of evidences would require *anecdotal records* for prompt, on the spot recording of the kind and degree of attainment.

16

Problem-Solving Method

Any method of solving a problem scientifically, involving thinking, reasoning planning and execution by following logical steps, is a scientific method. The process of problem-solving results in the development of *cognitive abilities, affective qualities, psycho-motor skills*. It is in this context that the 'Problem-Solving Method' is called a scientific method.

RISK explains problem-solving as "*a planned attack on a difficulty, perplexity or problem to find a satisfactory solution*". ROSS interprets problem-solving as an educational device whereby the teacher and the pupils attempt (in a conscious, planned and purposeful manner) to arrive at an explanation or solution to some educationally significant difficulty.

A problem occurs in a situation in which a felt difficulty to act is realised. It may be a mental difficulty or a physical one, slowing or blocking the path of progress for reaching the goal. It may, therefore, impress upon the learners (who may meet it) as needing a solution and is recognised and realised by them as a challenge to be picked up and squarely met.

Characteristics of a 'Problem'

A problem in an educational setting ought to possess and actually possesses some distinct characteristic spelled out below:

- *Emergence from a live educational setting*: The problem is normally related to life or education and is, therefore, normally within the ambit of common experience of the learners.
- *Focussed in nature*: The problem identified as the subject of instruction/ learning ought to be clear, definite, understandable, interesting, aligned to the age group of the pupils, within the capability of the learners to tackle through the knowledge they already possess. Above all, it ought to be thought provoking.
- *Of practical utility*: The problem should have a practical value and the outcomes/solutions ought to be taken to be of practical utility by the pupils. This would motivate the pupils to demonstrate diligence and

perseverance in investing efforts for solving them.

- *Related to the curriculum*: To be pursued purposefully the problem must be a part of the curriculum (objectives, content, content/support material, methodology and evaluation) to realise the goals which is the prime concern of the learners.
- *Within the operational range of the time budget and resources available*: The process of problem-solving as a method of teaching/learning should not put unnecessary strain on the finances of the institutions. At the same time it should also be possible to accomplish the total task, within the available time.

Approaches to Problem-Solving

Basically, there are two main approaches to problem-solving with different and contrasting procedures:

- the inductive method, and
- the deductive method.

The *Inductive Method* carries the thinking process from particular to general situations. Conclusions by way of generalisations are arrived at from particular principles and concrete situational examples. An example of inductive problem-solving could be that "As Vitamin C dissolves in water and is easily destroyed by heat, a generalisation could be drawn that all foods rich in Vitamin C should be cooked in minimum amount of water, for the least possible amount of time and with minimum possible heat."

The *Deductive Method* carries reflective thinking from general to particular/specific. For example, when learners find that in dry summer the desert coolers substantially bring down temperatures inside the rooms, they draw the inference, through deduction that the heat outside leads to the evaporation of the water of the cooler pads and thus, causes loss of heat which makes the air passing through the wet pads cooler, which in turn cools the rooms.

In classroom situations, simulated/hypothetical problematic situations could also lead to integrative learning and in this manner reinforce the knowledge and the skills among the learners.

Two other important methods also help reinforce the problem-solving method and could be safely mentioned here, in passing.

Heuristic Method: Heurism is derived from the Greek concept of 'Heurisken' which means finding out. This can be an important approach for problem-solving or for the discovery approach. It aims at making learners more observant, accurate, truthful, thoughtful and dexterous. The method lays the foundation of self-education and helps promote the spirit of enquiry and research among learners.

Discovery Method: Problem-solving involves scientific enquiry which is a search for truth and knowledge. The emphasis in problem-solving too is on discovery/search of something so far unknown or unfamiliar rather than mere acquisition of existing knowledge. This scientific method is also referred to as the discovery approach to teaching and learning. The method was spearheaded by Piaget in Switzerland and Brunner in Cambridge Massachusetts.

Learning by discovery also implies experiencing a sense of achievement and personal aggrandisement. Discovery is the identification and recognition of a relationship between:

- an idea and an observation
- two ideas
- two relationships

BRUNNER mentions four following advantages of learning by discovery:

- increase in intellectual potency
- shift from extrinsic to instrinsic rewards
- learning the heuristics of discovery
- memory processing

Steps of the Problem-Solving Method

The main steps involved in using the Problem-Solving Method could be listed as under :

- *Sensing or selecting the problem*: The teacher should help the learners to identify the problem to be solved by analysing the hurdles and handicaps posed by it. Necessary motivation for solving it should also, thus, be generated among the learners. Learners should also be enabled to be alert in spotting and recognising the problems as and when they crop up in different situations.
- *Defining (Interpreting and delimiting) the problem*: The problem selected should be fully understood by the learners. The nature of the problem should help in charting the path for overcoming it. The feasibility of the action plan is governed by the ability of the learners and the availability of the needed resources.

  Hullfish and Smith suggest the following questions to be raised in defining a problem:
  - What exactly is the problem? Can it be broken into sub-problems?
  - Does the problem bear any similarity to any of those encountered in the past?
  - In what fundamental ways is the problem similar to others?
  - In which ways does the particular problem differ from the others?
  - What do differences imply—new approaches?
  - Is it necessary to redefine the problem in view of the above?
- *Collecting and evaluating relevant information/data*: After the problem has been defined and interpreted in collaboration with the learners,

they should be prompted to list the information needed for solving it and to commence the process of its collection. With a view to initiating this, the teacher may identify:

- the sources from which the information can be collected—books, documents, reports, etc.
- the personnel—experts and functionaries to be consulted.

The collected information should then be checked for its:

- appropriateness and relevance,
- adequacy and
- applicability in the given situations of the problem.

- *Formulating alternative solutions and selecting the most suitable one*: Different possible approaches for solving the problem could then be listed and their pros and cons discussed. This process of churning would enable the identification of the one most suitable. Tentative solutions could also, thus, be arrived at.
- *Arriving at the final solution*: The next natural step is to pool together the possible solutions. These may then be discussed thread bare from different angles, for reaching a decision about the approach/solution to be pursued. At this point, teacher's indepth knowledge and ingenuity will be called for, for guiding learners to reach apt and appropriate judgemental inferences.
- *Testing the validity of the solution arrived at*: The validity of the solution finally reached at, could be arrived at through:
  - the application of the hypothesis to new situations
  - further exploration, experimentation and investigations
  - additional investigations for gathering new information.

  Teachers constructive help and guidance would but be necessary throughout the process of problem-solving.

Problem-Solving and Project Method

Inspite of a host of similarities the problem-solving and project methods do stand out prominently in respect of marked differences.

Problem-solving requires a solution in thought or action or both. Project Method on the other hand aims at the successful completion of a task or unit of work.

Problem-solving could be taken up as project work but a project cannot always be a problem-solving exercise.

Merits and Limitations of Problem-Solving Method

The pursuit of the Problem-Solving Method imparts valuable personality attributes to the learners. The limitations of this method, however, mainly relate to logistics and the perpetual paucity of resources.

The Problem-Solving Method prompts pupils to learn by doing, a process through which they learn to think, to reason and in the process to develop initiative. They also acquire valuably desirable work habits and self-reliance. As problem-solving requires a higher order of mental abilities, it also helps learners develop mental self-discipline.

The main *limitations of the problem-solving method* are that it is time consuming both for the teachers and the learners and hence, cannot be used extensively and frequently. Paucity of resources too often become hurdles in using it. Quite often when problem-solving is used as a method of teaching the elaborate and intensive focus it requires, turn out to be the only mental activity with others relegated into the background and in fact they get grossly neglected.

The teacher has, therefore, to use his discretion in establishing the needed balance among different methodologies of instruction. He has particularly to guard against the situation when he may assign problems without the problems coming from the learners as that kills their interest.

17

The Herbartian Steps

Historical Overview

John Friedrich Herbart (1776-1841), the German educational philosopher was both by birth and education an educationist. His grandfather was the Rector of a Gymnasium (a German School) at Oldenburg, Herbart's native town. His father was a lawyer and Privy Counsellor there. Herbart's mother is known to be a rare and a wonderful woman, who was able to assist her son with Greek and Mathematics and provide direction to his educational pursuits.

Just before graduation he became a tutor to the three sons of a Swiss Governor. During this span of two years (1797-1799) he was required by his patron to prepare a bi-monthly written report about the methods he used and about the progress and conduct of his learners. This was Herbart's only experience in Pedagogy.

While in Switzerland Herbart met Pestalozzi and was greatly impressed by the educational principles propounded by him.

Then on resuming his interrupted university course he developed his own ideas from Pestalozzianism and put them into writing as well.

Following this, he lectured on pedagogy at the University of Gottingen from 1802 to 1809 and brought out his book 'General Pedagogy'. In 1809, Herbart was called upon to the chair of philosophy at Konigsberg as practically the successor of the illustrious Immanuel Kant. Kant died in 1804 and was succeeded by Traugott who resigned in 1809 to accept the chair at Leipzig.

It was at Konigsberg that Herbart took to documenting his ideas to become the first example of being an educational psychologist and philosopher, developing the educational process from the point of view of a teacher with the evolution of his concept of the '*apperceptive mass*' as the core doctrine of his educational philosophy. According to him, it is in accordance with apperception that a teacher can secure the interest and attention of the pupil to any new idea and have him retain it. The teacher can make or modify his apperception masses or system of ideas in such a way that it can be apperceived or incorporated with the old in educative instruction.

Originally Proposed Steps

The spirit of Herbartian steps to instruction propounded by the philosopher are widely used in different parts of the world until this day. They are:

- clearness (absorption)
- association (reflection)
- system (coherence)
- method (application/active reflection)

Subsequent Adaptations

Subsequently Herbart's noted disciple ZILLER divided the step of 'clearness' into 'preparation' and 'presentation' and a more recent Herbartian REIN added 'Aim' as a sub-step to preparation. The names of the other three processes have also now been changed by subsequent Herbartians for giving greater lucidity and significance to them. The formal steps of instruction are now given as:

- Statement of Aim
- Preparation
- Presentation
- Comparison and Association
- Generalisation
- Application

These steps are based on his concept of three primary functions of the mind as knowing, feeling and willing and incorporate Herbart's concepts of 'apperceptive mass', 'concentration' 'correlation' and multisided interests and project his philosophy that to 'instruct' the mind is to 'construct' it.

The above steps could be described as under:

- *The Statement of Aim:* What we today call the expected learning outcome is stated in clear terms. These are relevant to the subject of study, the age group of the pupils, and are to be both achievable and testable.
- *Preparation*: Before starting to introduce new ideas it is necessary to mentally prepare children for the new intake. What the children already know is to be related to what is planned to be taught to them. The most common and also the most appropriate method is to ask them some questions about their previous knowledge which may logically or sequentially lead them to the new one. This step has essentially to be a brief one.
- *Presentation:* It consists of relating and connecting new information with the old one, by dividing it into sections, if necessary. Links between what is already known and what is purported to become known, as also the subsequent areas of content, have thus to be

established. The degree and quantum of learning, desired to be imparted by the teacher and acquired by the learners is an important decision to be made at this stage.

The subject-matter becomes the focus of attention of both the teacher and the taughts. The presentation made by the teacher has but to be logical, sequential, clear, and focussed, involving lecturing, narration, description, demonstration and discussions participated by pupils. Repetition is also resorted to for internalisation of learning and the themes are also attempted to be integrated with those of other subjects and with life for creating, promoting and retaining the interest of the learners in the subject. Developmental questions play an important part in this process.

- *Comparison or Association* is the stage for consolidating learning by attempting to relate old knowledge with the new through comparisons and contrasts for establishing closer relationships between the two. The process is also aimed at arousing pupils motivation to know more, curiosity for learning more, about the theme as also for leading them to think creatively.
- *Generalisation* is the stage for putting together through *recapitulation* (revision) the facts and principles dealt with, during the earlier stages and for drawing of inferences and generalisations about them with the teacher remaining in the background. Such learner-based initiatives make learning abiding.
- *The Application stage* attempts to demonstrate to the learners that knowledge acquired has a vital relationship with life. The mind of the learners at this stage shuttles between specific facts and phenomenon to generalisations and back to the specifics. At this stage the learners ascend from the individual to the universal stage of knowledge and are enabled to acquire the ability for applying the generalised knowledge to specific unfamiliar individual situations.

Conclusion

Through these steps which go by his name Herbart, it is attempted to demonstrate that philosophy is not just a macro-level concept but can also be applied at the micro-level as well.

Herbartian steps, in fact, present a blended amalgam of the principles of teaching and learning. That is why, they have been holding the ground for nearly two centuries now. Being easy to understand and practice they are a valuable guide for the teacher in preparing a teaching plan. Based on psychological principles they present the outline of a sequential action plan of day-to-day teaching.

As they have been *tested by time, suitably modified with experience* they propose a practicable approach to teaching.

In course of time it has been realised that within the time available to the practicing teachers, it is not possible to follow the Herbartian Steps. Therefore, a simpler set of steps, incorporating the spirit of these steps has come to be evolved and is being followed even by a number of teacher training institutions. These are

1. Objectives
2. Activities
3. Evaluation

Just as with the passage of time modifications have been introduced in the steps, they can be further altered to suit emergent needs. Their value however, will still remain.

18

Activity Method

Activity Method is learning through activities. While the method has involvement of students and is, therefore, interesting to them, every subject or every topic therein cannot be taught through this method. But wherever teaching through the activity method is possible, learning is guaranteed.

For example, if children are required to pursue the activity of everyday noting down the direction of wind in the month of July and December in northern India, the direction of wind in these rainy months, the children will not need to memories that July rains are due to North-East monsoons and in December due to South, West monsoons.

Similarly, if they take some water in a trough and fix a lighted candle in this trough and then put an inverted glass tumbler on the candle and the water goes up when the candle gets extinguished and s/he observes that the water in the glass tumbler has gone up by one-fifth of the length of the tumbler from the level of water in the trough s/he will easily conclude that one-fifth of the air is oxygen because a candle needs oxygen to keep burning. This will certainly be a more effective method that telling children that one fifty of the atmospheric air is oxygen.

The *pre-requisites* of Activity Method are:

- a clear understanding of the targets,
- a defined road map,
- the methodology to be pursued,
- the resources/inputs to be marshalled to be pressed into service.

Characteristics

These pre-requisites impart the specific characteristics to the activity method, the main of which are:

- Self-planning of operational strategies,
- Self-monitoring,
- Self-designed approaches for overcoming road blocks,
- Choosing among alternative approaches.

Short Comings

The short comings of the Activity method are that

- **it is very time consuming.**
- **it needs constant individualized supervision which in view of the large classes is impossible.**
- **mistakes are all punished.**
- **failure can cause hearts breaking disappointments and discouragement for taking up individual projects in future.**

19

Peer Tutoring

It is a common experience that on Teachers, Day the Senior Teachers (or students) take charge of the teaching of their junior classes. But this kind of peer tutoring should not be just limited to this ritual but become a regular part of one of the activities of the activity day of the week of the school. In some schools, Saturday is a day reserved for such activities like project work, group projects, peer tutoring, etc.

Peer tutoring pays dividends to the senior students who act as teachers in consolidating their learning. The students who are taught feel greater freedom in asking questions for clarifying their doubts from the peers.

The students can also ask their seniors some simpler questions which they may be afraid of asking their teachers.

Peers can narrate their own experiences about the problems they themselves felt in such activities and how they overcome them. This will give the junior the confidence they need at crucial junctions.

Characteristics /Advantages of Peer Tutoring

- Collaboration from and cooperation of Peers makes the learning process an informal exercise, where the elements of fear is moving
- Peers find it easier to come down to the level of the learners
- Peer tutors know exactly the points where learners falters and being involved save debacles
- Peer tutors are always easily available for helps as compared to teachers
- Learners can more easily argue with the Peer tutors which can be an incentive for innovation

Shortfalls of Peer Tutoring

- Learners can take things passively and not bothered about keeping time targets
- Learners may over depend on Peer tutors
- Learners could undermine the advice of the Peer tutors
- Non-seriousness on the part of the Peer Tutors or the Learners could defeat the purposes of Peer Learning.

20

Joyful Learning

Once a goat tied to a rope was forcibly being taken, a child saw that and asked an elder as to where was the goat being taken? The man replied "to the Butcher House". The child said "I thought it was being taken to a School". So such could be the perception of the child about the school.

Such a School cannot be a place for joyful learning for which we need

- parental love from the Teacher
- reassuring pet at every point
- graded teaching activities for imparting a sense of achievement
- teachers patience for listening to the child and responding to him
- praise and never a public reprimand (unless absolutely necessary)
- giving leadership positions to everybody by turns in groups activities

Advantages of Joyful Learning

Joyful learning is like a fruit bearing tree. It yields both visible and invisible gains. It imparts

- motivation to learn on one's own
- desire to learn-how-to-learn and
- confidence in undertaking self-directed learning
- an inquisitiveness to know more
- a capacity to do more

Shortfalls of Joyful Learning

While we always try to make learning joyful, all learning is not possible to be imbued with joy.

Some learning requires rigour perseverance, concentration and a deligent long-term investment of time and effort. In such cases though the sense of achievement at the end of the journey, no doubt joyful, the journey itself is tedious.

21

Inter-disciplinary Teaching

Subjects of study do not stand alone, they are related to other subjects. These relationships cannot and should not be ignored and sidelined.

Language is the link between and among the subjects we study. In Geography we study rainfall, on which crops depend which are a subject of Botany. Crops determine Economy.

Every subject like transport has a History, a Geography, an Economics, a Physics, a Chemistry, a Biology and so on. To highlight these relationships in teaching will make them not only interesting but lead to permanent learning.

Such a treatment of subjects will also impart a holistic entity to the curriculum, to the environment and to the life.

This will also impart a very important message for life that it does not have islands in the ocean, but that these islands do have bridges.

Integrative teaching and learning will impart to children motivation to learn more by enabling children to draw their own conclusions from these realities.

Advantages of Inter-disciplinary Teaching

- The creation of a wider vision of the world around.
- The development of an idea that the subjects of study are not islands without bridges but in a way inter-dependent.
- That just as different topics of a subject of study are related even different subjects of study are.
- That the subjects of study of a course are related to life.
- That education as a whole prepares students for life.

Short Falls of Inter-disciplinary Teaching

- That there are some natural relationships among what is studied by the learners, which only need to be highlighted.
- That any attempts at stretching the concepts and connotations to establish inter-disciplinary teaching relationships is undesirable.

Some Unconventional Methods of Teaching and Learning

Introduction

Emancipation from Rigidities of Formal Education

Formal education, has somehow come to imply mainly the use of the traditional methods, the main of which have been discussed in the preceding section on conventional techniques of teaching. Besides, there are also some other *unconventional methods*, the use of which is more an exception than the rule. These approaches nevertheless possess a powerful potential for imparting learning, which is easily digestible by the learners, to become an internalised part of themselves. This is because most of them involve the active involvement of learners in the process of the acquisition of knowledge and other competencies. These methods also enrich the learners because they become *participatory crusades of learning*, where individuals are enabled to learn through the joint outcomes of their individual efforts or the labour of their teams and the contributions that each one makes to the learning programmes.

As the approaches are basically learner-based, the teachers stand to gain, by way of saving on their time and effort in dishing out information to the learners. This must, therefore, be an additional motivation for the teachers to use them for economising on their workload, and at the same time, successfully reaching their sole goal of ensuring abiding learning on the part of the learners.

Furthermore, the freedom and flexibility that these unconventional strategies allow to both the teachers and the taughts, does not shackle the learning process by any rigid rules or standardised procedures. This is something that often turns the frequently caused pain of learning into a joyful pursuit.

Some of the main of these approaches are attempted to be discussed in the following pages in general terms. The teacher should feel free to make the needed adaptations in them to suit the special needs of their specific situations.

22

Project Method

The Project Method is based on the pragmatic philosophy of experience and experimentation propounded by *John Dewey* and *Kilpatrick*, which brought a new dynamism in education. It transformed the dull monotonous and often purposeless classroom teaching into one that made it vibrant and imparted vitality to it. Dewey said that '*Education should not only be for life but through life*'. He was keenly aware of the gap between a pupil's life in school and his life in the society. He insisted that in an efficient educational system this gap should be bridged. The project method is an attempt to bring society and the local community closer into the school programmes.

William Kilpatrik defines the project as a "unit of whole hearted purposeful activity, proceeding in a social environment." *Stevenson* defines a project as "A problematic act carried to completion in its natural setting." *Ballard* states that "a project is a bit of real life that has been imported into the school." A *project is, thus, related to real life, its problems and their solutions in the social environment.*

Types of Projects

According to *Kilpatrick* projects can basically assume four forms:

Producers' Type: In a producers type of project the emphasis is on actual production or development of material, or an object or an article.

Consumers' Type: This type of project consists of various experiences like reading listening and evaluating things.

Problem Type: This type of projects involve problem-solving requiring the exercise of mental processes.

Drill Type: This type of projects involve learning mainly by repetition of the processes like learning vocabulary, spellings, etc.

Principles Involved in the Project Method

The principles governing the project method are:

Purposefulness: A project must be meaningful and purposeful to the learners. This offers incentive and motivation to the learners to learn and yields them the satisfaction and gratification at having been successful in accomplishing the tasks.

Activity centredness: A project is woven round some activity and offers opportunities to learners to learn by doing by getting involved in the activities. They are also required to plan, think, evolve strategies of functioning and in accomplishing tasks independently, with an urge for innovativeness in self-designed strategies culminating in a sense of achievement and fulfillment.

Life centredness: A project is planned around an actual life situation which is specially created/simulated in the school environment. The situations so created enable children to demonstrate their special abilities, competencies, ingenious capacities and talents.

Based on experience: Experiences lead to abiding learning, as the learning that so accrues, is self-acquired. The child also learns the value of team work and participatory learning and the resulting social and democratic values.

Freedom: The process of learning through the project method, offers full freedom to children to exercise their initiative and ingenuity in planning and executing the steps of the process on their own. Such freedom enables children to express themselves fully and freely. Incidentally this also helps them develop a sense of accountability for their activities.

Utility: Utility of the knowledge and experiences gained, through personally initiated and executed tasks, yields children the satisfaction of having realised something on their own, which is of utility in life. This imparts meaningfulness to the educational ventures undertaken.

Steps in the Project Method

Quite like some other approaches, in Project Method too children learn by doing. The teacher's job is to provide a situation which may give pupils a spontaneous urge, to carry out the project according to their interests, attitudes, aptitudes, competencies etc.

Project situations can be both inside the classroom and outside. Situations and settings for the execution of projects can be provided through:

- conversations on different topics
- discussions on different themes
- pictures
- video films
- story-telling
- excursions
- educational tours

With the seeds of situations sowed, the steps of proceeding on the projects have to be pursued, which are as under:

Proposing and Purposing a Project

The teacher proposes a project and enunciates the purpose. This serves as a motivating device as the children discover its usefulness and its compatibility with their respective interests and capacities to work for.

Planning the Project

Planning could be ideally done by the learners themselves but in regard to the younger folk, some hints could be offered by the teacher, who may keep on watching them do things on their own. In fact, the learners may be encouraged to think of alternative approaches for realising the same goal and then to select the one that they consider as most appropriate. This paves the way for the internalisation of the idea that there could be multiple solutions to a single problem. This serves well in later life situations where an individual has but to learn to be flexible in weighing situations for taking ones own decisions.

The learners also come to learn that whatever they may have planned, need not always be rigidly followed even if the plans do not work. The concept of 'mid-way corrections' for realising success is a valuable mental attitude of accepting the need for making changes in plans and finally making them.

Executing the Project

The freedom of project execution too is the prerogative of the learners. It gives them the joy of doing things on their own, as per their self-developed plans. Distribution of responsibilities among team mates is another valuable step which enables learners to contribute their best to their respective (often self-chosen) tasks. While the project execution goes on, the teacher mainly remains an observant on-looker, ensuring that the learners get all the materials they need and that all precautions are in place, so that they do not get hurt in any way. He has also to establish a balance between the over-enthusiastic and the comparatively less interested learners. Encouraging and guiding the latter can yield them confidence and enthusiasm to work and effectively contribute to team effort.

Evaluating the Project

While evaluation is considered to be a teacher's activity, the learners can also be motivated to assess their own efforts and the resulting outcomes themselves making them their own rivals in striving for excellence.

The teacher should try to evaluate the project from the academic angle, diagnosing and identifying the outcomes of the project in real terms by way of the development of competencies by the participants, cooperation in team work, voluntary willingness to make a contribution to the project, while in process, identification of gainful outcomes in terms of the developments and whetting of *interests* and *abilities*.

The learners too can undertake a self-evaluation of the gains, the new things learnt, the capacities enhanced, the insights into various operations gained, the improved level of confidence generated in oneself and motivation for further improving ones competencies. The teacher should, in fact, lead them to such realisations.

Shortcomings of the Project Method

Project method though a great educational innovation does suffer from some shortfalls the main of which are stated below:

It is a *time consuming* method of learning and teaching. It is also *not applicable in all the subjects and all the themes therein.* The teacher cannot always think of completely original themes for projects and therefore, quite often they become repetitive.

Conclusion

Inspite of the shortcomings, the project method remains a very useful method of imparting abiding learning through personal experiences. Its great value in concept formation and the development of valuable life-relevant attitudes cannot be underestimated.

23

The Laboratory Method

Learning by Doing

We all learn by doing. The laboratory method helps learners to learn by doing. In experimental subjects experience in the laboratory becomes an important segment of pupils' total experience. It is the best method of providing a clear understanding of any process. Laboratory experience under teachers' supervision is the first step for the development of manipulative and managerial skills among the learners. Personal involvement in experimentation promotes the development of a spirit of inquiry, capacity for reasoning, exploration for purposes of acquiring the needed information and objectivity in observation as also faithful recording of observations, and rational deduction of inferences.

Support Material for Laboratory Work

The laboratory method even in science subjects, suffers from the handicap of the availability of sufficient items of apparatus for offering hands-on experience to all learners but now thanks to the NCERT, some Science Kits have been developed. Each kit has apparatus for twenty learners to perform experiments individually. The basic idea behind prompting this venture is to provide inexpensive aids for experimental science education. In these kits, every item of glass apparatus which could be converted into plastic has been so converted, eliminating the fear for their replacement in case of breakage, if it was glass and thus, of repeated financial investments. The fundamental premise for developing these aids/items of experimentation is to educate learners in *concepts* rather than insisting on *accuracy* of results.

The Science kits are also a way of reaching the rural schools where adequate infrastructure is not available. The kit has taken the form of a box with a handle at the top, this can be bestowed in any corner of the classroom, thus, eliminating the need for a special cup-board for storing the equipment. The apparatus is all stored in the drawers and chemicals on the shelves of the kit box. The kit has two doors, both in the front. One has hinges that brings the inner door from top to bottom and this can serve as a demonstration table. The outer cover is hinged in a manner that it opens up on one side. This side that opens up is painted black and can be used as a black-board, where even that is not available. Now, however, things have improved. The innovation of the development of science kits, however, still remains an ingenious thing for overcoming constraints and handicaps.

As experimentation is usually time consuming, it is desirable to allot two consecutive class periods for it.

Types of Laboratory Methods

The laboratory method could assume three forms:

- Experimentational
- Observational
- Productive

The *experimental mode* helps explain, illustrate or to prove principles by enabling learners to explore, experiment and draw conclusions on their own. These conclusions become abiding acquisitions of the learners. This mode also helps in creating in learners an instinct for verifying facts and phenomenon.

The *observational mode* is again based on personal deductions not just based on experimentation but also on personal observations. Exploration becomes the chief means for making observations. Observations of this type could be illustrated by the inferences on characteristics of growing children of different age groups.

The *productive mode* consists of creating a tangible outcome like the production of a simple item like a pin tray in wood work, a candle in wax-work or a frock in tailoring (home science).

The laboratory method starts and ends with activities. It starts with an introduction by the teacher establishing a relationship between theory and practice. The pupils are enthused to make and promptly put down their observations as they make them. The laboratory method could be used both for individual and group teaching. The latter, however, is a common practice.

A *first aid kit* is, however, a perpetual part of all laboratories for meeting emergencies.

Process of Laboratory Work

In performing experiments, learners are always advised to go strictly by the oral instructions given by the teachers and the directions contained in the manuals and instruction cards.

In the process of experimentation, the teacher goes round and supervises the work of individuals or groups and helps those that need it. If there is a common mistake being committed, he draws everybody's attention and makes necessary suggestions.

Post Experiment Discussion

After the process of experimentation is over, discussions are the concluding step. The common experiences and differences of opinion are discussed and the teacher finally helps them to get to accurate conclusions.

24

Programmed Instruction

Purpose of Programmed Instruction

Programmed Instruction promises to increase the effectiveness of mass instruction. Through this approach individualised instruction is possible to be provided to pupils in a more effective manner than what is possible for any single teacher to do.

The uniqueness of programmed instruction lies in the fact of its not just being a device of teaching but more so as a scientific approach applicable to different levels and sectors of education.

Skinner and his colleagues at the Harvard University conducted research experiments to study the behaviours of pigeons. They managed to teach these docile little creatures to master certain tricks and also to play a form of Table Tennis.

The basic principles guiding the experiment of teaching pigeons were:

- If rewarded whenever a pigeon made a right move, it learns a new one more quickly.
- A complicated feat must be taught through small steps and just one at a time with each subsequent step being graded to become an easy one.

Structure of Programmed Instruction

Skinner once visited his daughter's fifth grade Mathematics class and noticed that pupils' attention wandered away from the inefficient classroom instruction. He grew indignant at what he saw in the classroom and developed a fifth grade Mathematics course based on the principles used in teaching pigeons and other small animals.

In programmed instruction, *the subject-matter is broken down into a sequence of small learning steps*. The sequence and steps must be determined much more carefully and skilfully than what is possible for an ordinary learner to do. The steps must be small enough for the learner to move from an easier one to the next more difficult one easily, with a minimum of error. *Mistakes are costly, as they have to be unlearned.* Trial and error learning must be reduced to a minimum. The ideal programmes would result in no mistakes. Constant success reinforces past learning and motivates further effort.

Programmed instruction may take many forms depending upon the subject, and the objectives desired to be achieved. The most common form in academic subjects is to present certain carefully-worded data in a '*Frame*' or viewing space. Each Frame calls for a response.

In programmed teaching/learning, a school subject is broken into simple, easy, graded, progressive steps and presented as questions, which the pupil must answer. The pupil would be kept active with the process of continuously answering the questions. The reward would be that of knowing at once if he was right or wrong, and if the subject was programmed in its sequential logical order, he would rarely be wrong. The learner would need to work alone, concentrating on the questions as they emerge, writing his own answers. A mechanical device or a '*teaching machine*' is a device used for the purpose. It presents an exercise or a problem to the learner, induces him to respond and reveals to him whether or not his response is correct. Many machines require that incorrect responses be corrected before the learner can be allowed to continue and move ahead. Most teaching machines use the tutorial or the *Socratic method*. They ask questions, wait for answers and then let the learner know whether or not he is right. They induce the learner to think and work for himself. This is how the 'Teaching Machine Movement' came into existence. Instruction by '*Teaching machines*' *is called programmed learning or self-instruction*. The material may be presented through any device—a machine or a book.

Operations of Programmed Instruction

In general, programmed material consists of a series of small units called '*Frames*'. Each Frame is based on the previous knowledge already possessed by the learner and each Frame attempts to add a small increment to this knowledge. Each Frame contains one or more blanks to be filled in by the learner in a sentence—completion fashion. The blank in a Frame calls for a response that the learner is able to offer either because he learned how to make it, in the settings of the previous Frames or because it is made possible by the study of the Frame currently confronting him. The learner reads each Frame and then fills in the blanks. The learner type of reading required by a Frame ensures active and continuous manipulation of the ideas, described through it. This type of concentrated and focussed reading reinforces learning in contrast to passive reading, without a need for active manipulation of the ideas that make up the subject-matter.

The genesis of programmed learning can be summarised, thus:

- Small steps
- Thoughtful reading
- Active responding
- Immediate confirmation
- Reinforcement
- Self-paced learning

There are different styles or systems of programming. The *'linear'* programming, associated with the work of *Skinner*, is a single track programme because the learner goes directly in a straight line through the material from beginning to end. The *'intrinsic'* programming associated with the work of *Crowder* is a branching programme. It is a method of programming material that directs the erring pupil along certain corrective pathways, before he is permitted to proceed to the next step in the programme. Introducing remedial or explanatory loops of review introduced into a programme helps the learners who need them, while the swifter learners can skip the entire practice.

Research findings show that programmed instruction helps to accomplish *consolidation of learning at every level*, from pre-school to graduate or professional level. It is useful for slow learners as well as mature superior learners. It can teach a variety of subject-matter, such as mathematics, statistics and language and a variety of skilled, behaviours like rote-learning, paired associated learning, application of formulae, formation of concepts and 'thoughtful' reading, etc.

Conclusion

Developing a 'programme' is not easy. It requires not only mastery of and insight into the subject but also meticulous planning thorough preparation and sound training. The nature of the programmed instructional material is such that *it cannot be easily transplanted from one setting/environment or country to another*.

One of the important factors in the use of programmed material is, that programmed material *need not substitute the textbooks or the teacher* as only certain parts of a text is programmed. The textbook could, thus, remain largely intact.

Teaching machines can never replace human teachers, however indispensable they may become. Factual learning which comprises the content of most programmes is only one means to some important cognitive processes, associated with intuitive, judgemental and problem-solving behaviour.

25

Think-Tank Sessions

Connotation

Think-tank sessions imply joint/*collective loud thinking* by a group on a common issue or problem. The theme selected could be real or hypothetical.

Requirements

Normally placards, with questions, phrases and statements or slogans on the selected topic are prepared with the help of learners. These are such as to force people to think.

Physical Arrangements

Learners sit in groups (circles or semi-circles) to deliberate in-depth on the parts of the given theme. Each group has its own placards on the same theme.

Purpose

Reflecting in-depth on an issue or a problem, analysing it, delving into the causes (if any), discussing implications, suggesting alternative solutions, pondering on the pros and cons of each solution in terms of immediate outcomes as also long range impact and identifying the most suitable one, pre-occupy the learners as they engage themselves in dialogues to exchange views without any heated debate or argumentation.

Process

Learners are divided into groups of 10 or 15. The purpose is explained to them along with the working dynamics. The learners are required to do reflective thinking. Each learner may explain the meaning and connotation of the contents of his/her placard. Placards are also circulated among different groups for encouraging different viewpoints on the same issue. New ideas also, thus, get generated.

Expected Gains

It is possible to get different viewpoints on the different facets of the same theme. With every learner desirous of saying something new, it becomes a *race in creativity of thought and speech.* Learners are also enabled to appreciate about how the same problem, can be viewed from different angles. It also helps impart to the learners the most valuable *conviction that theirs is not the only view*, and also not essentially the only correct one. With no inhibitions, learners are also able to come out with their thoughts which they may not normally express. This prompts them to experience the exercise their right present without any reservations their own respective opinions about different facts and phenomenon.

Think-Tank Sessions basically are exercises in collective thinking on a given issue. Though different members of the team may hold different view-points, because of the different exposures and experiences they may have had, they entertain the common mission of charting the most appropriate road map for reaching the same goal. In fact, different viewpoints enrich the thinking process, as the suggestions are invariably constructive and forward looking.

The realisation of likely pitfalls and a discussion about the gravity of each, in regard to their potential for dislocating the proposed plans, gives valuable pointers for avoiding them through care in advance planning.

The development of placards on different facets of the identified theme also becomes a valuable training ground for being *creative with eye and ear catching brevity.* To squeeze the content of many sentences into a small slogan like statements is by itself a valuable ability to inculcate, which can stand people, in good stead, in life.

Furthermore, when one coins a catchy statement for a placard, he follows a particular line of thinking the interactions that follow enable the individual to learn about other possible meanings and interpretations of what he has written as well. This process and the discussions that follow, enlighten everybody in the group and by so learning from others, one acquires a greater clarity about his own notions.

Furthermore, 'Think-Tank Sessions" also successfully offer to each member of the group, a sense of cohesion and unity as a team working towards the same goal. The outcome, in terms of conclusions thus does not remain any single individuals work but that of the entire group. The group as a whole, takes it to be its work with a sense of achievement and satisfaction.

This also creates a sense of interdependence among members who then have *no egoistic hesitation in consulting others*. Such attitudes are conducive to welfare of the institution, agency or organisation the individuals work for. The so emanating personal harmony also naturally results in professional harmony.

26

Seminars

Connotation

A seminar is an in-depth discussion on a topic under the guidance of a teacher or a leader.

Requirements

Being an in-depth discussion, a seminar is normally preceded by an extensive, in-depth study of the theme in advance from different sources.

Physical Arrangements

A circular or a semi-circular seating arrangement for an in-house seminar is considered appropriate. For formal seminars, there may be a dais for experts to sit and rows or round table seats for the audience in the front.

Operational Steps

The date for the seminar and the topic are announced in advance. Normally, the learners jot down their misgivings (if any) about the different aspects of the theme earlier. Some of them may even prepare a brief presentation about their explorations.

Process

The teacher or the leader briefly introduces the topic and coordinates the discussions, allowing time to everybody to have a chance to speak. The thematic organisation is also the leader's responsibility. S/he also makes inputs/ corrections, wherever needed, and ensures that the major aspects of the theme are covered.

Different ideas and points of view are then presented and discussed thread-bare, covering the minutest of details. For everybody, it is also an opportunity for clarifying ones conceptual confusions.

Expected Gains

Even though the whole class/group may participate, the situation in seminars is informal, and learners have no reservations about expressing their opinions. The cross-fertilisation of ideas is very educative as everybody is eager to share whatever new s/he may be knowing about the topic, or whatever opinions s/he may be holding about it.

The theme being a part of the curriculum, the learning so acquired is unique and more enriching and abiding than any classroom teaching or individualised learning.

Seminars normally display an academic inclination. With the prior timely announcement of the theme everybody may have had an opportunity to study the theme. In the process, he may also have jotted down his own misgivings about which he needs classifications.

The study of different books and materials by the learners may also have exposed them to different viewpoints of the authors. The presentation of these viewpoints naturally enriches the deliberations of the seminar.

While a consensus may or may not be possible, to be arrived at, a seminar does become a platform for participatory learning. The discussion at the seminar becomes such an enriching experience that no learner normally wants to miss a seminar while he may not mind missing a lecture.

The threadbare analysis of the theme in question, through contribution pouring in form all sides, enables the participants to gain from the labour and explorations of their other peers, which they on their own may never be able to do.

It is always useful to ask each learner to write briefly about the points they may have made in the course of the seminar. A small group could then be constituted to arrange the ideas sequentially in a logical order in the form of a summary paper. The sources from which different ideas may have been culled out will be valuable reference points for those who may like to know about the particular aspects of the theme.

Seminars offer a valuable opportunity for *library research* and help inculcate the ability of *learning how to learn and self directed learning*. The ample scope for showing off ones own exploits, is by itself a powerful motivation for the learners to acquire indepth knowledge and to present it before the whole group/class/seminarians. These presentations of individuals, often leave good impressions on others about the deligent and intelligent homework done by the individual and enhances his prestige in the group. This becomes an incidental gain.

27

Panel Discussions

Connotation

A small group of persons are selected to discuss an issue among themselves. The panelists could be both outside experts and/or faculty members.

Physical Arrangements

There is normally a dias where the coordinator and the panelists sit, and there is the audience. Panelists normally do not exceed five.

Requirements

The chairman/coordinator directs the presentations. He also sets time limits for the panelists to speak, and provides the links between the presentations of different panelists. He initiates the discussions and also concludes it.

Process

A topic is decided in advance. Panelists who are experts in the field are selected and invited to present their viewpoints on the identified theme. After the chairman has introduced the panelists and the theme, he asks each one of them to make brief presentations. Threads from the ideas expressed are then picked up, and discussions start among panalists. Sometimes even after the introduction of the theme, if it admits different viewpoints or controversies, the discussion starts straight away with inputs coming from different panelists. Towards the close, sometimes, the audience is also permitted to ask questions which are responded to by the panelists.

Expected Gains

It is an opportunity to hear experts speak out their ideas on a theme. The differences of opinion on the subject come to the fore, and as points are normally made with reasons they become very enriching.

'Panel' discussions are normally organised on themes where view-points may be varied. A Panel Discussion provides an opportunity to the members of the audience who could be learners, to analyse the ideas and facts for themselves and draw their own conclusions.

Panel discussions are held on specialized themes and the panelists are experts in that field. Quite naturally, the experts would be having different experiences and backgrounds which will come to bear on the presentations they make.

Sometimes as a matter of planning the different panelists may be requested to focus on specific facets of the theme of discussion which may be allocated to them in advance. This helps avoid avoidable duplication. However, the main theme being the same, some overlap is bound to be there. But, the panelists, on their own, try to avoid it on the basis of the presentations of earlier panelists.

The discussions among the panelists after the presentations are basically technical and the learners as the members of the audience have to pick up things relevant to their needs. Sometimes when the panelists enter into technicalities quite a few things go over the heads of the audience, the learners. It is, therefore, desirable to brief the panelists in advance for remaining within the range of understanding of the learners for whom really the panel discussion has been arranged.

It is, however, always desirable to record the presentations and the deliberations. These presentations being by specialists are surely likely to be of interest and use to others working in the field. With the permission of the panelists, these could be widely circulated, after editing by the panelists themselves.

While selecting the panelists it is always desirable, in the setting of an educational institutions, not to include known rivals among the panelists who may contradict everything that the rival may state. This vitiates the ethos and destroys the purpose of the discussion by becoming a wordy battle ground.

After the presentations, discussion and the question-answer session, time must be saved for brief concluding statements by the chairman.

28

Symposium

Connotation

A symposium is a discussion on essays prepared and presented by some selected individuals (learners or experts) on a particular theme/topic.

Physical Arrangement

It could be a semi-circular arrangement or a classroom setting.

Requirements

Learners or experts are selected, and after being assigned the topic, are asked to prepare brief papers for presentation. As normally the total time available for a symposium is limited, they are asked to prepare brief presentations as per the time budget.

Process

The learners or experts who have prepared the essays on the theme make presentations one by one, as called upon. As the presentations are made, the others jot down the things to remember and the questions to ask. The rest of the period is devoted to questions and answers.

Gains

The topic being the same, each speaker is anxious to prepare the best essay by consulting the largest possible number of sources. The exercise, thus, motivates learners (in an institutional symposium) to undertake library research. As the time is limited, they also learn to be brief in their writings, so as to include everything that is relevant, in the smallest possible space. The essay has to be drafted as a speech and so has to have new facts, convincing arguments and reasoning. Stage shyness is also got over in such an exercise of public speaking/reading. Those who write and read papers also incidentally get the needed training in responding to questions orally. So, besides written expression, oral expression too finds an opportunity for being demonstrated, of which promptness to marshall arguments to respond is an important part.

It is desirable to ask learners to write essays by turns. The teacher could initially come to the help of those who may not be proficient in writing and speaking, and enable them to subsequently do things on their own.

A symposium is basically *an all learner affair*. The selection of a theme well in advance is necessary for the learners to prepare their own essays for presentation. In symposia the themes selected are mostly those of common interest reflecting common concerns/problems.

Quite naturally each learner selected to write an essay and to present his own point of view and the approach for solving the common problem. *Practicability of the suggested solutions* will, of course, be the central focus. No theoretical impracticable approaches will, therefore, be appreciated. As each one would have a stake in the solutions suggested he will analyse it in the context of his own interests. This will make it necessary for the suggestions to satisfy the majority, if not all.

As this will involve presentations on the basis of written essays those writing them will need to ensure all the requirements of written expression. To add to this, the ability to present a reasoned point of view, will also be called for. The pros and cons of different possible approaches will also need to be examined and the final solution suggested, will also have to be supported by arguments. This will be no easy task and need originality and creativity.

It will be desirable not to select the same learners for writing essays and presenting them every time. Learners should take turns in executing this valuable learning exercise which has many things to teach learners.

After the presentations have been made, there should also be an open house for the audience to raise questions. Those who may have made presentations could jot down the points raised related to their respective presentations and then each of the four or five should take turns to respond. The concluding note, however, should be given by one of the teachers. This teacher should try to balance different viewpoints and focus on points of agreement rather than points of disagreement.

A symposium, thus, becomes an instrument for training learners in library research for collecting and compiling information for drafting it in an organised manner and for making a public presentation.

29

Library Research

Connotation

Library Research implies systematic exploration and investigation for discovering/establishing facts on identified themes.

Requirements

Access to a library with books on the selected topic and access to internet as also availability of time for exploration are pre-requisites for library research is a pre-requisite and involves:

- Consultation
- Taking notes
- Systematic organisation
- Summarisation

Process

The theme is identified and given to the class. The class has then to be divided into groups not by choice but by selection. Each group is allotted a sub-theme to work on. Time-table for collection of material, group presentation, class discussion and summarisation is decided in advance and intimated. The groups then go about their business. Each learner takes his notes about significant points from the books/documents studied or from the internet surfed.

The learners then come back to their respective groups, where the collected material is pooled analysed, synthesised and evaluated for the preparation of the group report. The points of the group report are jotted down and the member of the group with a facile pen prepares the draft of the group report. The report is then read to the group and approved by it. This is then presented by the writer/group leader.

The Group Reports on different sub-topics are then presented by the Group Leaders to the total class and discussed. The suggestions made, and the ideas that emerge in the course of the discussions are incorporated in the group reports and a final report on the whole topic weaving-in the different group reports is prepared and formally written.

This report and any other material which may have been prepared by the groups is then put up in an exhibition.

Expected Gains

Library research is a valuable experience in both individual and participatory learning which saves teaching-learning time, and at the same time is enriching. It is good training for the concept of *Frontline Curriculum*, where say 90% syllabus remains relevant for four or five years and 10% changes every two years or so. As no books are available for this 10% of the syllabus, *teachers too become co-learners with learners in the process of exploration.* Learners, while browsing through books, journals, etc. are able to realise the richness of the topic. They also learn to analyse ideas, synthesise them and evaluate them. This also often motivates them to learn more about the theme.

Library Research is always an enriching exercise. In fact the old time practice of allocating library periods in the time-table, served a great motivating force for children to explore the world of books. He may not necessarily read every book in the library but "browse" through it. This will imply looking through the table of contents and turning the pages just like that for identifying an interesting chapter an attractive picture or an educative diagram. It is quite likely that the learners, would be able to identify some chapters of books or books themselves for further study.

This, in fact, will be the beginning of self-learning which is an important attribute for success in life.

Library Research is surely not an aimless exercise of browsing through the books but a focussed one, before the theme is taken up in class and necessarily after the theme has been completed. Collection of additional knowledge about the same theme will surely be an enriching exercise, as it would help the learner gain further insight into the topic which will make the content more meaningful to him,

Consultation of other textbooks for the same class and the same subject not prescribed by the school, could be a very valuable exercise. Learners, for example, could select the exercise in mathematics textbooks for purposes of drill for the mastery of the theme.

Consultation of children's encyclopaedias would surely be a useful exercise in widening the knowledge horizons of learners.

The magazines subscribed by the school library could lead the learner, to some interesting reading material which may motivate the learners for further whetting his interest in self-reading, self-learning and learning how to learn.

30

Photo-Language Session

Connotation

Photo-language sessions involve giving expression to thoughts, ideas, feelings, emotions evoked by photographs or pictures.

Requirements

The collection of photographs, pictures related to the selected topic is the first step, as everybody looks at the pictures attentively, and tries to mentally analyse what they depict and reflect on them in terms of the ethos of their contents. The atmosphere naturally is reflective, because what is attempted to be caught are thoughts and feelings that the pictures or photographs exhale.

The time for viewing these pictures or photographs is also *rationed*, say two or three minutes, so that all the learners are able to view them closely. The class is then divided into groups of say ten learners each, who are normally seated in a semi-circle for watching the set of pictures presented to each group.

Process

As mentioned, sets of pictures/photographs related to the central theme are given to each group. The leader of the group shows the pictures/photographs given to the group one by one. Learners are given time to observe them in silence and jot down in telegraphic language the things they observe. The leader then asks the learners to give their reactions to the details observed in the pictures without any inhibitions or reservations. The learners then individually write their observations. These observations are then compiled picture wise. The pictures and photographs are then circulated to the other groups where the same operation is repeated. All the groups then come together. Each picture or photograph is then presented one by one and each group presents its report on that one by one. The variation in the perception of different groups about the same picture or photograph are by themselves enriching experiences. If time permits, a discussion on each could also follow.

Gains

The exercise promotes the habit of close and critical observation and the ability to mentally translate the depictions/details into feelings, and these into words. The exercise empowers learners to reach out their thoughts to the affective domain and thereby to sensitise the learners to certain needs and situations. This also helps learners to channelise emotions and to communicate them.

Photo-language Sessions sound like something new but even in the good old days there used to be a question on *Picture composition* in language question papers.

The broad purpose in the two exercises is the same i.e. the translation of one form of presentation into another. Even in mathematics this type of translation exercises from one form of presentation to another among tables, diagrams and graphs bar/pie diagrams is quite common.

The Photo-language Session focus on language for interpreting the contents of pictures. The projective techniques in Psychological Testing like the *Thematic Apperception Test* uses the interpretation of pictures for judging attributes of personality.

Coming back to Photo-language Sessions, it could be said that this involves the varied interpretations of the contents of the pictures by different individuals. The exercises involve the power of intricate observation of pictures for giving them a meaning. The different observations on the same picture enable learners to learn about the points they missed to observe and interpret. Thus this by itself becomes a learning exercise in focussed observation.

With all the pictures, aligned to the common themes the scope for differences in interpretation does no doubt get narrowed down, but still some elements of it do remain unexplored.

The ability to write what one sees and feels about it is the main ability attempted to be developed.

The exercises become difficult because of the depiction of emotions and likely related activities. This requires not just close observation of details but also of the expressions and gestures depicted by the pictures.

To be able to do that, one must have a good backup acquaintance with vocabulary and usage for which extra reading becomes a stand-by asset.

31

Surveys

Connotation

Surveys connote detailed study by collecting information tabulating it and analysing it to discover some new facts, or to reinforce the existing knowledge, or to confirm and verify some stated idea or principle.

Requirements

Selecting a topic and allotting its facets to different groups for study.

Physical (Seating) Arrangement

Informal and flexible.

Process

Dividing the class into groups and the teacher holding separate meetings with different groups to explain to them the objectives, areas of exploration, places to be visited, information to be collected and people to be interviewed, tables to be prepared the diagrams to be drawn, etc.

The groups may be given *specific time budgets* for doing the job.

The learners may individually maintain notes of the things they observe, the things they learn and the conclusions they draw. Groups then make their presentations to the whole class (all the groups) and prepare a written report for exhibition along with tables, charts, etc. prepared in the course of their work.

Gains

The learners do not receive information collected by someone else but have to collect it on their own, which by itself is very aggrandising. They learn how to collect, tabulate, and interpret the information they may collect for drawing their own conclusions. This makes the inferences more meaningful to them. They experience the thrill of discovery and also come to realise that team work can do many things which individuals by themselves cannot singly do.

They also gain faith in their conclusions and take the established principles to be really true and valid, having been experimentally verified by themselves.

Surveys as such are a valuable teaching devices. They enable children to acquire first hand knowledge form *primary sources*, to compile and organise it and to draw their own conclusions form it. The so derived inferences become the self-earned part of an individual's knowledge and being so, turns out to be his abiding permanent treasure of knowledge. *The Engel's Law of Consumption in Economics*, for example, if memorised it can slip out of the memory after some time, but if it is derived though a survey of different levels of people (say an executive, an office assistant, a labourer) about the proportion of their income they spend on food, clothes, shelter, and entertainment, it will be never forgotten by the individual learner.

Furthermore, surveys bring learners closer to realities of life enabling them to personally gather information based on their own exploration and experiences about the life in their environment. This too is a permanent gain making the individual realistic in this statements or decisions.

The schedule through which data for surveys is collected and the hurdles that come in the way, yield insights which other situations cannot impart.

Furthermore, the learner also learns about the importance of little bits of information when he reaches a solution where for want of a small piece of information he may have felt disabled in reaching conclusions.

Surveys in fact become enjoyable when the learner has an eye on the end result and hopes to collect information for substantiating an existing tenet or for disproving it. In this process, exceptions always attract his attention and these prove the rule.

Surveys should not be undertaken as a formality but should be purposeful and the purpose when firstly understood by the learners would whet their motivation by igniting their interest in them.

32

Participatory/Group Learning

Introduction

Participatory learning is an innovation mothered by necessity. Even though an outcome of compulsions, it has started paying valuable dividends by way of:

- speeding up the process of collection of educational information as compared to individualised endeavours.
- consolidation and internalisation of self-acquired learning as compared to teacher dispensed information.
- reduction of teacher's workload and more particularly, his speaking load.

These gains are not just encouraging but enticing and tempting for being pursued as an instructional methodology.

Genesis of Participatory Learning

In 'Participatory Learning' it is not just that each learner pursues his course of action for deriving the gains of learning. It is the group or team as a whole that pursues learning as a joint venture by sharing responsibility, replicating the concept of 'division of labour'.

Pre-requisites of the Approach of Participatory Learning

A well-equipped School Library/Laboratory

Process of Participatory Learning

The process of participatory learning consists of the following flexible and adaptable steps:

- Announcement of the theme/topic to the class by the teacher.
- Taking the class to the library to browse through the books on the subject and identify those that deal with the given topic.
- Dividing the class into viable groups.

- Distributing the books to the groups.
- Loud reading of the concerned theme from the books by learners in their respective groups by taking reading turns. This could be done in the course of any decided span of time and at any place the group may decide, with each member of the group taking his/her own notes.
- Return of the groups to the class, in the next scheduled class period, when the teacher may, in consultation with the learners, draw-up on the black/white board, an outline of the sub-themes of the main theme and throws each one of them up for a discussion one by one.
- Taking up each such theme for a detailed discussion one by one, with learners contributing on the basis of the contents of whatever books they may have consulted. Different points of view or approaches could thus emerge.
- Simultaneous development of black/white board summary by the teacher.
- Concluding observation jointly by the team/group leaders and the teacher.

Participatory Learning has, infact, become the need of the hour, particularly because knowledge is growing every fast and becoming redundant faster. An individual cannot all by himself explore the many sources that contain related knowledge. Therefore, a division of labour is a valuable innovative approach. If a number of learners set out to collect information about a particular theme in a planned manner, almost everybody will be discovering something different. The compilation of this knowledge and its presentation to the group is enriching to one and all of them. Every member of the group will also, thus, derive a unique satisfaction for contributing to the common pool of knowledge. This will become a meaningful exercise to everybody, because of the eagerness that will automatically get generated in each one. There will, thus, be a beginning of both *competition for advancement and co-operation for strength.*

Participatory or team learning will not thus be restricted to only library research but could take the form of *surveys, projects, exploration, experimentations etc.* It will offer examples of situations where *learners will learn without being taught* even though the teacher will remain a planner and a guide in these activities. Even the teachers would stand to learn from these initiatives of the learners and he would always be looking forward to what new the learners may discover through their strides.

It needs to be specifically pointed out here that when there is a *teacher learner interaction* in the course of a teaching-learning session, the concentration level of the learners is minimal. When this becomes a *learner-*

learner interaction the level of this concentration improves and when it is the interaction of the learner with himself (as in self-learning and self-directed learning episodes) the concentration is at its highest level.

Conclusion

Thus, the aims stand more than realised with children learning much more than what they could ever have dreamt of, while pursuing learning individually. All the learners can take pride in contributing to the theme in his own way. The process leads to abiding learning, and the learners do not usually forget what they learn. The teacher too saves time and labour.

The approach is simple, easy, effective and economical. It is also an encouraging proposition aligned to the standard of the class. Institutions would, however, need to have a good library. The method could be usefully used from class VII/VIII onwards.

33

Action Research

Concept

Action Research is in fact a problem-solving strategy in the teaching process. Whenever and wherever a hard spot in learning is identified, that situation could become the starting point of Action Research. The problem that arises has first to be analysed for getting to its source or causation. Steps for overcoming it are then designed. The action is instant and so, it disallows any snow-balling of the confusion or lack of clarity, that may have emerged. Action research is not any theoretical construct but a practical approach specifically designed for the specific situation. The approach, therefore, is a *hand maid of the teacher*, who exercises full freedom and flexibility in designing and implementing a strategy specific to the situation for making teaching amenable to learning.

Designing of Steps

The teacher, being the master of the situation, designs the exercise as per his own thinking in the hope of solving the problem through it. In the process he often breaks down a complex situation into smaller sub-situations and helps pupils move on step-by-step for overcoming them, wherein the success they realise at each step, gives them the confidence for realising success in the subsequent steps. This also leads to a better consolidation of learning in the pupils. This approach for realising the goal is termed as Action Research Hypotheses.

Both the strategy and the targeted goals can change midway, at the discretion of the teacher, on the basis of the need for change experienced by him. Action Research, thus, admits immense flexibility and adaptability.

Success in a particular situation in Action Research does not go to enunciate a principle or a theory or a generalisation, particularly because it is based on situation specific ingenuity of the teacher. This characteristic differentiates it from basic or fundamental research as in Action Research the teacher and in some measure the learners become the sole judges of the effectiveness of the approach in realising the anticipated success.

Operation of Action Research

Action research, is an informal methodology and satisfaction of the teacher and the learners, is the measure of success which does not offer any quantitative enunciation.

The outcomes of Action Research are also not normally presented formally as the findings, result in self-assuring experiences, which may encourage other teachers to devise their own approaches for solving the problems they may face from time to time.

Unlike fundamental research where the findings are normally used subsequently by others, in action research there is no such time gap and the teacher is both the designer of the approach and its follower. Thus, he is both the producer and the consumer of the research. He also, thus, translates his knowledge of theories into practice.

Action Research admits a very wide operational scope. It can be used in any teaching, learning or testing situation and at any step or juncture. It can also serve as a useful tool of management of different operations for making them effective.

Action Research bears a striking similarity with *micro teaching*. In fact, the diagnoses of shortfalls is the starting point of both. In the former the purpose is transmission of ideas to others (learners whereas), in the latter it is for self-improvement. Improvement, however, is the common goal.

Though an invariably successful strategy it often turns out to be time consuming but the time spent becomes an investment because internalisation of learning, leads to faster learning of subsequent steps. The time saved at subsequent stages thus compensates for the extra time spent now.

Though the conceptual terminology of Action Research introduced by *Stephen Corey* sounds new, there is nothing new about it, as teachers have all along been using it for transmitting knowledge to the pupils. It is, in fact, common sense which is not uncommon in its utilisation. Corey, however, gave a formal shape to this informal approach.

34

Constructivism

Constructivism has its origin in the ideas incidentally mentioned by Jean Piaget, John Dewey and Lev Vygotsky as a part of their writings on some other subjects. None of the classical educationalists or psychologists including the above have, however, exclusively written on the subject in any detail.

Concept of Constructivism

These ideas have been picked up and written about by some academicians. The main ideas picked up by almost all of them are

- Human beings construct/generate their knowledge by reflecting and giving meaning to their experiences and hypotheses about the environment.
- Each Individual generates his own rules and models rather than acquiring their knowledge from others.
- Observations, experimentation and hands-on-experience are the main sources of these experiences, reflection on which yields knowledge
- Learning in the classroom has to be an active interactive process imbued with operational democracy
- Learning involves focussed attention interaction and communication
- Previous knowledge and experiences are the main determinants of the process of learning
- Initial learning which is the foundation of future learning is the immediate environment and its diverse facets
- The generation of knowledge is a continuous tireless striving
- Subsequent introspection can augment or change past knowledge
- Knowledge is best acquired when the learner becomes an active 'subject' in learning and not a passive object of learning. Experiences are supposed to replace formal tests and procedures.

Critical Estimate of Constructivism

Though constructivism professes to be a reaction to didactic approaches like

Behaviourism, it has failed to dethrone Behaviourism which still holds the reins of educational theories and practices.

Constructivism therefore has more critics than supporters. Some of the main criticisms are:

- Human beings in this ever-growing and changing scenario cannot start learning from a scratch ignoring the existing store of human knowledge.
- Constructivism is neither a philosophy nor a theory but is only a method of teaching, which focusses on experience-based learning by doing problem-solving which has all along been advocated by educationalists in the past.
- Self-experience cannot cover the entire expanse of knowledge and can be applied only to segments of knowledge and only in a few disciplines. Even where applicable the time available will not be adequate for using this method.
- The approach is more applicable to advanced learners.

Conclusion

When textbooks based on the constructivist approach funded by the government were experimentally introduced, it evoked criticism from teachers and parents.

It would, thus, be a mistake to accept constructivism as a rationale for accepting to use pure discovery as a method of instruction, as lack of guidance and support to the young learners, may create chaos.

SECTION IV
Evaluating People Performance

35

Concept of Evaluation

A fit conclusion of this book naturally is a description about the meaning of educational evaluation. Such a conclusion has to be brief and simple. This is what is attempted here.

Evaluation is a much broader concept than what is commonly thought of. In fact, it not only touches but also crosses the boundaries of different facets of education. The following diagram given by *Ralf Taylor* best explains this phenomenon:

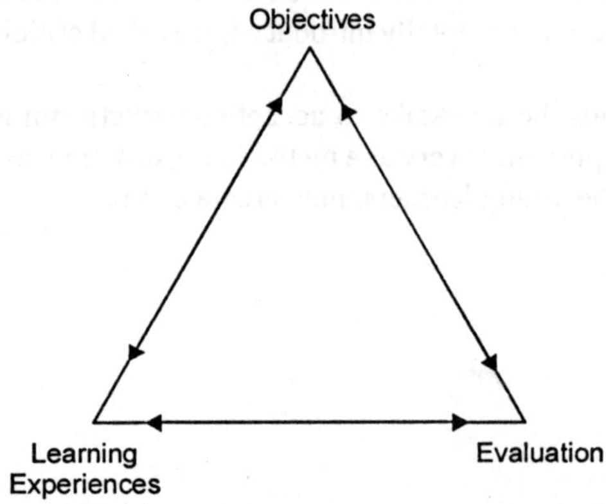

Concept of Evaluation

The above diagram has three nodal points:

- Objectives,
- Learning Experiences, and
- Evaluation

Each one of these is related to the other two through a two-way relationship. Let as first examine the connotation of each of the three nodal points.

Objectives denote the targets set to be realised through the educational programmes.

The *Learning Experiences* constitute the teaching-learning situations covering both the materials and methods deployed for realising the objectives.

Evaluation connotes the techniques, tools and procedures used for assessing the kind and degree of attainment realised through the inputs pressed into service and for further enhancing and improving their levels.

Process of Evaluation

Let us now focus attention on the three facets together and starting from the objectives move in the anti-clockwise direction. Having set the targets for realisation, we continue and evolve teaching-learning situations and strategies for realising them. As the targets have manifestations in different facets of personality (both scholastic and co-scholastic), the teaching-learning situations too have to be consciously tailored and devised *for each one of them individually and for all of them collectively*. These teaching-learning situations could assume different forms in different locations for learning—in the classroom or the laboratory or the library and so on. The focus of each one of them, however, shall be on the realisation of objectives set. After feeling 'apparently' satisfied that the content of the courses and the methodologies of curriculum transaction, have been apt and appropriate and that the objectives may have been realised, we revert to evaluation. Here, it is necessary to identify the suitable techniques and to design appropriate tools for evaluating the *kind and degree* of the level of attainment of the objectives, through the learning experiences offered to the students. While at the stage of learning experiences, we check whether appropriate teaching-learning situations have been provided for realising the objectives set, at the juncture of evaluation, we also try to judge whether and in what degree, have the objectives set been actually realised.

Now, if we find that certain objectives have not been possible to be realised by the students, we move in the *clock-wise direction* and again from the nodal point of objectives, to first find out whether the techniques of evaluation selected and the tools used were appropriate. In case of the detection of a shortfall, the necessary amendments are made. We then proceed to the learning experiences, to discover the facets of their inadequacy, if any, for realising the objectives and make necessary modifications here as well, wherever necessary. After the amendments are effected both in the content and/or the methodology, we again check on their potential for realising the objectives.

Evaluation, thus, attempts to judge the aptness adequacy and appropriateness of:

- the objectives in respect of different facets of personality for the age-group concerned,
- the learning experiences (the content, aids and the methodology of instruction used),

- the evaluation techniques and tools selected/devised and used in the educational programme, and
- the kind and degree of attainment recorded by the students.

The foregoing explanation of the Concept of Evaluation clarifies the meaning and the implication of the concept, which broadly covers the total gamut of educational pursuits, aimed at the growth and development of the students, who ought to be conceived as the 'subjects' and not the 'objects' of education.

Examination and Evaluation

It appears desirable at this point to subject this explanation to a further elaboration and clarification. The best way of doing this appears to be, to attempt a comparison of the concepts of Examinations and Evaluation because one is often confused with the other.

Examinations and Evaluation

Criteria	*Examinations*	*Evaluation*
Purpose facets covered	Assessment of the level of achievement'	Improvement of the level of achievement and growth. Diagnosis, remediation, enrichment and improvement of competencies.
Personality facets covered	Mainly scholastic aspects of personality-academic achieve-ment—covered	Both scholastic and co-scholastic aspects of personality covered-interests, attitudes, personal and social qualities, health status, as also proficiency in outdoor activities, etc. over and above academic achievement.
Evaluation Techniques	Mainly written and practical examination	Observation, interviews, and other unconventional techniques, besides written, oral and practical examinations.
Evaluation Tools	Mainly questions and question papers	Rating scales, inventories, interview schedules, profiles besides questions and question papers.
Periodicity	In periodical strokes as events	A continuous affair built into the total teaching-learning process as an integral part.
Student Status	An incognito roll number	An individual of flesh and blood.
Uses of Test Results	Assessment, classifica-tion and certification of students	Further improvement of performance levels of students.

It is hoped that the above table will not only clarify the common confusions but help us in understanding of the two concepts of Examinations and Evaluation, bringing to the fore the realisation that evaluation is a much broader term than examination, that it does not consist of only periodical events but is a continuous process, that it goes much beyond classification and certification of students only in regard to the academic achievement but aims at the diagnosis of the strengths and weaknesses of the students and the remediation/ enhancement and enrichment of achievement. Evaluation, thus, ought to be conceived as an exercise concerned with the process of engineering development and growth in the various facets of the personality of students in both scholastic and co-scholastic aspects because:

Evaluation = Measurement + Value Judgement about Growth

We will be discussing this last aspect in greater detail in the Chapter on Continuous and Comprehensive School-based Evaluation in the context of the coverage of the total personality of students (scholastic and co-scholastic) not just confining mainly to the assessment of academic achievement alone.

The most important thing in this regard which deserves to be emphasised, however, is that evaluation is not to be conceived just an end in itself, but a means of promoting growth.

Examination Reform

Educational Evaluation ought to be conceived as an on-going process of collecting evidences for judging the worth of educational inputs and outcomes, in all the three domains of human development (Cognitive, Affective and Psycho-motor) for purposes of making various types of decisions.

Ventures in Educational Evaluation, therefore, should be geared to critically judging the appropriateness of:

- objectives
- materials and methodology
- learner growth
- evaluation procedures and practices
- Impact making potential of educational programmes for not just identifying gaps but addressing them.

With a view to uncompromisingly ushering - in , *a shift of focus from 'examination-based education to education based examination*', the above paradigms would , in the area of learner evaluation , operationally imply:

- Use of Educational Evaluation 'for' learning, rather than merely 'of' learning.
- Disallowing examinations from passing a judgement on the 'total' personality on the basis of 'partial" evidences, through the introduction of Comprehensive and Continuous Institution -based Evaluation (CCE), with an independent certificate issued by the institution, followed by a foot-note about it in the certificate of external examinations.

- Use of a larger number and variety of techniques and tools for effective, accurate, dependable, just and practicable evaluation.
- Balanced coverage of content and objectives, de-emphasis of memorisation and containment of subjectivity.
- Use of 'Designs' and 'Blueprints' for preparing balanced question papers in written examinations; cognisance of 'Process of Performance' in practical examinations and extending the scope of oral examinations beyond 'content' to 'communication'.
- Abolition of the practice of declaring learners as 'pass' or 'fail' and declaration of examination results in terms of subject-wise 'Relative' (Stanine) grades.
- Increased use of technology in examination processes for making them fast and error-free.
- Strengthening the compulsory component of Educational Evaluation in Teacher Education Courses.
- Encouragement to innovative initiatives like 'On -Demand' and 'On-line' examinations.
- Training of question paper setters and moderators in the Concept and Techniques of Evaluation.
- Constructively tackling operational issues and problems of examinations through built-in research initiatives.

The learners going through such an achievement verification drill, could be justly expected to graduate:

- *From only being* consumers of knowledge *to becoming* creators of knowledge
- *From only being* human beings *to becoming* human resources
- *From only being* persons *to becoming* personalities with an identity.

A National Testing Service be established as an instrument of quality control (maintenance and improvement) of the standard of education. Testing Services may be available on voluntary basis.

Recommended Reform Measures and Gains from them

	Measures of Reform Recommended	*Expected Gains to Education from the Implementation of the Reform Measures*
1.	Conceiving examination reform in its totality with linkages between different stages.	Smooth implementation of reform measures.
2.	Use of examinations, to improve student's performance, besides assessing it.	Remediation of diagnosed short-falls to improve the standard of education.

(*Contd.*)

3.	Supplementation of external examinations with comprehensive and continuous school-based evaluation.	Attention by institutions to the investment of efforts for development of the total personality of students.
4.	Separate certificates for continuous comprehensive evaluation and external examinations.	Provision of insight into an individuals' personality and proficiency for use by the institutions of higher studies and employers.
5.	Coverage of co-scholastic aspects of personality through continuous and comprehensive evaluation.	Development of desirable personal and social qualities, interests, attitudes and values, etc. in students.
6.	Improvements in external examinations.	– Minimisation of subjectivity. – De-emphasis of memorization. – Discouragement of selective study. – Improvement of the teaching-learning process
7.	Abolition of the system of declaring results in terms of 'Pass' or 'Fail' and over-all divisions on the basis of pre-determined cut-scores and their presentation as subject-wise relative grades.	Containing the current over-importance of examination results and the mad motivation for malpractices that follow.
8.	Opportunity to improve upon ones grades through subsequent attempts.	Rectifying the situation of irreversible judgements of examination to be cleared in all subjects in one stroke.
9.	Opportunity for clearing examination by parts.	Reducing wastage due to a large number of failures.
10.	Flexibility in the content and operation of Continuous and Comprehensive Evaluation.	Applicability of the scheme in widely varying situations.
11.	No detention policy	Reduction in the incidence of drop-outs.
12	No public examination earlier than Class VIII	- Reduction of pressure on students and teachers. - Availability of greater freedom for self-paced learning.
13.	Decentralisation of the public examination machinery.	Efficiency in the management of examinations and an accelerated speed of operations.

14.	Introduction of Semester System	- Providing mobility to the students through periodical earning of credits by students. - Reducing pressure on students. - Ensuring continuous learning' throughout the period of education.
	Institution of Aptitude Tests for admission to courses of higher education and for jobs.	- Appropriate selection of suitable candidates. - Reducing the chances of failure in courses, resulting drop-outs and frustration on jobs.
16.	Establishment of a National Testing-Service to offer voluntary service for selection.	Equivalence in standards. - Opportunities to students to appear at a bench-marking examination when they feel they are ready.

36

Purpose of Evaluation

Some Important Purposes of Educational Evaluation

E.J. Furst lists some important purposes of educational evaluation as under:

- judging the effectiveness of learning
- tasting assumptions and practices
- classifying objectives
- selecting and appraising objectives
- planning instructional programmes
- motivating learners
- guidance of learners
- certification of candidates
- selection of candidates
- in-service development of workers

These purposes remain undeniably valid even after more than half a century of their enunciation, both in letter and spirit. However, when applied to the current testing scene they have functionally got shrink to

- Bench-marking and certification of the level of attainments of an individual used as an eligibility criteria for a variety of future academic and professional pursuits. This is reflected through the certification of candidates for degrees, diplomas, certificates, etc.

Selection Tests

Selection tests are now widely in use mainly for

- admission to courses of higher/professional education
- recruitment for jobs
- promotion and on-the-job elevation in institutions

In these instances though they are called aptitude tests, but in actual practice are just achievement tests.

The phenomenon has come into place because aptitude tests are difficult to construct and expertise for it is not easily available. Secondly because the number of candidate aspirants are many times more than the actual positions available and the tests in vogue also turn out to be *elimination* rather than *selection* tests.

It needs to be noted that while the bench-marking achievement tests are based on '*content*' the selection tests are based on "*proficiencies*".

The selection tests, by and large, have come to have the following components:

1. General awareness
2. Linguistic ability
3. Quantitative ability
4. Subject-matter competence
5. General mental ability (verbal and non-verbal)

This broad framework with some adaptations and varying weightages to different aspects is used in most situations.

The tests consist of multiple choice variety of items. The number of test items normally being more than what the candidates can possibly attempt in the given time, they just become *speed tests* rather than being *power tests*, even though they ought to be power tests, except in some special situations.

Furthermore, apart from the mistakes and shortfalls in the basic principles of constructing multiple choice test items, they often ask for *insignificant microscopic details*. This no doubt raises the difficulty level of the questions but imparts little predictive validity to the test.

The greatest shortcoming of these tests in most cases is that the test items test mainly memorisation (recall and reproduction of information).

The other higher abilities of understanding, application of acquired knowledge in unfamiliar situations, analysis and interpretation of information, synthesis and drawing of inferences, based on given information and overall evaluation of situations, are not attempted to be tested. This is because the prescribed *syllabus* mostly gives only topics to be covered and no indication about the *abilities* to be tested and the weightages to them.

These shortfalls pass off undetected and unquestioned particularly because the establishments needing to fill vacancies do not have specialists in testing/measurement/evaluation to man the operations related to testing and the decisions are taken administratively. A glaring example of this is the delayed announcement of the date of the tests and then expecting the tests to be prepared as a turnkey job. This makes test construction and its uploading a fire fighting exercise where many essential requirements like vetting of tests have often to be sidelined causing mistakes to creep into the tests.

Sometimes the agencies also require five alternatives in a multiple choice test, which is a long discarded practice. Another more grave cause of shortfalls is that the business of test construction is often outsourced on the basis of tenders where the establishments are obliged to select the cheapest and not the most efficient agency with experience and expertise in testing. In this game of sorts, many unqualified agencies have come into play. Many unemployed people too have found employment in this manner taking testing as a business and not as a field of specialised functioning.

Furthermore, the employers seldom undertake any *job analysis* of the positions required to be filled in and easy generalised solutions are attempted to be pressed into service for solving specialised problems.

In evaluation situations designs for tests are but necessary, in any case. This is being discussed in subsequent sections.

Class Promotions in Institutions

Both these are internal matters of the institutions and the employing establishments but the tests in the two situations, however, display quite a lot of similarity.

Promotion from One Class to Another in Institutions

These have some basic characteristics. They are based on "norms" set by the institutions, for example, in schools, they may be say the attainment of 30% marks in each subject of study, at the university level they may be 40% and in professional institutions they may be 50%.

Promotions from class to class should ideally be based on assessments done throughout the year. In higher education, it is usually based on the level of attainment mainly on the academic/scholastic front. At the school level, it normally covers both the scholastic and the co-scholastic areas of personality.

The concept of Comprehensive and Continuous Evaluation which is *institution-based* in school situations broadly covers—

- Health status like height, weight, chest expansion, eye-sight, hearing, etc. (which can be assessed by the teacher)
- Personal and social qualities like regularity, punctuality, habits of cleanliness, discipline, diligence, sense of responsibility, emotional stability, cooperation, civic consciousness, spirit of social service (for whichever evidences are available).
- Interests in the literary, artistic, scientific and cultural and social service areas (selected by the learner to be pursued)
- Attitudes towards studies, institutional programmes, public property as also towards societal issues.
- Values like dignity of labour, honesty, courage, courtesy, tolerance, forgiveness, team-spirit (for whichever evidences are available).
- Outdoor activities like games, sports, yoga, gymnastics, scouting, NCC, swimming, gardening, adventure activities, first aid (in whichever area a learner participates).

Besides

- Academic achievement where beside evaluation through questions, question papers, laboratory experiments, projects, assignments, surveys and case studies also become subjects of evaluation. The outcomes of learning are also evaluated not just in terms of marks but also in terms of symbolic grades through rating scales (usually five point) observation schedules, inventories, check-list, etc.

Being *comprehensive* covering both scholastic and co-scholastic aspects as enunciated above such evaluation has but to be *continuous*, spread over the total teaching—learning process as an integral part.

While in the co-scholastic areas, the outcomes of evaluation may not be aggregated, in the scholastic/academic areas they normally are aggregated and used for purposes of class promotions as presented through the following hypothetical diagrammatic representation. The diagram presumes that an academic session starts in July and ends in April.

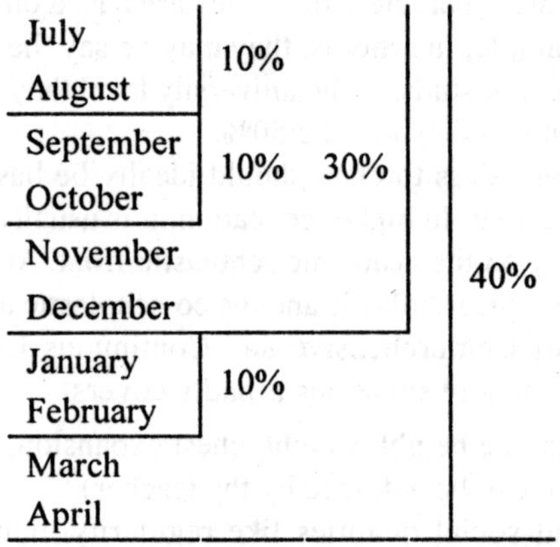

Test Time	*Weightage*	*Syllabus Covered*
Aug end	10%	Jul & Aug
Oct end	10%	Sep & Oct
Dec end	30%	July to Dec
Feb end	10%	Jan & Feb
April end	40%	Jul to Apr

The tests carrying 10% weightage are supposed to exclusively focus on the topics covered, within the time span concerned. The tests carrying 30% and 40% weightage, will in addition also focus on linkages between the topics covered during the concerned span without repetition.

At the terminal stages, *two different independent supplementary certificates*, one issued by the institution and another by the external examining and certifying agency are proposed. This is meant particularly for overcoming the malpractices which are likely to creap-in. The institutional certificate will be issued on a format prescribed by the examining agency. The Certificate of External Examination will carry a foot-note that the certificate issued by the institution may also be studied for judging the total personality of the learner.

Promotion in Jobs

There are two types of situations in vogue. In one case an individual moves to another job. In the other case the individual is given a new designation and a higher scale of pay but continues to do almost the same job in a supervisory capacity.

In both these cases, it is entirely an internal matter. In smaller establishments it is more of a subjective decision. In large scale establishments elaborate criteria, rules and procedures are used for imparting greater objectivity and transparency to the process.

Ideally, these promotions ought to be based on:

- The workers' self-evaluation report.
- The supervisor's report of individuals performance on the job covering both technical abilities and personal attributes.
- The peer evaluation report about things like cordiality, team spirit, etc.

In large-scale establishments, there are detailed proformas and procedures available for periodical performance evaluation.

Promotion tests both formal and informal are used in both job promotions and class promotions. In both cases observation turns out to be an important technique of evaluation.

In promotion on jobs the evaluation should be done regularly/periodically and a record maintained to be aggregated, instead of an individual evaluated on the basis of the last impression, to avoid subjectivity. It is desirable that an external expert is also involved in deriving the final ratings. To be objective and transparent, the methodology for quantifying qualitative information in terms of a numerical index like the PREP Index ought to be used. An independent chapter is devoted to this concept.

37

Preparing of Objective-based Questions of Different Forms

In any comprehensive programme of educational reform, improvement of examinations and the improvement in the quality of the question papers is a foregone conclusion. Individual questions would, therefore, have to be framed in such way that when put together in the form of a question paper, they fulfill the prerequisites of good measuring instruments. We may make use of essay type, short-answer type, very short answer type and objective type questions or their contributions combination of them, but they should all conform to and satisfy the basic characteristics of a good question of the given form. This is discussed below :

Characteristics of Good Questions

Objective-Based

A good question should be framed to test a predetermined objective and it should to able to test the concerned ability effectively. Questions may sometimes test more than one objective. They may also sometimes test one or more specifications of a particular objective on which that question is based. *In case a question attempts to test more than one objective, it is designated as the one testing the highest objective in the hierarchy which it aims to test.*

Content-Specific

The content or subject matter on which a question is based is closely related to the objective being tested. The framer of the question, has, therefore, to take into account the topic or the sub-topic he is going to prepare a question on. He should also ensure that a question samples exactly the same area of content, which is desired to be tested through it.

Form of Questions

Essay type, short-answer type, very short answer type and objective-type questions are the main forms of questions in use. In a question, the form depends considerably on the *kind of ability as well as the nature of the content desired to be tested.* Some forms are more suitable than others for testing certain abilities. Essay-type questions, for example, are more suitable for testing abilities like organisation of thoughts, analysis, interpretation, etc. through written expression. Therefore, a judicious mix of the appropriate question forms, will have to be attempted, while setting questions which may finally be woven into a question paper. A decision about this has to be made while preparing the design for the question paper itself.

Wording of Questions

To bring about objectivity in evaluation, there is need for using clear, precise and unambiguous language while framing questions. Use of unfamiliar and difficult terminology may be avoided so that the comprehension of the question itself, may not become a problem for the learners by and which may even influence the difficulty level of the question. A question should be so worded that by-and-large, all learners as also examiners may make the same meaning out of it, about the scope and length of the expected answer. Here special care is to be taken *to avoid the use of stock, phrases like describe, elucidate, discuss or write short notes on, write an account of, write a report on, what do you know, etc.* What is expected to be written by the learners as part of the answer has to be explained to them in unabiguous terms, while wording the questions themselves.

Structuring the Situation

In writing different questions, selection of an appropriate situation is an important step in the framing of questions. Textbook situations could be alright for testing knowledge. Other situations discussed in the class may be suitable for testing knowledge or understanding. But to test application of knowledge, some unfamiliar situations real or hypothetical will need to be identified or even concoted. Although in such cases situations are likely to go beyond the textbook, yet they should be in keeping with the ability levels of learners and related to the content studied by them. It will be advisable if the teacher collects such situations and keeps a record of these so that they may be available to him as and when needed.

Estimated Difficulty Level

While writing a question, the framer of the questions should be conscious of the estimated difficulty level of the question in relation to the ability of pupils for whom the question is meant. The difficulty level of a question usually depends upon the complexity of the mental processes involved (objectives) in responding to it, the standard of the area of the content desired to be tested and the time available which can be spent for answering it. The difficulty level of a particular question can be estimated fairly well in advance by an experienced teacher. Actual difficulty index can, however, be statistically calculated only after the question has been really tried out and its responses analysed. Established procedures are available for analysing responses of multiple choice type of question and calculating the difficulty level. However, an experienced teacher can easily estimate the difficulty level in approximately in broad terms. Such decision helps in deciding the distribution of questions of varying estimated difficulty while preparing question papers.

Discrimination Value

It is also not possible to estimate the discriminating value of a question unless it is tried out. Nevertheless when some novel situations are involved and common place questions are avoided, the questions definitely go a long way in discriminating the bright learners from the weaker ones. *Questions at either extremes of the difficulty continuum are poor discriminators, while those in the middle range are found to be more effective in this respect.*

Delimiting the Scope of the Answer

The question framer or paper setter should in respect of free response questions ensure that while constructing a question s/he gives due thought to the expected answer. S/he is also required to develop an outline of the expected answer alongwith the marks (value point) to be devoted to each part of the expected answer, as part of the marking scheme. This is desirable to be done at the same time as the preparation of the question. This would reveal the weaknesses (if any) in the wording of the question itself. It should be specific and precise in language so that the scope and length of the expected answer stands clearly delimited and defined. This would evoke the expected answer. In case the test constructor discovers that the question as worded is not likely to yield the expected answer, he would change its wording.

Key/Marking Scheme

In case of objective-type questions, the key must be prepared alongwith the questions. In case of long answer, short answer and very short answer questions, outlines of expected answers and the marking scheme has to be prepared. Weightage in terms of marks to each value-point or aspect of the expected answer has also be indicated.

A question framer or paper setter, while constructing each question, should be conscious of the various dimensions of questions discussed above as also the other considerations and rules for framing different forms of questions.

The keys and the marking schems should be prepared at the same time as the questions are framed.

Forms of Objective-Based Questions

Objective-based questions are questions designed to test definite objectives/ abilities of teaching and testing. They could assume different forms, of which objective type questions are one. The other three varieties being Essay Type (Long Answer Type), Short Answer Type and Very Short Answer Type. All the forms (types) of questions are used for testing, some objective/ability/ competency/proficiency beside some designated content. Thus, *all objective type questions are objective-based, though all objective-based questions are not objective type questions.* Questions could broadly be classified into different forms/types as under:

Classification of Question Forms

- Fixed response questions
  - Objective Type
    - True False Type
    - Matching Type
    - Fill-in-the blank Type
    - Multiple Choice Type
      - Only Correct Answer Type
      - Only Wrong Answer Type
      - Best Answer Type
      - Mixed Type
  - Very Short Answer Type
- Free response questions
  - Short Answer Type
  - Essay Type or Long Answer Type

It is intended here to discuss different forms of questions in terms of their characteristics, their strong and weak points and the rules governing their preparation.

It has already been mentioned that depending upon the objective (ability) and the content area (subject-matter) we can select the most suitable form of the question (essay type, short answer, very short answer or objective type).

The most commonly used tools of evaluation in the written tests are the questions which are generally of two types – the *free response* type and the *fixed responses* type. The long answer/essay type questions which are basically free response questions have been in use for quite some time. They used to be the sole variety of questions in traditional question papers. Now with the realisation of the shortcomings of these questions (as proved through research studies both in India and abroad) and their adverse effects on the accuracy, dependability and objectivity of examination results, short answer questions which also fall under this category are also being increasingly used. Fixed response questions (Very Short Answer type and Objective type) are those where the answer is fixed and any deviation from the expected answer is taken as incorrect. In free response questions as compared to this situation, the examinee exercises freedom to manipulate his answer in his own language.

The long answer or free response type questions are still being used but in limited numbers, only for testing those abilities which other forms of tests cannot effectively test.

Operational descriptions of questions of different forms are attempted below:

(i) Objective Type (*Multiple Choice* with four alternatives).

(ii) *Very Short Answer (VSA)* questions usually carrying one or two marks and requiring an answer in one word, one phrase or at the most one sentence or involving one or two steps of mathematical calculation. They should need about a minute to answer.

(iii) *Short Answer Questions (SA)* carrying two to four marks which require answers in about 25 to 50 words or involve four to six steps of mathematical calculation. Each of these questions usually require 3 to 5 minutes to answer.

(iv) *Long Answer or Essay Type Questions (LA/ET)* which require answers between 100 to 400 words or upto a maximum of ten steps of mathematical calculation. These may carry 5 to 15 marks.

(v) In languages the composition questions require the learners to discuss certain themes using their own vocabulary, usage, syntax with originality and in their own style. These questions would also need to be given a rough time limit based on the expected length of the answer. Therefore, the length of the answer will also be required to be approximately indicated preferably in terms of words and not lines or pages as part of the wording of the question itself in the question paper. In case a question paper carries 100 marks and 100 minutes are given as the time limit, then 50 seconds could be allowed for answering a question of one mark (leaving 10 seconds for revision). The length of the expected answer could also then be determined on the basis of the age group for which the question is meant in view of the marks devoted to a question.

Preparing Long Answer or Essay Type Questions

These questions are considered to be easy to prepare and administer in the traditional scene. They also offer quite a lot of freedom to the examinees who can use their own language and style of writing. These questions require examinees to choose the language, select the facts, organise the ideas for presenting a response to the question asked in the way they choose.

These questions provide examinees an opportunity *to analyse, synthesise, re-organise, integrate, synthesise and evaluate situations, as also to investigate, interpret them for drawing conclusions for justifying or negating a particular stand.*

They also have the potential of testing the originality and creativity of the particular examinee, Thus they can most effectively test those abilities and mental processes which are not possible to be tested through any other form of questions.

Shortcomings

Despite the positive points, the long answer or essay type questions are also imbued with some very serious shortcomings. While they provide freedom to the examinee, they also offer freedom to the examiner to go by his whims. Thus, they breed subjectivity in scoring. Quite often they are criticised and quite rightly so, for introducing a substantial element of unreliability in scoring.

Besides, there is also another serious shortcoming and that is that because they require long answers, they also need longer time to answer and because they need a long answering time, only a few of such type of questions can be asked in a given time. Again because only be few questions can find a place in a question paper, they are able to test only a small part of the prescribed syllabus. The use of such questions, in question papers, more often than not, encourage selective study and selective teaching, which in turn endangers the validity (or accuracy) and reliability (or dependability) of the result, because of restricted and poor sampling of the content.

In this background, therefore, while long answer questions are incorporated in the question papers, their number and the quantum of marks devoted to them are deliberately restricted to the barest minimum.

In spite of these shortcomings the long answer type questions continue to be used in examinations, because as already mentioned *they can test those abilities which no other form of question can effectively evaluate* e.g., the capacity to weigh ideas, to argue in favour or against a proposition, to establish relationships, to critically analyse situations, to judge the implications of a given phenomenon and so on. These questions also promote self-study with insight.

Some Guiding Principles for Preparing Long Answer Questions

Preparation of good essay type or long answer questions is by no means an easy task. Some tips for preparing this type of questions are spelt out below:

- Long Answer or Essay Type questions because of their limitations, should be set to test only those instructional objectives (abilities), which are not possible to be tested by other forms of questions.
- Essay questions should be prepared for specifically testing the mental processes or learning outcomes implied by the objectives in view.
- These questions ought to be so worded that the scope and approximate length of the expected answer is clear to the learners.
- Maturation level of the examinees must be taken into consideration while constructing an essay/long answer type question. Length and nature of expected answer will differ from class to class. For example, questions requiring discussion, interpretation, summarisation or evaluation may be asked in higher classes, whereas those testing abilities like listing, describing, selecting, etc. may be considered suitable for lower classes.

- Outline answers of each question with value points (the allocation of marks) to different parts of the expected answer, also needs to be specified as part of the marking scheme. This should be done at the same time as drafting the questions themselves. After framing each question the test constructor, should revert back to the language of the question and check that it would evoke the expected answer from the examinees. In case it does not do so, changes may be introduced in the wording of the question in question, so that it may be ensured to yield the expected answer.
- The use of directional words or phrases like the following need to be systematically avoided:

Or

Elucidate	Relate
Exemplify	Evaluate
Criticise	Weigh
Discuss	Examine
Justify	Write an essay on ....
	Write short notes on ....
	Write a report on ....
	What do you think of ....
	What do you know about ....

The purpose of these words or directions is not clearly understood by learners and also sometimes by examiners. What the learner is expected to write in the answer, should, therefore, be clearly and unambiguously stated instead of using these unintelligible directional words and phrases.

- This will also contain the tendency of the learners to write all that they know about that topic, instead of responding to the requirements of the questions.
- The questions ought to be worded in such a manner that each question presents a definite problem. Though the learner should be provided freedom to choose the language and style, this should be exercised within the dimensions and parameters which may be indicated by the wording of the questions.
- The marks that each question carries should not be indicated against them as a whole (e.g. 10). They should be clearly distributed among the various parts of the expected answer or various expected abilities attempted to be tested and indicated as say (2 + 4 + 4).
- The questions should not be repeated vertatim from among those asked in previous examinations or lifted from those given/listed at the end of the chapters of the books/work-books.

- The questions set may not just be direct questions, answers to which may be found directly in the books and could be lifted as such from a particular portion of a book and memorised. The questions should also invariably present situations or problems which *call for thinking* rather than just recall and reproduction of memorised information.

Scoring of Long Answer Questions

Essay/Long answer type questions in the traditional set-up are prepared quickly but they take a much longer time to answer. Furthermore, though easy to prepare, they are difficult to answer, mark and evaluate.

A detailed marking scheme, giving outline answers and value points in terms of marks for different aspects or facts of the expected answer (desired to be taken into consideration for purposes of evaluation) have to be prepared alongwith the framing of questions and adhered to in letter and spirit while evaluating answers as mentioned earlier.

The aspects of an answer required to be evaluated should be made known to the learners through the wording of the questions in the question paper itself e.g. there may be situations where spelling mistakes, may be taken into account for deducting marks and others where the opposite may be true.

Correction of a sample of scripts by at the time of Co-ordination Meetings and the modification of the marking scheme prepared by the paper setter, wherever considered necessary, needs to be meticulously done for finalising it. This would iron out ambiguities regarding the interpretation of the wording of a question and thus, ensure objectivity.

As far as possible scoring of essay/long answer type questions should be done on an *analytical* basis. *Impressionistic* scoring may be done only in cases where it is absolutely unavoidable.

However, the directions in the question paper may clearly indicate to the candidates, the major points of emphasis in the scoring pattern. They could even be built into the language of the questions themselves or form part of the general directions. Furthermore, if a *diagram* or an *example* is required to be given by the learners as part of the answer, it should be clearly mentioned in the question and not left by the paper setter to the initiative of the learner or the imagination of the evaluator.

In the marking scheme, which may be finalised for the evaluation of scripts, the aspects and the sub-aspects or the steps of the process of the expected answer be clearly spelt out. Each of these may be given a definite weightage e.g. in a given situation, and wherever applicable its analysis, interpretation and drawing of inferences may be allocated separate weightages. Similarly, if spellings, language, style, coherence, and unity of presentation deserve to be given independent weightages, these also should be made known to the learners. *In short the learners should know what is expected of them, what will enable them gain marks and what will make them to lose them.*

In Mathematics the steps of calculation and weightages to them be clearly indicated in the marking schemes.

Preparing Short Answer Type of Questions

Short answer questions present a compromise between the long answer and objective type questions. They enjoy the advantages of both the types of questions.

While the long answer questions suffer from lack of objectively and reliability, the short answer questions are technically better off in regard to these criteria.

On the other hand while the objective type questions are largely unable to test abilities like expression, organisation and synthesisation of ideas, the short answer questions possess, at least in a limited measure, the capability of testing these abilities.

As these questions enjoy the advantages of both essay and objective type questions, without their disadvantages, to some extent, the short answer questions have come to be increasingly used in examinations.

A rule of thumb used in many examinations is the provision of a weightage of 50% marks in a question paper to short answer questions with the remaining 50% be distributed between the long answer and the very short answer/objective type questions.

Short answer questions too have always to be carefully structured in wording, so as to evoke specific and to the point answers. They should not be vague in their wording and should not encourage or admit vague and global answers. This is what differentiates them from the traditional, open-ended *short note questions* indicating themes without enunciating the dimensions of the given themes expected to be tackled by the examinees, like "Write short notes on democracy", where a learner does not know as to how long or how short, the short note has got to be on such a topic like democracy, on which even books can be written. The intent of such a questions could be more than satisfied if we break-up the questions and structure it as under to give it an edge of specificity, "Define democracy. Give two merits of Indian democracy and two demerits of Indian democracy."

The construction of short answer questions also requires lesser level of competence in preparation as compared to the objective type questions.

As the limits in regard to length/dimensions of short answer type questions could vary quite a bit, they cannot be precisely defined. Still some rough and ready explanation of their physical dimensions is attempted here.

Short Answer Questions normally require:

- A 30 to 50 word answer
- An answer with upto 6 steps of mathematical calculations

They usually have 2 to 4 credit points and they approximately need 3 to 5 minutes for answering them.

Thus, there can be many short answer questions in a question paper covering a larger proportion of the syllabus, than what a few long answer questions can possibly accomplish. With this increase in the length of the test they tend to provide a more reliable/dependable estimate of an individual learner's proficiency and potential.

The following examples of short answer question could illustrate the above points and be worded as under :

History : Give two evidences to substantiate that Clive was the real founder of the British Empire in India.

English : Write a paragraph in about 40-50 words on trees. You could use some of the following words:

Beauty	Utility
Pleasure	Forest
Branches	Shade
Twigs	Fruits
Birds	Logs

A long answer question could also sometimes be converted into a number of short answer questions with great advantage as illustrated through the following example:

Usual Form of Long Answer Question

Give a brief account of various theories of organic evolution. (Essay-type question)

Modified Form (Short-Answer Questions)

(i) Name the various theories of organic evolution.

(ii) Which theory better explains the mechanism of organic evolution? Give two reasons.

(iii) Write two fundamental principles on which the theory of Lamarck is based.

(iv) How does d'Vries' theory differ from that of Weismann's?

Such questions can be profitably used in both external and internal examinations. They also ensure better reliability, because such questions are more definite and specific and can be scored more objectively. They also cover a larger segment of the syllabus as we can have a number of such questions in place of a single long answer type question. Therefore, they draw upon a wider range of learners' achievements than the usual long answer question do. They also ensure adequate sampling of content and thereby help improve the validity of the question paper.

It is, therefore, desirable that we should encourage the use of such questions in our examinations to improve their validity and reliability and objectivity.

Preparing Very Short Answer Type Questions

Very short answer type of questions have been discovered as a possible substitute to objective type questions. While they can be assessed as objectively as objective type questions, they do not require as many conditions or rules to be satisfied in construction as the objective type questions do.

Very short answer type questions require an answer in one word, one phrase or at the most one sentence. They have *just one or two testing points and* thus, ensure almost the same level of *objectively* in scoring, as exists in the objective type of questions. Normally they are assigned just one or two marks and need about a minute to answer.

In view of the small answering time and low mark weightage, many such questions can be set in a question paper by using a very small quantum of marks. They can also, therefore, be spread over a larger chunk of the prescribed syllabus, thus, improving upon the *reliability* of a question paper.

Sometimes when the forms of questions are classified as *Selection type* and *Supply type questions*, the very short answer type of questions are classified among the 'supply type questions' because unlike most of the objective type questions, the answer has to be supplied by the learner and not just selected from out of the given ones.

Very Short Answer type questions could assume a number of forms. Some examples of these related to English are given below :

Fill-in-the-blank type:

I am not satisfied .... your answer.

Completion type:

I was so worried ....

Analogy type:

Soyabean: Protein :: Rice:

Location type:

Show the location of Sydney on the outline map of the world

Transformation type:

Questions on
– Reported speech
– Voices
– Synthesis
– Transformation of Sentences

Usage type:

Use the following words/phrases in your own sentences :
– Break/Break-up
– Look/Look-after

Question type:

What is a mole?

Preparing Objective Type (Multiple Choice) Questions

Objective-based and objective type tests are often confused with each other.

It, therefore, needs to be stated again that when a question is framed with deliberate attention to the objective (ability), which we want to specifically assess, it is an *objective-based question.*

But when a question is designed to provide a measure of learner's achievement in an objective rather than a subjective manner, we call it an objective type question.

There are various forms of objective type items. Two alternative questions, which are commonly known as *true/false* or yes/no type is the oldest of the objective type of questions in use. *Fill-in-the-blank type* questions are the other commonly used variety of objective type questions. *Matching type* items have two or more columns. In a two-column matching question, for example, we can give principles on one side and the illustrations-based on those principles on the other. The learner is required to write the matching number of the principle involved against the related illustration or example given. Among these the *master-list type* of questions consists of two parts. One is the list of closely related terms, concepts, etc. which form the alternative and are called the master-list. Then it is followed by another often a longer list consisting of a number of statements related to the master-list and the learner is required to relate each statement with the corresponding one, of the master-list for identifying the right response. *Multiple Choice Items* are those in which a statement or question is followed by normally four alternatives out of which the learner is to select the only correct one.

The form of objective type tests commonly used for examination purposes is the multiple choice type of question. It consists of a *stem* which may be in *the question form or in the form of an incomplete statement* followed by a number of words, phrases or statements which answer the question or complete the statement. The learners' task is to select from the given alternatives, the one which correctly gives the answer. The effectiveness of the item should depend on how well the item has been framed, to test the desired objective. The following points may be kept in view while structuring a good multiple choice test item.

Suggestions for Writing Multiple Choice Test Items (questions)

A multiple choice type of item, as already mentioned comprises a '*Stem*' in the form of a statement or a question followed by usually four *alternative* choices or distractors. The whole item when constructed must make complete sense and be accurate in respect of language and information.

The following are some suggestions for framing such items:

1. It should be ensured that there is only one choice/alternative which is correct or the best. Alternatives which are overlapping with one another should be avoided. The response should be agreed upon as the best or the most suitable one, from among the plausible ones given, by competent critics.

2. The stem of the item should be comprehensive enough to contain the central problem by including in it as much of the item as possible. The alternatives should not contain anything which could have been put in the stem.
3. The pupil should not be required to copy the correct response but only mark or write the serial number of the alternative to answer the question.
4. The use of the text-book language should be avoided. The rote learner should be mislead by using familiar or stereotyped phrases as distracters.
5. The stem and all the alternatives should be made as succinct and consistent as possible.
6. It should be explored if a better item can be obtained by turning round a partly formulated question into an answer and the answer into the question.
7. All the choices provided ought to be sufficiently plausible to be selected by a fair proportion of the examinees. Both correct and incorrect choices, should be homogeneous in their mode of linguistic expression, physical length and other external characteristics. The distracters should represent errors commonly made by the learners, who are to be tested.
8. Each choice (alternative) should be studied for any possible irrelevant clues. For doing this the following steps are suggested:
   (a) The correct response should not be consistently longer or consistently shorter in length than the incorrect ones.
   (b) All choices should be grammatically correct and grammatically consistent with the stem. The use of singular and plural number, or tenses, etc. should not be allowed to serve as clues.
   (c) The choices may be arranged in a logical order, if one exists; otherwise they should be arranged in the alphabetical order.
   (d) The position of the correct answer in the series ought to be chosen entirely at random. The first and last places should be used as often as any of the intermediate places.
   (e) No part of the stem should follow the distracters.
   (f) All the above or none of the above should not be used as distractors.

To conclude, it may be said that while the multiple choice type of questions are used in examinations, other form of *objective type questions could be effectively used as teaching devices* for initiating discussions in class. Such discussions could greatly help in consolidating ideas. These objective type questions, other than the multiple choice questions, however, can surely be used upto class two even in examination situations as well.

The multiple choice type of questions are particularly used in examinations because, there are a variety of statistical measures available for calculating their characteristics/qualities like the Difficulty and Discrimination indices. Various types of sophisticated statistical analysis approaches have also been evolved.

38

Written Examinations — Preparation of Balanced Question Papers

Backdrop

There are various *techniques* of testing like Written Examinations, Oral Examinations, Practical Examinations, Observation. Each of these techniques uses different tools of 'testing'. For example, we use observation schedules, check-lists, inventories, rating scales and question papers as *tools* of evaluation in different techniques as per need. Among these the question papers and tests are the most commonly used of the tools.

While tests and question papers are the basic tools of evaluation in written examinations, they are also used for other techniques.

As public/external examinations are the most common types of examinations used and since they are pre-dominantly written examinations, question papers have become the most important of the tools of testing the situation needs to be studied in greater detail.

The traditional form of question papers used to suffer from a variety of flaws which have been attempted to be overcome as a part of the Movement of Examination Reform Programme of the NCERT, wherein the author played a crucial note. These reforms, however, have been by and large confined to the education sector. Now testing is also being widely used for purposes of selection, promotion recruitment, etc. in trade and commerce, business and industry, science and technology with evaluation as a scientific approach having also diversified into project evaluation, programme evaluation, etc.

Examination Reform at the school stage has been influenced by the latest developments in the science of evaluation which have revolutionised education in respect of its concept, content and process. Earlier it was thought that anybody who knows a subject can teach it, anybody who can teach can also test. These notions no more hold ground with the evolution of the Science of Pedagogy and the Technology of Evaluation. In fact, both pedagogy and evaluation have germs of both science and art.

Without getting way-laid into the wider realms of pedagogy and evaluation let us revert to the central theme of Setting Balanced Question Papers/Full Tests.

Shortcomings of Traditional Question Papers and their Remediation

Some of the main shortcomings that had come to infest the traditional written examinations particularly because of the pattern of question papers are:

- Over-emphasis on memorisation
- Subjectivity
- Poor Content Coverage and
- Some administrative shortfalls

Let us now take up these, one by one and analyse the nature of each shortfall its implications for teaching and testing and the measures for overcoming them.

Over-Emphasis on Memorisation

The questions contained in the traditional question papers used to be mainly focussed on content where the examinees were supposed to *memorise and reproduce information.*

Since we tended to *teach what was tested rather than tested what we taught*, the development of higher abilities like understanding, application analysis, synthesis, critical thinking, evaluation were almost completely overlooked. Education so imparted, turned children into parrots and mechanical beings rather than creative individuals not just in examinations but also often in their future lives. While this served the needs of the foreign rulers for developing lower and middle level workforce, for running a colonial administration, they have turned out to be utterly inadequate for the emerging demands of independent India.

It has been because of this that the *ability* dimension has been added to the *content* facet in testing. In addition to the sub-division of the content (topics and sub-topics), objectives (abilities/competencies) too have been identified in respect of each subject and these have been further sub-divided into *specifications*. For example, the objective of comprehension/understanding has been divided into its constituent components (specifications) like discrimination, classification, comparison and contrast, identification of relationships, giving examples, detecting and correcting errors, giving examples, etc. These ability sub-divisions have, thus, now become integral and focal components of testing devices (questions) besides content. The phenomenon has encouraged educational institutions to try to develop the higher mental abilities also, besides memorisation—recognition, recall and reproduction—which in the good old days used to be almost the sole ability tested because of the main focus on the memorisation of content.

Furthermore, in the traditional scheme of things, the focus was predominantly on the mental facets. The reformed system also attempts to cover the *total personality consisting of the abilities of the head (intellectual cognitive abilities), of the heart (attitudinal or affective abilities) and those of the hands (actional or psycho-motor abilities)*. Taxonomies of these objectives too now stand developed as discussed earlier in the chapter on objectives. Evaluation of different cognitive, affective and psycho-motor abilities is being taken up as a part of *Comprehensive and Continuous School-based Evaluation.*

Testing in written examinations through question papers, however, mainly covers the Cognitive area and only partly the Psycho-motor and the Affective areas of personality. In developing balanced question papers, objectives desired to be tested in the concerned subject are listed and weightages allocated to each of them (in terms of marks) on the basis of the relevance and importance of a particular objective in the subject in question. For example, in subjects like Geography and Biology, a substantial chunk of marks would be devoted to 'skills', in subjects like Physics and Chemistry, to Application of Knowledge, in History to Knowledge and so on.

The next step is to construct questions equivalent to the allocated weightages allocated to content and objectives. In this process the choice of the form of question will be an important criteria, for example, for testing the ability of expression, a long answer/essay type question and not an objective type question, has to be chosen to be constructed. Furthermore, each form of question has to follow some rules which have already been discussed separately in the chapter on preparing questions of different forms.

All these measures help overcome the over-emphasis on memorisation by systematically including questions testing higher abilities in the question papers in due proportion.

The steps will also help improve the *validity* of the question papers.

Subjectivity

Traditionally subjectivity too has been a great shortcoming of the written examinations. It operates mainly at three levels. *Subjectivity of the question paper setter* used to operate in a wild manner particularly because the question paper setters enjoyed complete unrestricted freedom to pick up or drop any part from the syllabus for setting question papers and nobody could question their authority. *The questions were basically factual and the directive words like 'elucidate', 'illustrate', 'elaborate' were indiscriminately used.* Invariably there was a short note question giving themes like 'Democracy' on which books could be written.

This unlimited freedom stands checked now because the paper setter is now given a '*Design*' (Format appended) of the question paper to be set and clear instructions given about the language of the questions, their unambiguous/specific wording indicating the precise scope and length of the expected answer. The paper setter is also now required to develop a *marking scheme* indicating the parts and outline of the expected answer and the marks to be allocated to each part. This curbs the paper setter's vagaries and helps him correct many mistakes in the questions on their own.

While the format of the design is appended to the chapter, it is pertinent to mention here its main parts which are:

- Weightage to objectives
- Weightage to major areas of content
- Weightage to different forms of questions
- Scheme of sections
- Pattern of options

In addition to this, the paper setter is also required to prepare a '*Blueprint*' (Format enclosed) for setting the question papers. This indicates the precise placement of each question in respect of objective and topic attempted to be tested by it, the form in which it is to be framed, and the marks it is supposed to carry. These requirements make him check the comparability/compatibility of the design of a question paper with its blueprint, and of the blueprint with the questions, and of the questions with the marking scheme. The question paper setter besides preparing the blueprint, the questions, the marking scheme is also required to prepare a *question-wise analysis* (format appended) which is yet another confirmatory device for him to conform to the paradigms of each question he has prepared. This table of question-wise analysis incorporates the following details *about each question or part thereof*:

1. Objective and specification tested
2. Content Area (topic & sub-topic) covered/tested
3. Form of the question
4. Marks carried by the question
5. Estimated difficulty level (easy/average/difficult)
6. Estimated time for answering

Subjectivity of the Examinee

This too is a common phenomenon and occurs mainly because of the vague wording of the questions where the learner himself has to interpret about what he has to write. In response to the questions in the traditional question papers anything and everything could be written. *Learners, therefore, chose to write all that they knew about that topic rather than answering the question as such.*

With restrictions on the language of the questions which has now to be precise and pinpointed, exactly spelling out the scope and length of the expected answer, the examinee now precisely knows what is expected of him to write and what the parts of the answer have to be, how long the answer has to be and what marks each part of the answer would carry. In the new question papers the marks carried by different questions are not given in the margin as say 10 in all, but the marks to parts of the expected answer as well like (2 + 4 + 4).

Subjectivity of the Examiner

This too has been a common phenomenon and one which stands scientifically proved. The technical term ' Standard Error of Measurement' owes its origin into it.

Edwin Harper's study 'Hundred Marking Ten' in 1967 done at Allahabad proved that marking variations operate within a range of 5% and 8% and in more than 50% of the cases, they are likely to be more than 5%.

The NCERT study of 1988 where 20 examiner evaluated the same 10 History answer scripts of Class XII of CBSE, did not have any different story to tell. The scripts and the examiners were both randomly selected. The examiners evaluated these photostated scripts when they were actually evaluating the actual answer scripts of the same subject, of the same examination, using the same marking scheme, which they were expected to follow in evaluating these photostated scripts.

The marks awarded out of 100 by the most lenient and the most strict of the *twenty examiners* to the same ten scripts were as under:

Script No. / *Examiner*	1	2	3	4	5	6	7	8	9	10	*Mean*
Marks Awarded by the Most Lenient Examiner	50	66	23	35	37	74	54	53	39	37	46.8
Marks Awarded by the Most Strict Examiner	21	28	02	10	14	43	23	19	05	07	17.2
Difference Between the Two	29	38	31	25	23	31	31	34	34	30	29.6

The position could only be worse thirty years back. Though things have no doubt improved with double checking, a lot still needs to be done.

A concrete measure taken by the *Council for the Indian School Certificate Examination (CISCE)* is that though a marking scheme already stands developed by the paper setter, each Deputy Head Examiner is required to evaluate 20 or so randomly selected scripts himself. This is followed by a discussion in the course of the *Coordination Meetings,* only after which the marking scheme to be used is finalised. Another suggestion could be for the Boards and Universities to make it compulsory for all affiliated institutions to dispute teachers for purposes of evaluation for continuation of their affiliation to the Board. This is because the good institutions do not send their teachers for evaluation. The non-availability of examiners in adequate numbers also forces the Boards and Universities give more scripts for evaluation to each examiner than what should ordinarily be given for doing justice.

There should also be a provision for appointing some *additional hands at the evaluation centres,* who may *only check that the totals are correct, that all parts of answers have been evaluated, that marks to all parts of answers have been individually awarded and that the marks have been correctly posted on the cover page of the script and also on the mark sheet.* They should also check that the member of *supplementary sheets* indicated are all there. The Deputy Head Examiners in-charge of evaluation centres should also actually check the sample of scripts they are supposed to check and not just initial them as a formality. He and the checker should ensure that the marking scheme is being followed for evaluation in letter and spirit so that the errors of measurement can be minimised.

With the above measures the *objectivity* the testing instrument (the question paper) will become possible to be ensured to a large extent.

Inadequate Content Coverage

When no 'Designs' and 'Blueprints' were used the situation was alarming. It among other things, led to *poor content coverage prompting selective study and selective teaching.* The provision of *options* further aggravates the problem. Suppose there are 20 topics in the syllabus, 16 are covered by the question paper and a learner can attempt full 100 mark-questions if he attempts questions on 12 topics and he can pass, if he gives correct answers to 5 questions on say topics. In this case

20 Topics	imply	100%	Full coverage of content
16 Topics in the question paper	imply	80%	Apparent coverage of content
12 Topics which can yield full marks	imply	60%	Actual coverage of content
5 Topics for passing the examination	imply	20%	Real coverage for passing

In this commonly witnessed situation, a learner can easily omit 40% of the syllabus and yet aspire to get the highest possible marks. One needs to study just 20% of the course content to pass. Is the situation not shocking?

This is not all about options, which do lead to selective study and selective teaching. They also make examinations a farce.

The traditional question papers normally used to have about 8 questions or so and the instructions used to be "All questions carry equal marks, attempt any five". These *overall options* meant that any question could be substituted for any other. The presumptions that the situation made were that:

- if an examinee knew one topic, it was taken that he knew any other.
- all questions tested the same ability and same content.
- all questions needed the same answering time.
- all questions were pitched at the same estimated level of difficulty.
- all of which could not stand any of the above tests.

In addition, in such a situation, different learners may attempt different sets of questions – in effect, different question papers. If A got 40 marks, B got 50 and the C got 60, it *could not be said* that C is first, B is second, and A is third even though all the three of them have not been subjected to the same tests and have been tested on very different tasks/exercises. The situation is similar to the one when a learner X does 1.83 m. long jump, Y does 1.22 m. high jump and Z 2.44 m. high pole vault, where one cannot say who is first, who is second and who is third.

Options could, therefore, be provided if the questions given as options.

- cover/test the same content/topic
- test the same objective/ability
- are of the same form
- are pitched at the same estimated level of difficulty
- take the same approximate time for answering
- carry the same marks

Satisfying all these conditions at the same time is not just difficult but near impossible for ensuring equivalence among options.

There are *Overall options* like 'All questions carry equal marks, attempt any five', *Internal option* within questions like 'Write short notes on any three of the given five' and *Alternate options* of *the 'This or this* type.'

A rule of thumb in this regard if options have to be offered is:

Type	Options
Objective Type Very Short Answer Type Short Answer Type	No options
Long Answer Type	Alternate internal equivalent options

It, therefore, appears necessary that major areas of content may be identified and each given an appropriate weightage (marks) out of the total marks for the question paper for preparing questions equal to these weightages which could be determined on the basis of :

- the importance of the particular area in the subject
- the difficulty level of the area
- the time needed for covering the theme in teaching and learning

These weightages would stand indicated in the '*Design' prepared by the examining agency* and should be appropriately reflected in the grid of the '*Blueprint*' *prepared by the question paper setters*. Questions could then be framed on that basis. This is a technical exercise and cannot be done appropriately by anyone and everyone without training in the concept and techniques of evaluation with particular reference to setting of question papers, which should be arranged to be organised and become essential eligibility criteria for being appointed as question paper setters.

Administrative Inadequacies

Question paper setters, and moderators/vetters have but to be trained in the Concept and Techniques of Evaluation with particular reference to the Technology of Setting Question Papers to execute the technical job assigned to them.

Detailed instructions should also be prepared and issued to the question paper setters, besides of course the design.

Three question papers based on the same design should be prepared at the same time. This should be a team task with the team of three consisting of *a content expert*, a *pedagogue and a practising teacher*. All the three should be given the same design for preparing their own blueprints and question papers marking schemes and question-wise analysis on them. The three of them should then come together to discuss and finalise the three question papers, their respective marking schemes and question-wise analysis of their papers. The *content expert* would be able to check the accuracy of content of the questions, the *pedagogue* the technique of framing questions and the *practising teacher* the appropriateness of standard of the questions. The three sets of such question papers and related material be then packed and sealed separately. One of these question papers may be picked up for the annual examination, the other for the supplementary examination and the third may be kept for a possible emergency. The three papers based on the same design will be *parallel at the level of the design and hence substitutable.*

Another administrative measure relates to the situation where a significant portion of the question paper/test may be consisting of objective type and very short answer type questions with some questions of the other forms (short answer and long-answer type) as well. In this situation, if the section with objective type and very short answer type questions remains with the examinees for longer than necessary, there could be a likelihood that they may try to check their answers with their neighbours. It is, therefore, desirable that the question paper be divided into two sectional booklets, section one with objective type (Multiple Choice) and Very Short Answer Type questions and the other section may have Short Answer and Long Answer questions. Both the sections may be administered together but the one with objective type and very short answer type questions be collected earlier at the end of the prescribed *tight time limit.* In case it is an *on-line test,* this section should not be available for the candidates to see beyond the stipulated him.

Adequate publicity about this strategy will also be necessary for a general acquaintance about the merits of the proposal.

Steps of the Action Plan

In respect of each question paper/test the following action points related to different sequential steps will need to be taken:

1. Preparation of a *Design* (Policy statement about the paradigms of the question paper) to be prepared by the examining agency/institutions.
2. Preparation of a Blueprint based on the Design to be prepared by the question paper setter. Format to be supplied by the examining agency alongwith instructions. This presumes that the question papersetter/test constructor will be trained in the concept and techniques of evaluation with particular reference to the preparation of balanced tests/question paper.
3. Transfer of blueprint details on to the *item sheets* with one question to be written on each answer sheet with the details about objectives,

specifications, topic, sub-topic, form, marks, expected, answering time and estimated difficulty level in respect of each question filled in. The key for the multiple choice questions and marking scheme with expected outline answers and marks to different parts of the expected answer written on the backside of the item sheet in case of question requiring description answers. Adequate number of item sheets to be provided by the examining agency alongwith instructions.

4. Papers for writing the consolidated question paper and consolidated marking scheme to be also provided to the paper setter.
5. Format/Proforma for the preparation of question-wise analysis be also supplied to the paper setter alongwith the instructions.

FORMAT OF A DESIGN OF A QUESTION PAPER/TEST

Subject	:	Physics
Unit/paper	:	Refracton Dispersion and Lense
Time	:	40 Minutes
Marks	:	25 Marks

Weightage to Objectives:

Objective	K/KE	U/CO	A/EX	S/AP	Total
Percentage of marks	40	40	15	10	100
Marks	10	10	3	2	25

Weightage to Forms of Questions:

Forms of Questions	E/LA	SA	VSA	O	Total
No. of Questions	1	5	4	6	16
Marks Allotted	5	10	4	6	25
Estimated Time	10	15	6	9	90

Weightage to Major Content Areas:

	Units/Sub-Units	*Marks*
1.	Refraction	9
2.	Dispersion	4
3.	Lenses	12
	....	....

Scheme of Sections : Nil ....

Pattern of options : No option ....

Estimated difficulty level: Difficult : .... % marks.
Average : .... % marks.
Easy : .... % marks.

Abbreviations : K (Knowledge), U (Understanding), A (Application), S (Skill)
KE (Knowledge of Elements of Language), CO (Comprehension), EX (Expression), APP (Appreciation)
E (Essay or Long Answer Type), SA (Short Answer Type), VSA (Very Short Answer Type), O (Objective Type – Multiple Choice)

SAMPLE MINI TEST IN PHYSICS

UNIT: REFRACTION, DISPERSION AND LENSES

Time: 40 Minutes M.M.: 25

Objectives / Forms of Questions / Units/Sub-Units	*Elements of Language Knowledge*				*Comprehension Understanding*				*Expression Application*				*Appreciation Skill*		*Total*
	LA	*SA*	*VSA*	*MCQ*	*LA*	*SA*	*VSA*	*MCQ*	*LA*	*SA*	*VSA*	*MCQ*	*LA*	*SA*	
Refraction		(11) 2(1)	(7) 1(1)	(1,2) 2(2)		(13) 2(1)	(8) 1(1)	(3) 1(1)							9(7)
Dispersion		(12) 2(1)				(14) 2(1)									4(2)
Lenses	(16) 3(1)*						(9,10) 2(2)	(4,5) 2(2)		(15) 2(1)		(6) 1(1)	2(–)*		12(7)
Totals															

Note: Figures within brackets indicate the number of questions and figures outside the brackets indicate marks.

* Denote instances where a question tests more than one ability (objective) and gives the division of marks of the particular question among the different objects tested by it.

* Entries within circles indicate the serial numbers of question in the test.

Summary:		*No.*	*Marks*	
	Essay (E)	1	5	Scheme of Options: NIL
	Short Answer (SA)	5	10	
	Very Short Answer (VSA)	4	4	Scheme of Options: NIL
	Objective (O)	6	6	

TEST ON REFRACTION, DISPERSION AND LENSES

CLASS X

Time: 40 Minutes M.M.: 25

General Instructions

(a) All questions are compulsory.

(b) Each question from 1 to 10 carries one mark. Marks for the remaining questions are shown in the right-hand margin.

(c) In each of the questions from 1 to 6 there are five answers marked (A), (B), (C), (D) and (E). Only one of these answers is correct or best. The letter indicating the correct or best answer should be written in bold letters against the Question Number in the answer book. In respect of the rest of the questions also answers be written in your answer book with the serial number of the question.

1. Refractive index can be determined by the formula (with usual notations):

A. $\frac{i}{r}$ B. $\frac{\sin i}{\sin r}$ C. $\frac{\sin i}{\sin e}$ D. $\frac{r}{i}$ E. $\frac{\sin r}{\sin i}$

2.

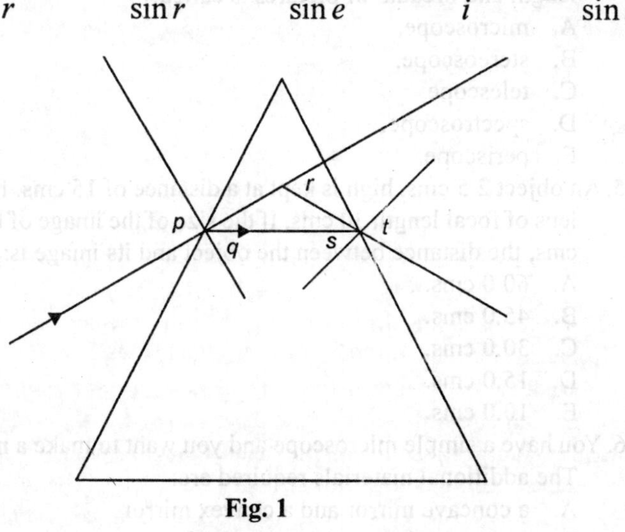

Fig. 1

In the above figure, the angle of deviation is:

A. p

B. q

C. r

D. s

E. t

3.

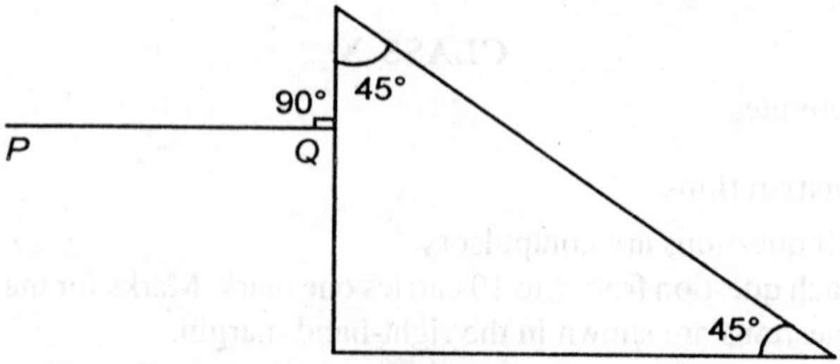

Fig. 2

In the above diagram, PQ shows the path of a ray of light. A prism intercepts it. Then there will be:

A. reflection only.
B. refraction only.
C. total internal reflection only.
D. reflection and total internal reflection.
E. refraction and total internal reflection.

4. The optical instrument that gives the idea of depth along with that of length and breadth of pictures is called:

A. microscope.
B. stereoscope.
C. telescope.
D. spectroscope.
E. periscope.

5. An object 2.5 cms. high is kept at a distance of 15 cms. from a convex lens of focal length 30 cms. If the size of the image of the object is 5 cms, the distance between the object and its image is:

A. 60.0 cms.
B. 45.0 cms.
C. 30.0 cms.
D. 15.0 cms.
E. 10.0 cms.

6. You have a simple microscope and you want to make a magic lantern. The additional materials required are:

A. a concave mirror and a convex mirror.
B. a concave lens and a convex mirror.
C. a concave mirror and a convex lens.
D. a concave lens and a convex mirror.
E. a plane mirror and a convex lens.

7.

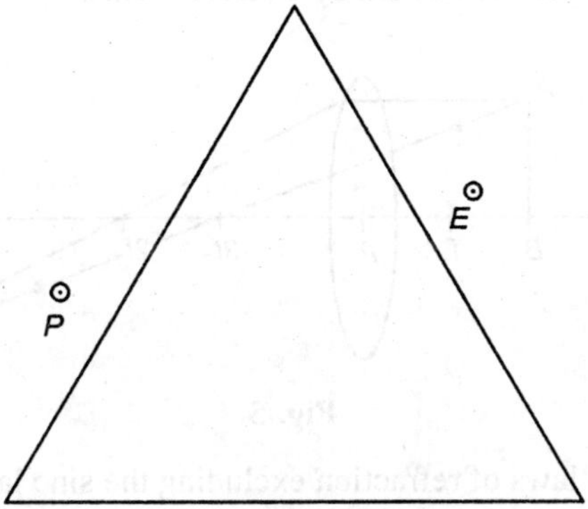

Fig. 3

An observer placing his eye at E and seeing through the prism tries to touch the pin P. Explain why he is not successful?

8.

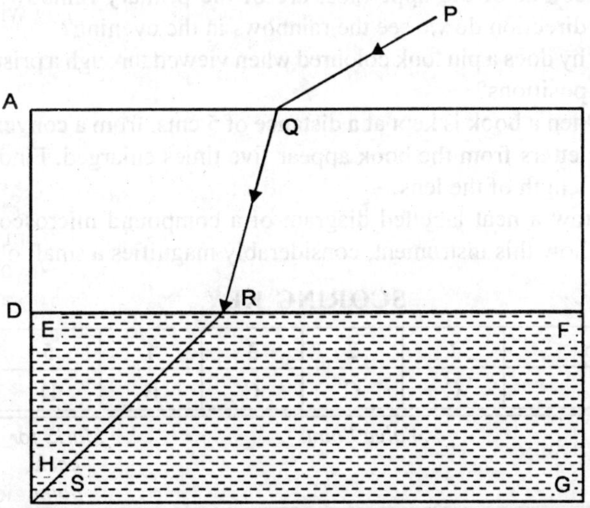

Fig. 4

In the above diagram, PQRS is the path of a ray of light passing through a glass slab ABCD. If a rectangular vessel EFGH of very thin glass containing water is kept alongside as shown in the figure, what change, in the direction of RS, will take place in water?

9. **You are given two lenses mounted on stands-one is a convex lens and the other a concave. How will you know without touching them as to which one is a convex lens?**

10. Find out two errors in the following diagram of an image 'AB' of the object AB formed by a convex lens.

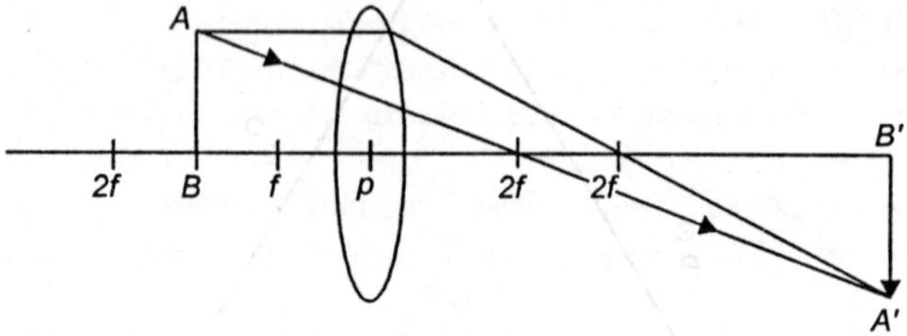

Fig. 5

11. State the laws of refraction excluding the sine law.
12. Give two points of distinction between the images formed by a concave lens and a convex lens when an object is placed between *f* and 2*f*.
13. State the principle underlying the formation of a rainbow. Name the colour of the uppermost arc of the primary rainbow. In which direction do we see the rainbows in the evening?
14. Why does a pin look coloured when viewed through a prism in some positions?
15. When a book is kept at a distance of 5 cms. from a convex lens, the letters from the book appear five times enlarged. Find the focal length of the lens.
16. Draw a neat labelled diagram of a compound microscope. Show how this instrument, considerably magnifies a small object.

SCORING KEY

Q. No.	1	2	3	4	5	6
Key	C	C	C	B	D	C

Q. No.	*Value Points*	*Marks for each point*	*Total Marks*
7.	Due to refraction	1	1
8.	Bends towards normal drawn at point *R*.	1	1
9.	By taking the image of a distant object on a screen	1	1
10. (a)	The ray passing through 2*f* should pass through '*f*'.	½	
(b)	The ray passing through *f* should pass through *p*.	½	1

(*Contd.*)

Q. No.		*Value Points*	*Marks for each point*	*Total Marks*
11.	(a)	First law	1	
	(b)	Second law	1	2
12.	(a)	In a concave lens, the image is virtual, erect, and diminished 1+⊙.	1	
	(b)	In a convex lens the image is real, inverted and magnified. × ⊙.	1	2
13.	(a)	Dispersion or total internal reflection	1	
	(b)	Red	½	
	(c)	East	½	
14.	(a)	Due to dispersion	1	
	(b)	Only some rays enter our eyes	1	2
15.	(a)	$\frac{I}{0} > 0 \;\;] \;\; \frac{I}{0} > 5$ $] \;\; V = 5 \times 5 = 25$ cms	1	
	(b)	$\frac{I}{f} > \frac{I}{v}.\frac{I}{u} > \frac{I}{25}.\frac{I}{5} \;\;] \;\; f = 6.25\, cms.$	1	2
16.	(a)	Correct labelled diagram	2	
	(b)	Position of the object with reference to the object lens	½	
	(c)	Formation of the image by object lens.	1	
	(d)	Position of the first image with reference to the eye lens.	½	
	(e)	Formation of the final image	1	5

QUESTION-WISE ANALYSIS

S. No.	*Objective+*	*Specification*	*Topic*	*Form*	*Marks*	*Est. Time*	*Est. Diff. Level*
1.	K	Recalls	Refraction	O	1	1 m.	C
2.	K	Recognises	Refraction	O	1	1 m.	B
3.	A	Predicts	Refraction	O	1	1 m.	B
4.	U	Selects	Lenses	O	1	1 m.	B
5.	U	Identifies relationship	Lenses	O	1	1 m.	B
6.	A	Suggests modification	Lenses	O	1	1 m.	B
7.	U	Sees cause	Refraction	VSA	1	1 m.	B
8.	A	Predicts	Refraction	VSA	1	1 m.	A
9.	U	Selects	Lenses	VSA	1	1 m.	B
10.	U	Locates errors	Lenses	VSA	1	1 m.	B

(Contd.)

S. No.	*Objective+*	*Specification*	*Topic*	*Form*	*Marks*	*Est. Time*	*Est. Diff. Level*
11.	K	Recalls	Refraction	S	2	3 m.	C
12.	U	Sees dissimilarity	Refraction	S	2	3 m.	B
13.	K	Recalls	Dispersion	S	2	3 m.	B
14.	U	Sees cause	Dispersion	S	2	3 m.	B
15.	A	Predicts	Lenses	S	2	3 m.	A
16.	K and Skill	Recalls and Draws	Lenses	E	5	15 m.	B

* A = Difficult B = Average and C = Easy
+K = Knowledge U = Understanding A = Application S = Skill

39

Oral and Practical Examinations

Oral and Practical Examinations have somehow not received their due place in educational programmes. These aspects are, therefore, being discussed here.

Oral Tests

While oral examinations are almost a continuous and an ongoing exercise in institution-based evaluation, they usually take the form of a supplementary test in external examinations. They usually supplement the practical tests in some Science, Home Science, Crafts, etc. Questions in oral tests, as parts of external examinations, are in a way confirmatory tests. These probing questions and cross questions attempt to dig out the degree of real assimilation of learning where a learner cannot easily dodge.

In the institutional (class-room) situation, oral tests usually serve a very valuable diagnostic purpose for the teacher to ascertain the hard spots as well as the strong points in the learning of a learner. These enable the teachers to develop remedial programmes for the weak and enrichment programmes for the bright learners. They also enable teachers to get an understanding of the level of success that they may have themselves attained in teaching his learners and where he needs to invest alternative inputs or more intensive inputs or where he needs to change the strategy for better realisation of his goals.

In institutional situations oral examinations assume a very special importance particularly in language subjects where there are important aspects of learning which are beyond any other form of examinations to evaluate. In this context, content for oral examinations is provided by:

- day-to-day life experiences
- immediate environment
- current affairs and
- hobbies and interests
- subject of study

Evaluation Situations can be offered through:

- Conversations
- Short speeches and
- Question Answers

The competencies which need to be inculcated and assessed are:

- Pronunciation
- Grammatical accuracy
- Vocabulary and usage
- Ideational content and its organisation
- Manners and Etiquette
- Fluency
- Delivery
- Effect

The usual tools of evaluation are:

- Check-lists
- Rating Scales

It will, therefore, be incorrect to try to test the same things through oral examinations as we do with written examinations. Oral examinations can test many things which written examinations cannot.

In view of the above it will be incorrect to ask learners the same or similar question in oral examinations that are asked through say written examinations for eliciting information.

Conducting Science Practical Examinations

It is in the realm of practical skills in some subjects, that written tests are not usable and hence, practical tests should essentially be supplemented to measure the acquired practical skills, although other objectives, such as knowledge, understanding or application need not be entirely overlooked. For this purpose *practical skill, was mainly conceived as a combination of two components*:

(a) the process of performance, and
(b) the product of performance.

They were further sub-divided in respect of each aspect of the subject to delimit their scope.

Process of Performance

To demonstrate the skills related to process of performance, the learner:

- selects appropriate apparatus tools, etc.
- checks apparatus, tools, regarding their working condition.
- detects error and limitations in the fitting of apparatus.
- rectifies errors, if possible, under laboratory situations.
- cleans apparatus, tools, etc.
- sets up apparatus, tools, etc.

- sketches the arrangement of apparatus, (if necessary, at the very outset).
- prepares and follows a systematic and sequential plan of action for taking observations and prepares proformas for the same.
- states the principle/formula (explaining the symbols, etc., useful in the experiment).
- manipulates apparatus, tools, etc., while performing the experiment.
- measures quantities and accurately reads instruments, apparatus, etc.
- takes precautions in handling instruments, substances, etc.
- makes accurate observations of parts, specimens, processes, etc.
- records observations and makes calculations where necessary.
- verifies observations.
- performs experiments with reasonable speed.
- performs experiments with reasonable accuracy.
- performs experiments with neatness taking necessary precautions.
- adapts himself to somewhat new and different apparatus in setting novel experiments.
- explains orally the procedures, principles, etc. involved in the experiments.

Product of Performance

To demonstrate the *abilities related to 'product of performance' the learner*:

- summarises observations.
- calculates and finalises the results.
- interprets data and draws conclusions.
- records experimental procedure and conclusions.
- dismantles and cleans the apparatus after the experiment.
- arranges the apparatus, substances, etc., and stores them at their appropriate places at the end of the work.

Sessional Practical Work

Some of the skills that may be appraised from this aspect of practical work are:

- drawing of diagrams and sketches from observed facts.
- collection of specimens like ores, minerals, crystals, etc.
- display of material collected.
- improvisation of simple apparatus.
- construction of models.

Development of a New Pattern

For the purpose of improving the validity and reliability, the practical examinations are to be modified in the following respects:

- *Increasing the Number of Exercises*: Instead of giving a few long exercises, a number of short exercises may be introduced, e.g., in Physics one major comprehensive experiment may be retained and the other replaced by four or five short experiments. The maximum marks and the time, however, may be kept the same.

- *Making the Exercises Objective-based*: Exercises may be set to test predetermined specific aspects of skill (or understanding) as laid down in the objective and as defined as part of the process and the product of performance. This is likely improve the *validity* of the practical examination.
- *Improve the Sampling of Abilities and Content*: Increase in the number or exercises which enables the test to cover many different abilities as specified under the specifications of the skill objective and also to cover a variety of content areas. This helps in improving the coverage and consequently tends to improve reliability and validity.
- *Improving Scoring Procedures*: Developing detailed marking schemes giving minute analytical details of assessment of performance not only for major and short exercises but also for sessional work and viva. Detailed instructions for the use of examiners and candidates for this purpose be also developed. This helps in improving objectivity of scoring and controlling inter-rater reliability by minimising the variability in scoring by examiners emerging from extraneous factors like personal likes and dislikes.
- *Improving the Reporting and Interpreting Procedures*: Detailed proformas end instructions may be developed for the use of examiners. When these reports would be properly used by institutions, they will be able to improve science teaching in many respects.

Experimental Try-outs

The above ideas were experimentally tried out and it is desirable to present the outcomes for developing faith and confidence in them. Four examiners in each of the subjects of Physics, Chemistry and Biology, who were involved in the development of the new pattern, tried out these procedures, three times in actual situations specially arranged for this purpose. In the first try-out 10 candidates and in the second and third try-outs 15 to 20 candidates were involved in all the three subjects. In all the try-outs the four examiners made observations simultaneously and marked independently. The experience of earlier try-out was always invariably used to improve the exercises and to refine the scoring procedures of the subsequent try-outs. The results of assessments were then studied and correlations found. The findings in the try-outs of *Biology* are given here as an illustration. In other subjects also findings were similar.

Comparative Study of Three Sets of Examiner Inter-correlation, in Biology Practical Examination in Three Try-Outs where A, B, C and D are examiners.

Averaged across questions

Examiner/Try-out	*AB*	*AC*	*AD*	*BC*	*BD*	*CD*	*N*
I.	.78	.65	.67	.83	.74	.68	12
II.	.94	.95	.95	.92	.94	.93	15
III.	1.00	1.00	1.00	.99	.99	.99	15

Based on total test scores

Examiner/Try-out	*AB*	*AC*	*AD*	*BC*	*BD*	*CD*	*N*
I.	.89	.88	.59	.78	.82	.63	12
II.	.87	.45	.84	.55	.90	.45	15
III.	.97	.99	.98	.98	.98	.97	15

Based on ranking of difficulty indices of questions

Examiner/Try-out	*AB*	*AC*	*AD*	*BC*	*BD*	*CD*	*N*
I.	.88	.90	.90	.98	.78	.75	9
II.	.93	1.00	.90	.93	.97	.98	9
III.	.98	1.00	1.00	.98	.98	1.00	9

Significance levels of Rhos:

When N = 9 : .05 = .600; .01 = .783

When N = 12 : .05 =.506; .01 = .712 and

When N = 15 : .05 =.439; .01 = .623

In this subject (Biology) during the first try-out three out of six examiner inter-correlations are not significant at the .01 level but are significant at the .05 level. The agreement among the examiners in try-out II is at or above .92. All the inter-correlations substantially increased in try-out II. Again in try-out III, the examiner inter-correlations averaged across the questions reached unity in 3 out of 6 cases, and in the rest they were at .99. Thus, the inter-examiner agreement in Biology practical tests reached almost the optimum level as a result of intensive training, practice and development of well-designed scoring procedures.

Implementation of the Scheme

Preparation

Encouraged by the above findings, it was decided to launch the reform programme on a large scale. Brochures were then developed by the Examination Reform Division of NCERT in each subject entitled 'Improved

Pattern of Practical Examination', through the examiners who participated in the try-outs, and circulated to schools. New examiners were also trained in the new pattern of practical examination in the three science subjects. They were given training in the theory of conducting the examinations through four-day workshops organised for the purpose. They acquired practical experience in conducting the new type of practical tests in actual examinations, which were specially arranged at various places as a part of the training programme.

Implementation

With these and other preparatory steps carefully and systematically executed, the-Boards of School Education introduced the new pattern in the Higher Secondary Examinations of 1968. Its impact on school practices has been found to be quite encouraging according to the follow-up studies the outcomes of which are outlined below:

Some Problems

During implementation some problems were faced which were already anticipated.

Lack of Adequately Equipped Laboratories

Many schools do not have good laboratories. For want of such laboratories, it becomes difficult to conduct the practical examinations effectively. This also proves to be a serious handicap in traditional pattern of examination also.

Some laboratories do not also have trained laboratory assistants. Services of trained assistants are essential.

Number of Candidates Per Examiner

This pattern envisages close observation of ongoing pupil performance during the period of examination. One examiner cannot obviously cope up with 40 candidates at a time as is, the practice, in vogue. Perhaps, 20 may be a manageable number.

Trained Examiners

Not only in the initial stages but even afterwards, it will have to be ensured that practical examiners are acquainted with the new pattern, as also the spirit and technique of the new pattern of examination, before being entrusted with the job.

Implications

For the efficacy of this new examination pattern, co-operation from different agenda will also be needed. Some implications of the scheme for such agencies are indicated below:

State Departments of Education and Boards of School Education

(a) School laboratories will have to be better equipped.
(b) Syllabus of practical work in science subjects may be detailed.

(c) Flexible time-table will have to be permitted.
(d) Better inspection and guidance programme will have to be developed.
(e) Only qualified and trained examiners will have to be selected.
(f) Examiners' reports will have to be scrutinised and the findings reported to schools for action.

Schools

(a) Greater initiative on the part of individual, teachers and pupils will be needed.
(b) Rigidity of time-tables will have to be reduced.
(c) The evaluation data should be used for remediation and improvement.

Teachers

(a) Variety of practical activities will have to be designed and organised to develop specific skills among pupils and to discourage the tendency of mechanical repetition of standard experiments.
(b) Initiative on the part of pupils will be required to be encouraged.

Practical work in science subjects is aimed at the realisation of some specific purposes, which cannot be otherwise achieved successfully through other means. Practical examinations, therefore, have to be so planned that they measure the degree of success achieved by practical work, as a contribution towards the multi-faceted development of learners' innate capacities and subsequent achievements. The new pattern suggested here aims at this. It defines the outcomes of the process and the product of performance, stresses the need for developing valid and reliable tools of measurement and builds-in ways of evaluating the results of measurement. It also envisages sound feed-back procedure for utilising the results of evaluation in improving school practices. It is hoped that given a fair trial this pattern will work as a catalytic agent in making science education a dynamic process and a creative activity in our educational institutions.

It may be mentioned that the scheme as developed through this experiment as outlined above has attracted the attention of science teachers and experts and is of great help in their effort at making evaluation of practical work as an integral part of science teaching and they have been increasingly using the above approach.

40

Grading Learner's Performance

Emergence of the IDEA of Grading in India

A discussion about grades has but to start from the concept of marks, as a shift from which, grades are taken to be a more desirable departure.

Marks and grades are both approaches for identifying/determining presenting/declaring the judged level of attainment or competency or potential of an individual in a particular activity/area.

Apart from this similarity both the concepts have marked differences.

'Marks' are points on the spread of a distribution while *'Grades' indicate the slots or ranges* within which the proficiency level of an individual is judged to lie in respect of a given quality or ability.

When we use 'Marks' as indices of the level of performance, we normally use a 101 point scale (0-100). In using 'Grades' we use a much smaller scale say a nine or a five or a three-point one. In the situation, where marks are used the likelihood of mis-classification of the levels of competencies of individuals, or of their potential is also, therefore, much greater than when we use a much smaller number of grades.

In awarding 'grades' as compared to marks, we are also much more confident about the accuracy of our decisions. The swinging in decisions which often generate chance elements, also naturally get crossed over. It is because of this that *approximations* in terms of 'grades' are considered as more valid and reliable than 'marks' which proclaim *precision.* One cannot just vouchsafe that an individuals' mathematical or linguistic ability is exactly say 57% and nothing more or less or that the honesty of an individual is say precisely 68%. One can only be general and not specific in such assessments.

There are, of course, human attributes that lie beyond the range of any technique or tool of evaluation to assess. *Grading, therefore, is an honest confession of our inability to assess human qualities with precision.*

Why Grading?

To just say that the National Policy on Education NPE 1986/92 has recommended the replacement of marks with grades is not enough for convincing others to advocate and practice it. One has to go into the reasons that have led to this recommendation. In fact, there are variations in the clientele taking the same examination in different years. Teachers always say that a particular year's batch of learners is better or not so good, as that of the previous year. Clear evidences of this were found when learners pursuing a 10+2 pattern went to colleges as compared to the previous batches who had been educated in the 8+3 pattern.

Apart from the variations in the clientele taking the same examination, there are also always marked variations in the *ranges of marks* obtained by the learners in different subjects due to the *mark yielding nature of the subject* (e.g. English 30-80 marks out of 100 and Mathematics 0-100). Furthermore, the standard of question papers in the same subject also vary from year to year. This goes against the sacrosanct use of the same cut off scores (33%, 45%, 60%), year after year in all subjects for classifying learners into different categories on the basis of their attainment level.

Grading and Concept of Pass and Fail and Award of Divisions

In view of the above logic the perpetual use of a 33% level of attainment for clearing the examination in each subject, also does not stand the logic.

The concept of pass and fail and of the award of 'Divisions' is alien to the concept of grading, as grades are awarded subject-wise without aggregation.

Grade Point Average

When the practice of awarding grades in place of marks is adopted grade-point averages could be calculated, if it is necessary for granting *admissions* or for awarding *scholarships*. Even raw scores could be used, if necessary, in such instances. In such a situation the numerical values (5, 4, 3, 2, 1, etc.) of the obtained symbolic grades (A, B, C, D, E etc.) in all subjects is added up and divided by the number of subjects graded.

Suppose the symbolic grades and their corresponding numerical value on a nine-point scale is as under. It needs to be observed that letter/symbolic grades could assume different forms.

Symbolic Grade	I	H	G	F	E	D	C	B	A
	E	DE	D	CD	C	BC	B	AB	A
	E	D_2	D_1	C_2	C_1	B_2	B_1	A_2	A_1
Numerical Value of Grades	1	2	3	4	5	6	7	8	9

Also, suppose that there are six subjects and the symbolic/letter grades on a nine-point scale obtained by a learner in the six subjects are as under:

Subject	*No. 1*	*No. 2*	*No. 3*	*No. 4*	*No. 5*	*No. 6*
Obtained Symbolic Grade	B	C	A	D	C	B
Numerical Value of Grade	8	7	9	6	7	8

$$GPA = \frac{\text{Sum of the numerical value of the letter grades in all subjects}}{\text{Number of subjects graded}}$$

$$= \frac{8+7+9+6+7+8}{6} = \frac{45}{6} = 7.5$$

A GPA will be able to give a value upto two decimal points which should satisfy the usual needs.

In special cases as per need some additional weightages could be provided to one or more subjects. The procedure of calculating GPA with cognisance to the weightages will, however, remain the same.

Methods of Awarding Grades

There are various approaches of awarding grades which deserve to be explained for the choice of the one to be adopted in a particular situation.

Diagrammatically these approaches can be presented as under:

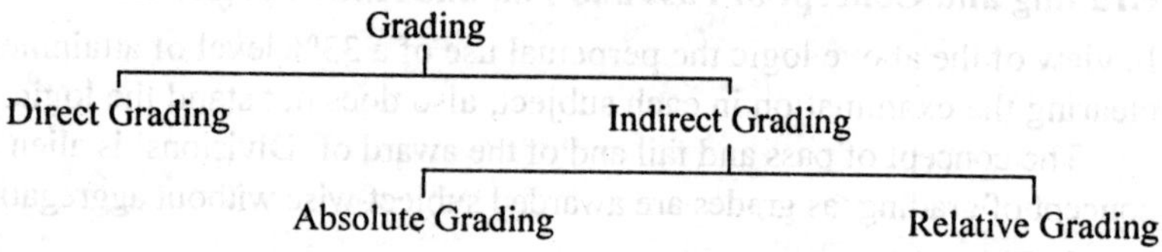

Deciding about the Scale to Follow

In each of the above situations, it is desirable to first decide upon the scale to follow.

The scales normally used have *middle points* as in a three-point or a five-point or a nine-point scale.

A Three-Point Scale

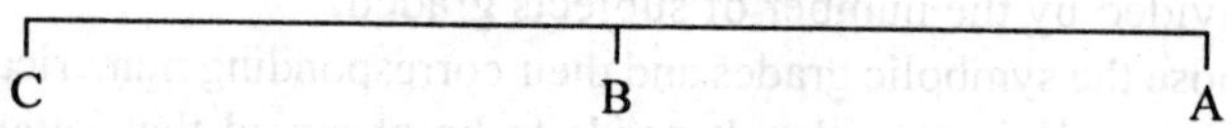

A Five-Point Scale

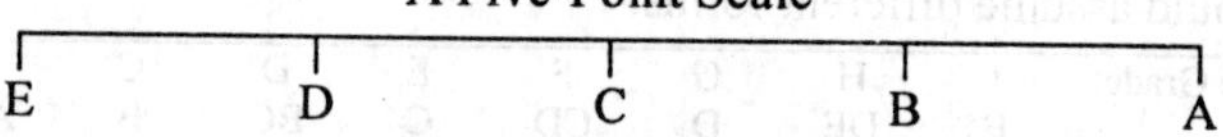

A Nine-Point Scale

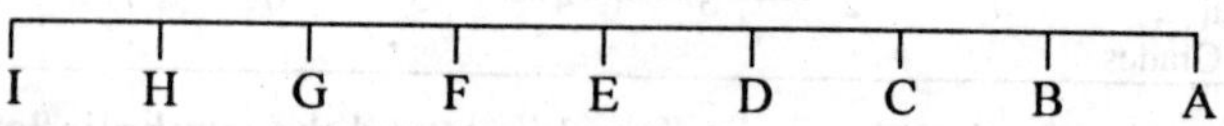

With the increase in the number of points in a scale the discrimination becomes finer. While choosing the scale one has therefore to take a decision on the basis of the fineness of discrimination desired.

Direct Grading

In direct grading *each piece of performance or a part thereof, is required to be individually graded.* Grading is done on the basis of the criteria evolved by the evaluators or on the basis of those forwarded to them by the examining agency (University or Board). Usually letter or symbolic grades (A B C D …) are used in Direct Grading.

After the award of Direct Letter Grades, the numerical value of each grade (as per the scale selected) is often tabulated and added up. This sum of the numerical values of obtained grades is then divided with the number of questions or parts evaluated in an answer script, for the calculation of GPAs. This total is again converted into a letter grade for obtaining an overall index of performance of the learner in that particular question paper in terms of a symbolic grade.

Use of Rating Scales

Rating scales are the main tools of evaluation for assessing co-scholastic aspects of pupil growth. Five point rating scales are recommended to be used. In such a rating scale (A, B, C, D, & E). A rating of "E" which is supposed to correspond to failure is not considered to be used at all and the learners may be classified into only four categories (ranges of competencies).

In some cases, e.g., in Personal and Social Qualities only one Rating scale will be required to be used as illustrated below in respect of 'Discipline'.

RATING SCALE FOR DISCIPLINE

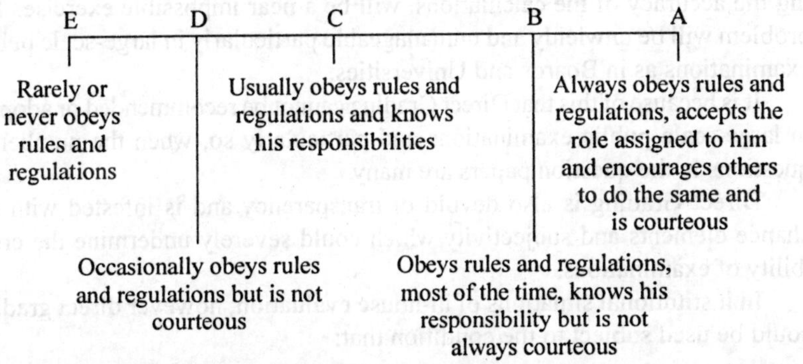

In some other cases as in activities related to interests and other co-curricular activities, there may be more than one evaluative criteria on which it may need to be evaluated through different Rating Scales, for example, in 'Dramatics' they may be:

- Make up
- Acting
- Dialogues
- Emotional Appeal

In such cases rating scales would need to be developed for each evaluative criteria and for arriving at the composite overall grade in respect of the activity to be recorded in the certificate the following procedure could be used :

Numerical Value of Different Symbolic Grades	*Symbolic Grades Obtained by a Student on the four Evaluative Criteria*		*Numerical Grades Corresponding to the Symbolic Grades obtained by a Student*	*Derivation of a Symbolic overall Grade*
A = 5	Make-up	B	4	4 + 4 + 5 + 4 = 17
B = 4	Acting	B	4	17 + 4
C = 3	Dialogues	A	5	= 4.25
D = 2	Emotional Appeal	B	4	= B
E = 1				

GRADE RANGES

E	D	C	B	A
0.6←→1.5	1.6←→2.5	2.6←→	3.6←→4.5	4.6←→5.5

As 4.25 falls within the grade range of grade B, the final symbolic grade for recording in the certificate is B.

With a view to ensuring uniformity in the standards of assessment, the rating scales may be developed centrally by the examining agencies and supplied to the teachers.

This by itself is a tedious process and it is difficult to check and make needed corrections. The current practice of awarding marks on the other hand is itself infested with mistakes of totalling calculation, etc. In the event of the introduction of Direct Grading such mistakes are bound to multiply and checking the accuracy of the calculations, will be a near impossible exercise. The problem will be unwieldy and unmanageable particularly in large-scale public examinations as in Boards and Universities.

It is because of this that Direct Grading cannot be recommended or adopted in large-scale public examinations and particularly so, when the number of questions in the question papers are many.

Direct Grading is also devoid of transparency and is infested with the chance elements and subjectivity which could severely undermine the credibility of examinations.

In institutional situations of in-house evaluation, however direct grading could be used subject to the condition that:

- the number of items to be evaluated are few.
- the number of learners whose performance is to be evaluated too are few and manageable.
- the grades awarded have to stay as such without the need for making necessary calculations for obtaining a GPA and again converting the same into grades.
- comparisons are not required to be made.

Situations like project work which have an independent identity could admit direct grading. However, if it is a part of a subject with a particular weightage for it out of the total marks of a subject, the problem would become difficult.

A similar problem would also arise in respect of question papers, where questions may carry different marks.

Indirect Grading

Indirect grading is *grading through marks*. In this practice the usual procedure of awarding marks to the units of performance continues. This being something to which the evaluators and teachers are already used, this is not likely to create any problem.

Indirect Grading can assume two forms:

- Absolute Grading and
- Relative Grading

Absolute Grading

Absolute grading is the one where the boundary scores for different grades stand *decided in advance of the examination.*

In fact, the practice of declaring learners as pass or fail and of awarding divisions and distinctions is a familiar example of Absolute Grading as illustrated below:

75% and above marks	Distinction
60% to less than 75% marks	First Division
45% to less than 60% marks	Second Division
33% to less than 45% marks	Third Division
Below 33% marks	Failure

As mentioned earlier the indicators of overall levels of performance will not be comparable because of reasons for which the replacement of marks by grades has been recommended.

Such decisions about boundary scores for different grades will invariably be *ad hoc and arbitrary because they would be decided in advance of the examinations and normally for all subjects alike, particularly because the same score in different subjects is not equivalent and comparable.* In fact, the recommendation of the NPE for the replacement of marks with grades is a reaction against the practice of absolute grading using sacrosanct cut of scores for all subjects and all examinations uniformly.

The procedure takes raw marks on their face value irrespective of the errors of measurement due to chance element and subjectivity.

Even though the procedure has a diagnostic value and the learners can make efforts for achieving the highest grades, the system of absolute grading cannot be technically recommended or accepted for adoption as it has evident shortfalls whose remediation was indeed called for, while suggesting the replacement of marks by grades. Any cut-off boundary scores for grades, decided in advance of the examination, does not take into account the actual performance of the learners in a particular subject of a particular examination which is likely to vastly.

An example of Absolute Grading on a nine-point scale is given below:

Symbolic/ Letter Grade	*Numerical Value of the Grade*	*Range of Marks*	*Description*
A	9	90% and above	Outstanding
B	8	80% to less than 90%	Excellent
C	7	70% to less than 80%	Very Good
D	6	60% to less than 70%	Good
E	5	50% to less than 60%	Above Average
F	4	40% to less than 50%	Average
G	3	30% to less than 40%	Below Average
H	2	20% to less than 30%	Marginal
I	1	Below 20%	Unsatisfactory

Evidently, in such a scheme of things, there may be no top grades in some subjects and more of them in some others implying thereby that only some subjects can breed talented learners and not others.

Relative Grading

Relative Grading is another approach of Indirect Grading through marks but is quite a contrast to its sibling of Absolute Grading.

Unlike Absolute Grading where grade ranges are decided in advance of the examinations and applied to all subjects, for all years, *the boundary scores in Relative Grading are determined*:

- after the examination has already been held.
- on the basis of the range and distribution of the obtained scores.
- for every subject at each examination separately

In relative grading, therefore, grade ranges could keep on changing for each subject, in each examination, of each year, as they are based on the range and pattern of distribution of obtained scores.

Decided in this manner, *Relative Grades, successfully overcome problems of the variations in the mark yielding nature of different subjects, variations in the standards of question papers of different years and differences in the groups of examinees taking the examination in different years.*

Relative Grading is based on the premise that whenever any population of learners is subjected to a particular test for testing any attribute/s ability or abilities through any mode—written, oral or practical—using any tool and their scores plotted on a graph, the true level of achievement in this graph would take the form of a symmetrical bell—shaped Normal Probability Curve.

In actual practice, however, there are *errors of measurement* which lead to differences in the 'true' and the 'perceived' levels of attainments and the obtained curve is not usually 'normal' but a 'skewed' one. This also happens because we usually work on samples (rather than populations) which are much smaller than the population, which would have yielded a normal curve of distribution. The obtained curves, therefore, are invariably found to be skewed positively or negatively. These obtained curves are negatively skewed, if a larger number examinees obtain higher marks and are *positively skewed* when a larger number of candidates obtain lower scores.

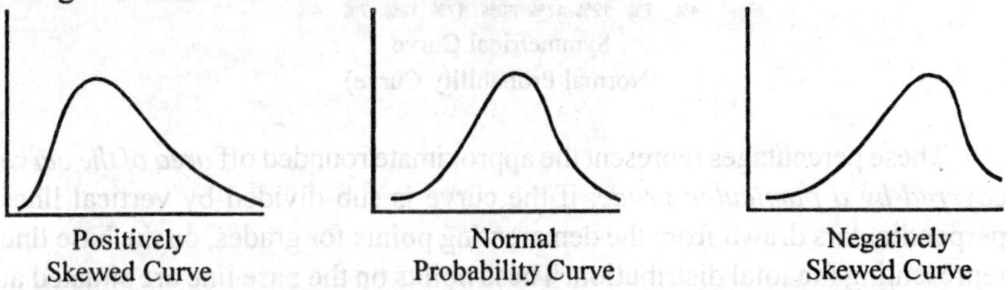

If then the obtained curve were to be converted into a normal curve it would allow us to scientifically categorise the candidates on the basis of the obtained curve, into grades. It is *because the obtained curve is infected with a number of shortfalls (errors of measurement) explained earlier which account for differences between the perceived and the true attainments of candidates, the element of skewness is ignored for practical purposes of awarding grades and taken as if it is a normal one.*

In regard to the choice of a scale for categorising (classifying) learners attainments or potentials, our choice in large-scale public examinations falls on the *Stanine Scale.* This term is a contraction of 'standard nine'. It is a scale evolved by the Air Force in World War II for categorising professional levels of proficiency of its workforce on different abilities on a nine point scale (into nine grades). The scale has come to be widely used in educational and many other situations.

In using this scale the entire distribution of obtained scores is divided into nine parts 1 to 9 with a mean of 5 and a Standard Deviation of approximately 2 units. The Stanine scale, clusters and clubs together the two tail categories at either end of the distribution for bringing the categories to the convenient number of nine instead of eleven. The measure does not make any significant difference because the number of learners whose performance falls in the two tail-end categories is insignificantly small.

The percentage-wise distribution of learners falling in each of the nine grades in a Stanine Scale follows a symmetrical pattern representative of a normal curve and from either the top or bottom it is

4% 7% 12% 17% 20% 17% 12% 7% 4%

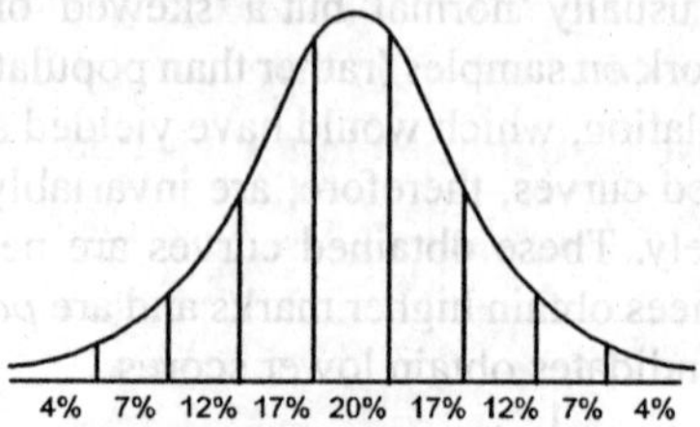

Symmetrical Curve
(Normal Probability Curve)

These percentages represent the approximate rounded off *area of the curve covered by a particular grade*, if the curve is sub-divided by vertical lines perpendiculars drawn from the demarcating points for grades, on the base line representing the total distribution. These points on the base line are situated at a distance of ½ a Standard Deviation from one another in a stanine scale.

These are proportions (rounded off to the nearest whole value) which would be formed in the corresponding ½σ intervals in a normal distribution. The area relationship under the normal curve would show that 9.9 per cent of the area lies between the Median and a point, one quarter of a Standard Deviation away. Hence, $2 \times 9.9 = 19.8$ per cent or 20 per cent lies in the Median interval.

The percentage to be assigned to grade D is similarly determined from the tables. The area from the mean to three quarters of a standard deviation above the mean contains 27.3 per cent of the area under the normal curve. Subtracting 9.9 per cent from this it is found that 17 per cent of the scores above the Median lie in this slot. The other percentages are determined similarity.

In the case of a Stanine scale the grade-wise distribution will be as under:

Grade-wise Distribution in a Stanine Scale

Symbolic or Letter Grade	*Interval*	*No. of Cases*	*Numerical Grade Value*
A	1.75 σ to ∝	4%	9
B	1.25 σ to 1.75 σ	7%	8
C	0.75 σ to 1.25 σ	12%	7
D	0.25 σ to 0.75 σ	17%	6
E	-0.25 σ to 0.25 σ	20%	5
F	-0.75 σ to -0.25 σ	17%	4
G	-1.25 σ to -0.75 σ	12%	3
H	-1.75 σ to -1.25 σ	7%	2
I	- ∝ to -1.75 σ	4%	1

In case, however, we decide to use a five-point scale, again, in a large population, the measurement scale will have to be divided into five parts where the numerical grade values for the symbolic grades will range from 1 to 5 with a mean of 3 and a Standard Deviation of approximately one unit. Grade-wise percentage of cases in this situation will be as under:

Grade-wise Distribution in a Five-Point Scale

Symbolic or Letter Grade	*Interval*	*No. of Cases*	*Numerical Grade Value*
A	$1.5\ \sigma$ to ∞	7%	5
B	$0.5\ \sigma$ to $1.5\ \sigma$	24%	4
C	$-0.5\ \sigma$ to $1.5\ \sigma$	38%	3
D	$-1.5\ \sigma$ to $-0.5\ \sigma$	24%	2
E	$-\infty$ to $-1.5\ \sigma$	7%	1

It could be mentioned that even though the Stanine Scale is widely accepted to be used, examining agencies could devise their own scales on the basis of their curves of distribution e.g. one examining agency has decided on the following scale for relative grading:

A +	Top	2%	
A	Next	6%	20%
A –	Next	12%	
B +	Next	15%	
B	Next	20%	50%
B –	Next	15%	
C +	Next	12%	
C	Next	10%	30%
C –	Next	8%	

However, a rule of thumb for determining the percentage of candidates falling in different grade ranges on a nine point scale is to use a table of 4.

Grade	I	H	G	F	E	D	C	B	A
	4%	8%	12%	16%	20%	16%	12%	8%	4%

In respect of a five point scale a table 10 could be used for determining the percentage of candidates falling within each grade

Grade	E	D	C	B	A
% of students	10%	20%	40%	20%	10%

Grading in Institutional Examinations

The differences between the parameters and paradigms of External Public Examinations and Institution-based testing are quite well known. The most prominent of these to be underlined in the context of awarding grades to different levels of learner performance or attainments, is that the former work with 'population' and the latter with 'samples'.

With a view to branding and tagging different performance levels different approaches examined for their facility and appropriateness in institutional settings.

Direct grading is considered suitable for lower classes (say upto standard II) this is because the groups to be evaluated are small and comparisons are not required to be made imperative. From class III towards, however, one does start experiencing the need for discrimatory comparisons for purposes of identifying the points of intervention and for determining the nature and quantum of inputs of remedial and enrichment material for enabling the learner to read their optimum level of growth in terms of attainmemnts.

It is at this juncture that we should examine the comparative practicability and applicability of absolute and relative grading in institutional settings. Relative grading presents the level/status of performance of learners/candidates in the context of total groups based on pecentiles. These groups are presumably large (samples) for justifiably adopting and using a nine point scale for purposes of classifying the candidates possessing different kinds and levels of abilities. We will, therefore, have to be content with using only a two point scale.

On the other hand Absolute Grading, while it does present the attained level of performance of individual learners, it unfortunately displays a rectangular distribution which is unnatural and unscientific as distributions always take the shape of curves irrespective of what is being evaluated and the tool used for the purpose.

In actual life situations the curves depecting the levels of performance assume a skewed form either positively or negatively, deluding the ideal vision of a symmetrical bell-shaped form.

Furthermore, absolute grading is invariably based on adhoc and arbitrary presumption about fixing boundary scores of different grades, in advance of the examination disregarding the realities related to variations in the abilities of candidates taking the test, difficulty level of the particular test and above all the mark yielding nature of different subjects.

It is in view of the above backdrop that the following compromise formulae which is neither fully correct scientifically nor completely wrong, is being suggested as a convenient rule of thumb.

As high grades may often elude candidates when a full range of marks (0-100) is used, particularly because of the marks yielding nature of the subjects is different (0-100 in Mathematics and say 30-80 in English) we propose that the actually obtained range of marks be used for deciding grade ranges. Thus, if in a particular subject in a particular class at a particular examinations conducted by an educational institution the highest score is 87 and the lowest one is 24, the actual range of obtained marks is 87–24 = 63.

As we have zeroed in on using a five point scale, we will divide this range (63) into five parts. We would then get the width of the range for each grade as 63 ÷ 5 = 12.6. We now take only the whole number of 12 ignoring the .6 figure as the range for each grade. Successively subtracting 12 from the highest score we obtain the operational grade ranges as under:

87–12 = 75	Grade range for grade A = 87 to 75
74 – 12 = 63	Grade range for grade A = 75 to 63
63 – 12 = 51	Grade range for grade A = 63 to 51
51 –12 = 39	Grade range for grade A = 51 to 39
39 – 12 = 27	Grade range for grade A = 39 to below 27

The strong point of this procedure is that.

- it uses only the actual obtained range
- by ignoring the fraction .6 it enables a lesser number of learners get an E-grade

41

School-based Evaluation

Historical Overview

Education aims at promoting alround development of the individual. This alround development involves both scholastic and co-scholastic aspects of personality. However, because our examinations take cognisance of mainly the scholastic areas, all attention and efforts of both pupils and teachers are primarily invested on this area alone.

The NPE 1986/92 has pinpointed, this shortcoming of our education system and given a directive about the introduction of Continuous and Comprehensive Evaluation (CCE) covering both scholastic and non-scholastic areas of the personality of the students. The logic behind this directive is that if some abilities, skills and qualities of the students are to be evaluated and reported for public consumption, it will prompt the institutions to initiate concrete action about offering the needed inputs and activities for encouraging their development.

CCE is aimed at correcting the current imbalance in our educational pursuits. The term '*Continuous*' emphasises that the evaluation of the identified areas of personality is a continuous '*process*' rather than a combination of isolated unconnected '*events*'; that it is built into the total teaching-learning process as its integral part and is thus spread over the entire span of an academic session. The second term '*Comprehensive*' implies that it attempts to cover different aspects of personality beyond the academic ones i.e., abilities, skills, qualities, interests, attitudes, values outdoor activities, etc. and not just academic achievement. The third term '*Evaluation*' implies that the purpose of the total endeavour is not just the measurement of the level of achievement and proficiency of students but also their improvement through diagnosis and remediation/enrichment.

Such a scheme of school-based evaluation, in addition to stimulating the pupils' scholastic growth, aims at promoting his physical health, developing in him desirable personal and social qualities, building in him desirable attitudes and values, helping him cultivate and nurture his interests by providing opportunities of acquiring skills and proficiencies through participation in various co-curricular activities.

While the concept of Comprehensive and Continuous School-based Evaluation, (CCE) crystallised in the 20th century, we are already in the 21st century and still at a talking stage in many places.

Even in some places, where CCE has been introduced after the incorporation of the concept in the National Policy on Education 1986/92, our impatient post-haste has sometimes prompted us to by-pass the inescapable trial run and the unavoidable training of teachers. This has created confusion where clarity should have prevailed.

The concept and implications of CCE are attempted to be explained here under:

Dimensions of the Scheme

Scholastic Aspects

Curricular Areas

Techniques of Evaluation
- Written Examinations
- Oral Examinations
- Practical Examinations

Tools of Evaluation
- Question papers
- Unit tests
- Projects
- Surveys

Periodicity of Evaluation
- Twice in an academic session

Coverage
- For all students

Co-scholastic Areas

Health Status
- Height in relation to age
- Weight in relation to height
- Chest Expansion
- Eyesight
- Hearing

Techniques of Evaluation
- Medical Check-up
- Observation by the teacher

Tools of Assessment
- Height and weight charts weighing machine, measuring tapes

Periodicity of Assessment
- Twice in an Academic Session

Coverage
- For all Students

Personal and Social Qualities

- Regularity
- Punctuality
- Discipline
- Habits of cleanliness
- Initiative
- Co-operation
- Sense of Responsibility
- Deligence
- Civic Consciousness
- Spirit of Social Service

Interests

Literary Interests
- Recitation
- Debates
- Creative writing
- Extra Reading

Scientific Interests
- Exploration
- Experimentation
- Science Club activities

Cultural Interests
- Music
- Dance
- Dramatics

Artistic Interests
- Drawing
- Painting
- Sculpture
- Artistic Embroidery

Techniques of Evaluation
- Observation

Tools of Evaluation
- Anecdotal records
- Rating Scales

Periodicity of Evaluation
- Twice in an Academic Session.

Coverage
- The first four personal and Social Qualities to be assessed in respect of all students and the rest only when evidences are available.
- A student may choose only one activity from any one of the areas of *interest* for being evaluated, though he may participate in as many as he likes.
- A student is to be rated on all *identified attitudes.*
- In regard to *values* a student will be evaluated only on those for which evidences are available.
- In regard to co-curricular activities Yoga and *Games and Sports* are to be compulsory for all students and they will be rated on any one of them selected by the student.

  In addition a student can choose any one other activity for evaluation, available in school for being rated.

Attitudes

- Towards teachers
- Towards school-mates
- Towards school programmes
- Towards school property

– A student could participate in additional activities other than those selected for evaluation. While these will not be rated, his participation in them will be indicated in the certificate.

Values

- Dignity of labour
- Honesty
- Courage
- Courtesy
- Tolerance
- Forgiveness
- Team Spirit

Co-Curricular Activities

- Yoga
- Games and Sports
- Gymnastics
- First Aid
- Swimming
- Scouting / Girl Guiding
- Gardening
- Craft
- Adventure Activities
- Artistic Embroidery

Note: *Evaluation in respect of Academic Achievement and Health status will be in numerical terms. In the rest of the areas proficiency will be evaluated in terms of grades on a five point scale (ABCDE). The grade "E" will, however, not be awarded to any student as it indicates failure.*

Operational Strategy

The schemes envisage the issue of an *independent certificate* by the school. The scheme will cover :

- Level of academic achievement attained in school
- Health Status
- Personal and Social Qualities
- Interests
- Attitudes and values
- Proficiency in outdoor co-curricular activities

The Certificate of School-based Evaluation will be issued as a supplement to that of Board Examinations, on a format prescribed by the Board.

The Board's certificate of external examination will contain a footnote stating that "*There is another certificate of School-based Evaluation being issued by the school on a format prescribed by the Board, attempts to cover those aspects of personality which though important for success in life are not, possible to be covered through external examinations. This certificate also, therefore, be taken cognisance of in judging the total personality of the student.*"

Salient Features of the Scheme

The scheme elevates the status of the schools by making them equal partners with the Board, in evaluating (and certifying students for public consumption), the abilities and potentials of the students through an independent certificate.

The official recognition given to the school certificate through the footnote on the certificate of external examinations, will naturally lead to an extensive use of this certificate by the institutes of higher education as also the prospective employers.

The delegation of the aforesaid authority to the schools for issuing a certificate for public consumption, as a supplement to that of Board Examinations, will also go a long way in improving the tone of the institutions.

The scheme successfully counters the common criticism of public examinations that they focus only on scholastic areas by bringing different co-scholastic facets of personality within the gamut of evaluation.

The *scheme also does away with the innumerable malpractices associated with internal assessment (where the marks awarded by the schools are arithmetically added to those of external examination for determining the students' final level of achievement)* by providing for a separate presentation of external and school evaluation through two independent certificates.

The simplicity and built-in flexibility of the scheme makes it applicable to all types of schools and does not increase the work-load of the teachers as it only means systematisation of the tasks they are already doing.

The scheme also pursues and toes the age-old dictum that those who teach must also test.

Evaluating Growth in Co-Scholastic Areas

Tools of Assessment

Two assessments are proposed in an academic session, for purposes of being recorded in the certificate, with Anecdotal Record Form and Rating Scales as the main tools.

Use of Anecdotal Records

Anecdotal Record Forms are basically used for collection of evidences. They ought to be freely available in the Principal's office and the staff room. They can be filled in by any member of the staff of the school on the observation of a particular noteworthy behaviour. They could assume the following form :

The Anecdotal Record Forms are basically aids to memory and spread the observation-net wider. They assume special importance because many of the facets of personality have only to be rated when evidences about them are available.

Use of Rating Scales

Rating scales are the main tools of evaluation for assessing co-scholastic aspects of pupil growth. Five point rating scales are recommended to be used. In such a rating scale (A, B, C, D, & E) are to be used. A rating of "E" which is supposed to correspond to failure is not proposed to be used at all and the students may be classified into only four categories (ranges of competencies).

In some cases, e.g., in Personal and Social Qualities only one Rating scale will be required to be used as illustrated below in respect of 'Discipline'.

RATING SCALE FOR DISCIPLINE

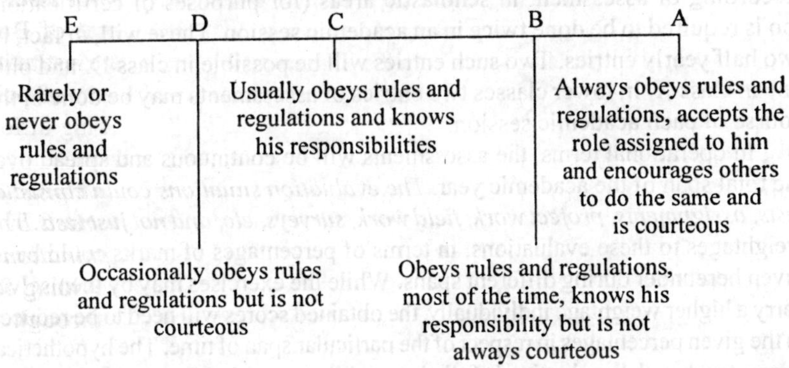

In some other cases as in activities related to interests and other co-curricular activities, there may be more than one evaluative criteria on which it may need to be evaluated, for example in '*Dramatics*' they may be:

- Make up
- Acting
- Dialogues
- Emotional Appeal

In such cases rating scales would need to be developed for each evaluative criteria and for arriving at the composite overall grade in respect of the activity to be recorded in the certificate the following procedure could be used :

Numerical Value of Different Symbolic Grades	*Symbolic Grades Obtained by a Student on the four Evaluative Criteria*		*Numerical Grades Corresponding to the Symbolic Grades obtained by a Student*	*Derivation of a Symbolic overall Grade*
A = 5	Make-up	B	4	4 + 4 + 5 + 4 = 17
B = 4	Acting	B	4	17 ÷ 4
C = 3	Dialogues	A	5	= 4.25
D = 2	Emotional Appeal	B	4	= B
E = 1				

GRADE RANGES

E	D	C	B	A
0.6←→1.5	1.6←→2.5	2.6←→3.5	3.6←→4.5	4.6←→5.5

As 4.25 falls within the grade range of grade B, the final symbolic grade for being recorded in the certificate is B.

With a view to ensuring uniformity in the standards of assessment, the rating scales may be developed centrally by the examining agencies and supplied to the teachers.

Assessment in Scholastic Areas

Recording of assessment in scholastic areas (for purposes of certification) too is required to be done twice in an academic session. These will, in fact, be two half yearly entries. Two such entries will be possible in class IX and only one in class X. In lower classes two entries of assessments may be done in the course of each academic session.

In operational terms, the assessments will be continuous and spread over the total span of the academic year. *The evaluation situations could consist of tests, assignments, project work, field work, surveys, etc. and not just tests.* The weightages to these evaluations, in terms of percentages of marks could be as given hereunder during different spans. While the exercises may by themselves carry a higher weightage individually, the obtained scores will need to be reduced to the given percentages in respect of the particular span of time. The hypothetical example when the evaluation is fully internal supposes that the academic session would start in July and end in April with May and June as the period of summer vacations. The horizontal lines show the points of time for recording of evaluation results and the vertical lines the spans of attainments to be covered and their respective weightages. In institution level evaluation, 50% marks could be taken as the level of eligibility for promotion to the next class.

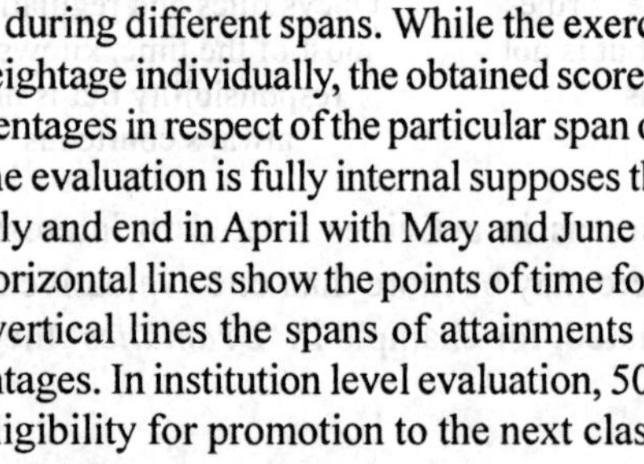

Assessment of Health Status

This will be done twice a year and will basically consist of those aspects which a teacher can manage on his own. A measuring tape and a weighing machine are the only instruments to be used. Height and chest measurements will be done in terms of meters and centimeters and weight in terms of kilograms and grams.

Charts giving age and height in respect of males and females and those giving norms height and corresponding weight will be required to be used and these could be supplied to the schools by the Department of Education.

In the remarks column any special thing like a physical deformity could be mentioned.

If a Medical Examination by a Doctor is done, the aspects needing the attention of the parents could be communicated to the parents by the class teacher/Head of the school on the basis of medical advice.

Ratings of Interests, Attitudes, Values and Co-Curricular Activities

These will be evaluated through rating scales and the ratings entered in the certificate.

Administrative Procedure for Determining Ratings for Entry in the Certificate

While objective evaluations will be available in some cases like height, weight, academic achievement and in some physically measurable co-curricular activities, it is desirable to minimize subjectively in evaluation to as great an extent as possible. While in some cases Anecdotal Record Forms will be available and in other cases the general observations may be the basis of assessment of participation and proficiency in different activities. It is, therefore, proposed that for deriving/determining the final ratings for certificate entry, the head of the school may nominate another teacher for working with the class-teacher.

42

Anecdotal Record Forms

Anecdotal Record Forms are instruments of data collection in regard to fleeting evidences of observation.

Purpose/Need

The purpose of the Anecdotal Record Form is to preserve an account of observed behavior from which important inferences about an individual's personality attributes can be drawn and which are likely to be forgotten at the time of stock taking.

Anecdotal Record Forms are pre-requisites of institution based evaluation intended to cover the co-scholastic facets of personality.

Characteristics

The Anecdotal Record Forms have the following characteristics:

- They can be written by any member of the academic faculty about any student of any class.
- They are supposed to give an objective account of the incident/event observed by the faculty member of the incident.
- The entries of Anecdotal Record Form should only give *facts and not opinions* or personality deserved conclusions.
- The entries of Anecdotal Record Form should provide significant details of the setting in which the particular behaviour or action was observed.
- The Anecdotal Record should contain the date and time of the observation along with the signatures of the faculty member who observed the particular anecdote.

Method of Preservation and Use of Anecdotal Record Forms

It is of utmost importance that entries of the Anecdotal Record Forms are safely preserved and appropriately used in filling in the entries related to the observed things. Towards this end:

- Whenever a faculty member of the Academic Staff of the institution observes a significant behaviour on the part of a student, he should fill in the details in an Anecdotal Record Form objectively.

- The Anecdotal Record Form should then be passed on to the class teacher who should be the custodian of these forms.
- The class teacher should maintain a register for receiving these Forms. The class teacher should give a serial number to each Anecdotal Record Form. While the Anecdotal Record Forms be maintained in a separate file, at the particular serial number the entries in the Register, maintained by the class teacher, should include in respect of each Anecdotal Record Form:
  - the academic session and date of observation
  - the name, class section of the student
  - the signatures of the submitting teacher
  - the signatures of the class teacher

The periodicity of entries in the cumulative Record Form should be twice in an academic session.

In regard to the items observed and recorded in the Anecdotal Record Forms an interpretation is required for entries in the *Cumulative Record Forms or the Certificate of School-based Evaluation* of candidates. At this time the Head of the institution should nominate one other faculty member to team-up with the class teacher to interpret the entries of the Anecdotal Record Forms for being entered in the final certificate/Cumulative Record which is a document for public consumption. This is a measure for overcoming subjectivity and the likely bias of the class teacher.

It may be mentioned that the observations made and recorded in the Anecdotal Record Forms could be evidences of both desirable and undesirable behaviour while in the certificate only the positive things be only mentioned.

Anecdotal Record Forms should be available in the Staff Room as bank slips are in the banks.

FORMAT OF AN ANECDOTAL RECORD FORM

<table>
<tr><td colspan="2">ACADEMIC SESSION --------------

Name of the Student -------------------------- Class ------ Section -------</td></tr>
<tr><td>Occasion and Place</td><td>A Factual Account of the Incident as Observed by the Teacher</td></tr>
<tr><td></td><td></td></tr>
<tr><td colspan="2">Teacher's Signature
and Date</td></tr>
</table>

43

Formats of Cumulative Record Cards and Pupil Records

Format

School Profile

- School Logo
- Name of the School
- Full Addresses and Fax Number/Email ID
- Board to which affiliated with Affiliation Number
- A brief description of the School
  - Year of Establishment
  - Type of School
  - Physical and Social surroundings and the school campus
  - The type of population being catered to

Pupil Profile

- Name of the Student
- Admission/Enrolment No.
- External Examination (if any) cleared with year and Roll No.
- Sex (Boy/Girl)
- Date of Birth
- Guardian's Name (Father/Mother)
- Permanent Address

Level of Academic Achievement (In Percentage)

Class / *Assessment* / *Subject*	*Class ....*	
	First Assessment	*Second Assessment*
I Language		
II Language		
Social Sciences		
Sciences		
Mathematics		
Additional Subject (If any)		

Health Status

Aspect / Assessment / Class	Class							
	First Assessment				*Second Assessment*			
	Height (in cms)	*Weight (in kg)*	*Chest Normal (in cms)*	*Chest Expanded (in cms)*	*Height (in cms)*	*Weight (in kg)*	*Chest Normal (in cms)*	*Chest Expanded (in cms)*
Additional Remarks (If any)								

Personal and Social Qualities

Sl. No.	Quality / Assessment / Class	Class	
		First Assessment	*Second Assessment*
1.	Regularity		
2.	Punctuality		
3.	Discipline		
4.	Habits of Cleanliness		
5.			
6.			
7.			

Interests

Types of Interest Literary/Scientific/ Cultural/Artistic, etc.	*Selected Activity*	*Class... ... ...*	
		First Assessment	*Second Assessment*

Additional Interest Related Activity/Activities in which Participated (Without Rating)

Type of Interest	*Activity / Activities*

Attitudes and Values

ATTITUDES

Sl. No.	Class / Assessment / Attitudes	Class... ... ... First Assessment	Second Assessment
1.	Towards Teachers		
2.	Towards School Programmes		
3.	Towards Schoolmates		
4.	Towards School Property		

VALUES

Sl. No.	Class / Assessment / Value	Class... ... ... First Assessment	Second Assessment
1.			
2.			
3.			
4.			
5.			

Outdoor Curricular Activities

Sl. No.	Class / Assessment / Activities	Class... ... ... First Assessment	Second Assessment
1.			
2.			
3.			
4.			

ADDITIONAL CO-CURRICULAR ACTIVITY/ACTIVITIES IN WHICH PARTICIPATED

Sl. No.	*Activities*
1.	
2.	
3.	
4.	
5.	
6.	

Dated:....................

Overall Remarks

Signature of Class Teacher

Principal's Observations

Principal's Signature

Pre-conditions for the Success of School Based Evaluation

- Development of an academically sound and a practically feasible scheme by a group consisting of
  - a pedagogue
  - an evaluation expert
  - a practicing teacher
  - an educational administrator
- Development of a Manual of Instructions for implementation of the scheme with guidelines for
  - educational administrators
  - needs of institutions
  - teachers

- Training of teachers with the help of the manuals with own infrastructure trained master trainers and trainees.
- A Trial Run of the total scheme for one full academic session.
- Review and finalization of the scheme on the basis of the experience of the Trial Run.
- Public Announcement of the scheme for mental preparation of students, teachers and parents highlighting its merits and advantages for the students.
- Making necessary changes in rules and procedures for the issue of an independent certificate of CCE through school evaluator as a supplement to that of external examination.

Pupil Profiles

Details about students stand preserved in different school registers. And at a glance description does need to be kept giving important *items of permanent information and longitudinal data about a pupil at different junctures in an academic session as also over the years of study in school.*

Schools have their own formats which are different in:

- Day and Boarding Schools
- Government/Private Schools
- Rural/Urban Schools

However, by and large the custom of maintaining in Government/ Municipal Schools is conspicuous by its absence.

Broadly some usual items included in Pupil Profiles are:

1. Scholar's Register Number in the School
2. Name
3. Date of Birth
4. Father's name and work address with phone number
5. Mother's name and work address with telephone /mobile number
6. Permanent postal address with Pin code
7. E-mail address
8. Address for correspondence
9. Date of admission in School

Educational Progress Record

Academic Session	*Class And Section*	*Result*	*Any Other Proficiency*

44

Preparing Objective-Based Questions of Different Forms: Some Examples

Questions are the basic tools used in written examinations which are the most common of the techniques of evaluation in vogue. They have different characteristics and they perform a number of functions for ensuring *validity* (accuracy), *reliability* (dependability), *objectivity* (justice), *practicability* (viability/feasibility) and for ensuring the credibility of evaluation operations. The preparation of questions, therefore, assumes crucial importance.

Physical Dimensions of Questions

In preparing questions it has to be appreciated that each question has three nodal dimensions:

Objective	–	(Ability tested)
Content	–	(Topic covered)
Type	–	(Physical form)

It has also to be realised at the same time that:

- Questions of different types or of different forms can be framed to test the same objective.
- Questions of different forms and testing different objectives can be framed for testing the same topic.
- Questions for testing different objectives and based on different topics can be framed in the same form.

Ramifications of the above particulars will help clarify the issue further:

- Questions based on different topics can be framed for testing the *same objective.*
- Questions of different forms can be framed for testing the *same objective.*
- Questions testing different objectives can be framed for testing the *same topic.*

- Questions testing different objectives can be constructed in the *same form.*
- Questions testing different topics can be constructed in the *same form.*

Some Examples of Objective-based Questions of Different Forms

It will be possible to understand the above postulates through the following concrete examples of questions:

Questions based on different topics testing the same objective (Application of Knowledge)

Arithmetic: Ramesh's salary was reduced by 10%. By what percentage should his salary be now raised to bring it to the original level?

Geometry: Two parallel lines *AB* and *CD* cut across through the triangle *EFG* with *EF* intersected by *AB* at *P* and at *Q* by *CD* and *EG* intersected by *AB* at *M* and by *CD* at *N*. If the angle *GND* = 50° and the angle *NQF* = 120°, of how many degrees will the angle *PEM* be?

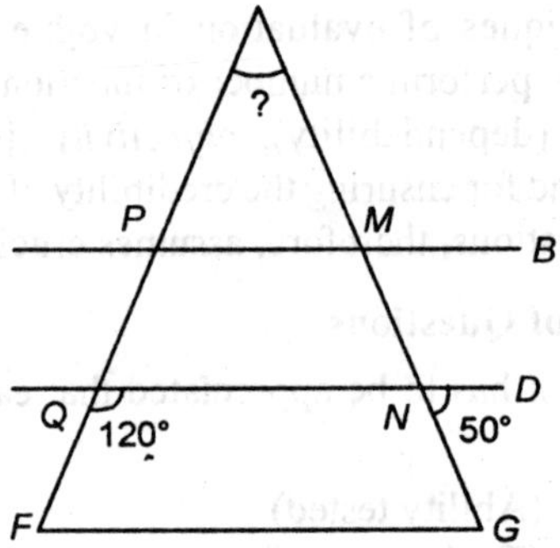

Fig. 44.1

Questions of Different Forms Testing the Same Objective (Understanding)

Short Answer Type: Why is it that even though 'fish' and a 'rose plant' represent the same individual level of organisation, yet fish are considered to be possessing a more complex organisation than a rose plant?

Multiple Choice Type: Which among the following tissues is of a different type than the rest of the three?

A. Tendons
B. Muscles
C. Ligaments
D. Blood

Questions Testing Different Objectives Covering the Same Topic (Periodic Table)

Application of Knowledge: If the classification of elements is done on the basis of 'atomic numbers', how many places will be occupied by the isotopes of carbon. Give reasons to justify your answer.

Understanding: State the Periodic Law and justify the replacement of "atomic weight" by "atomic numbers" as the basis of the classification of elements.

Questions of Different Forms (Types) Testing the Same Topic (Figures of Speech)

Classification: Each of the following sentences reflects a "Figure of Speech". Classify the sentences into two groups each, containing a particular figure of speech:

The ship got wrecked by a fierce wave.
Death lays its icy hand on kings and subjects alike.
He struggled against the storm of fate.
The sky smiled on him.
The lesson has much food for thought.

Identification: Point out the Figure of Speech contained in each of the following sentences:

She is as shrewd as a fox.
Death stared at him in his face.
He was a lion in the fight.
The sun smiled.

Questions Testing Different Objectives Couched in the Same Form (Short Answer Type)

अभिव्यक्ति (Expression)

निम्नलिखित वाक्यों को शुद्ध रूप में लिखिये:
मुझे आज रात का खाना नहीं खाना है।
यह पुस्तक बड़ी छोटी है।

भाषा ज्ञान (Elements of Language)

निम्नलिखित वाक्यों में से किस वाक्य में 'क्रिया' कर्म के अनुसार और किस वाक्य में कर्ता के अनुसार है–

पिताजी रमेश को रोज़ दो घंटे तीन पुस्तकें पढ़ाते हैं।
हमने कल लाल चौक से किताबें खरीदी।
मुझसे अब चला नहीं जाता।

Questions Based on Different Topics can be Couched in the Same Form (Very Short Answer Type)

Direction of Winds: Give one effect on the deviation, in the direction of winds if the pressure of air, at all places on the earth were the same.

Climatic Regions: Climatic regions can be defined according to fixed values of temperature and rainfall. In which elements of climate does such a classification not refer?

The above discussion does give a broad idea about *objectives, content and form* as the three dimensions of a question. While a topic attempted to be covered by a question is quite well understood by an average teacher and the common man, the aspects related to forms of questions and abilities tested by them, however, do deserve to be elaborated particularly because *while all the questions of all the forms have to have some basic characteristics, each form has also to follow a definite set of principles* and rules in its formulation. We will be discussing the different forms that questions can assume in the following pages of the present chapter.

Classification of Question Forms

In this context it is desirable to understand as to how questions stand classified into different categories. Even at the cost of repetition the diagram of classification of question forms is being given again to serve as a ready reference in the present context.

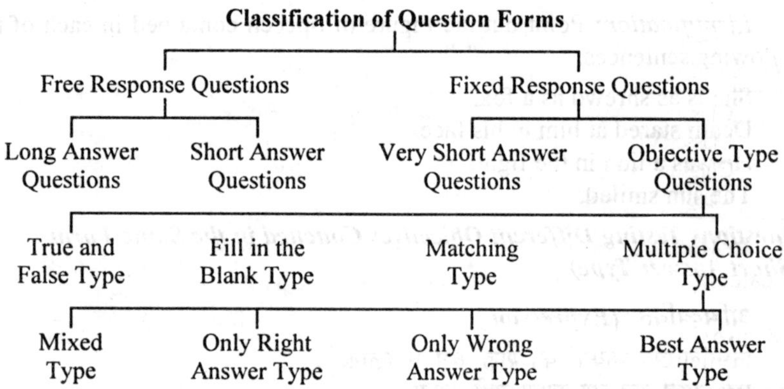

Fig. 44.2

Let us now briefly deliberate on the above diagram. As we see, questions stand briefly classified into

- Free Response Questions and
- Fixed Response Questions

Free Response Questions are those, in response to *which* the student is required to formulate his own response to the requirements of the question choosing his own words. In doing so he retrieves facts, organises ideas and marshalls arguments to support or oppose propositions, decides on the sequence of the presentation of ideas, facts, arguments and so on.

Free Response Questions stand divided into the long answer type questions and the short answer type questions. This sub-classification is basically related to the *length of the expected answer* and the length is basically related to the age-group/maturity level of the students besides the depth and dimensions of abilities and content desired to be tested.

Fixed Response Questions are those where the answers are definite and only these are expected to be identified or given by the students. Objective type and very short answer type questions fall in this category. Objective type questions admit different forms expecting different, Types of responses from the examinees. Very short answer questions expect answers in one word, one phrase or at the most one sentence.

Length of Free Response Questions

While *there can be no rigid rule* about the length of the answers, this can only be broadly stated in an ad-hoc manner just as an approximation. Being suggestions and not prescriptions, necessary changes could be freely made as per need, determined by a rational discretion.

Approximate Lengths of Expected Answers to Different Free Response Question Forms at Different Levels

Question Type / *Level of Education*	*Long Answer Type*	*Short Answer Type*
Classes I - V	50 - 100 Words	5 - 10 Words
Classes VI - VIII	100 - 150 Words	10 - 15 Words
Classes IX - X	150 - 200 Words	15 - 20 Words
Classes XI - XII	200 - 250 Words	20 - 25 Words

In *Mathematics* and other allied subjects, the length of the expected answer is calculated in terms of the *steps of calculation.*

Approximate Steps of Calculation in the Expected Answers in Mathematics Questions of Different Forms at Different Levels

Question Type / *Level of Education*	*Long Answer Type*	*Short Answer Type*
Classes I – V	1 – 2 Steps of Calculation	1 – 2 Steps of Calculation
Classes VI – VIII	2 – 3 Steps of Calculation	1 – 2 Steps of Calculation
Classes IX – X	3 – 5 Steps of Calculation	2 – 3 Steps of calculation
Classes XI – XII	5 – 8 Steps of Calculation	2 – 3 Steps of Calculation

Among the *fixed response questions,* the answer to a Very Short Answer Type of Question as mentioned earlier is usually limited to *one word, one phrase or at the most one sentence* and there is only *one correct answer* in multiple choice questions.

This classification of questions could, in fact, be taken to be a continuum of length of the expected answers.

A word also needs to be said here about the use of the forms of objective type questions, other than the multiple choice ones. *The general rule in this connection is that only the multiple choice questions should be used in examination situations and the other forms as teaching devices.*

However, a compromise arrived at (due to special reasons) is that the true and false, fill-in-the-blank and matching questions can be used upto Class **II** subject to certain conditions that:

- the questions framed should be original ones prepared by the teacher for use in that particular examination only.
- the language should not be bodily lifted from the book/s or earlier question papers.
- the fill-in-the-blank questions should require words/phrases containing 'basic' and not 'base' (insignificant) information for being filled in.
- the matching questions should have homogeneous words/phrases on each of the two sides and one side may have three or more of these which may not admit being matched.

Characteristics of Good Questions

All questions irrespective of their form or the objective tested/attempted to be tested or the topic intended to be covered ought to display the following basic characteristics:

The questions ought to:

- be *specifically worded* so as to clearly indicate the scope and length of the expected answer. This clarity and unambiguity would avoid breeding any misinterpretation about the points to be included in the answer, also whether the answer has to be reinforced by an example or a diagram besides, and of course, the length of the expected answer.
- ensure compatibility between the *time* required to be devoted for answering the question and the *marks* allocated to it.
- also ensure that the *ability/competency (objective) desired to be tested is actually being attempted to be tested.* Very often the framers of questions entertain gross misconceptions about this aspect and tend to feel that a particular question tests a higher ability than what it actually does. Sometimes apparently a question may look to be testing "application of knowledge" but because the question has already been solved earlier or discussed with the students earlier, it gets reduced to nothing, more than a "recall" (knowledge) question. It has, therefore, to be ensured that the situation on which a particular application question has been framed is "unfamiliar" to the students of that age-group.
- appropriately sample, the content area desired to be tested. It should

thus, bear a direct relationship with the teaching-learning situations. This is possible in evaluation within schools, where those who teach also test. The testing situations in external examinations, on which questions are framed, are, however, based on experiences of the question paper setters.

- consider that the form selected for garbing a particular question in, is the most suitable one for testing both the ability and the content desired to be tested. For example, if it is desired to test "expression", a fixed response question will be completely unsuitable. On this count itself a multiple choice question will be inappropriate for testing psycho-motor skills related to experimentation. Sometimes, however, a long answer type question could also incorporate within itself a component of drawing a diagram or map which will involve psycho-motor skills.
- basically test just one objective, but in case it is testing more than one objective, the question will be designated as the one testing the highest of the objectives from among those being tested by it.
- be aligned to the Maturity level of the students in terms of the complexity and its estimated difficulty level. Even though the content (topic) may be the same, the objective tested may be higher or lower. In regard to the content as well, the level of specificity of a question, as also the depth and dimension of the content tested, will be the main determinant of the estimated difficulty level at which the question may be pitched.

Rules for Framing Different Forms of Questions

It is also equally necessary for us to be familiar with the rules for framing different forms of questions. The discussion that follows will be restricted to only four forms of questions which are commonly used in question papers tests:

Long Answer or Essay Type Questions

A long answer question is basically an extended free response question, which can specially help assess one or more of the following vital abilities:

- to express one's ideas/beliefs
- to present facts in a unique manner characterising the degree and depth of knowledge possessed by an individual
- to interpret facts, phenomenon
- to analyse information
- to creatively present arguments in support of a proposition or against it.
- to relate and evaluate things, ideas, principles, events, trends, movements, etc.
- to weigh pros and cons for drawing conclusions.

- to apply knowledge in unfamiliar situations.

Thus, a long answer question is capable of helping the evaluation of intricate mental capabilities in various permutations and combinations.

Furthermore, in answering long answer type questions, a student has to select his own language, style and the mode of presentation, which also clearly reflects the internal processes within the brain and the degree of effectiveness of the assimilation and the ability of presentation of the individual student.

Shortcomings: The long answer questions, with such great potential as above, do also have some shortcomings.

- Long Answer Questions require longer time to answer and because they require longer time, they can only be few in a question paper. Hence, if there are all long answer questions in a question paper, only a small part of the syllabus can be covered which may lead to selective study and selective teaching, endangering reliability and validity of the tests.
- Responses to long answer questions can only be manually and personally evaluated and thus need longer time for evaluating answers.
- While it is true that long answer questions succeed in evaluating some of those abilities which other forms of questions cannot, it is also true that they are not able to test all the desired abilities in a particular solution. Thus, they also put the reliability of examinations at stake.
- The frequent inclusion of "Options" among long answer questions in question papers, not only encourages selective study and selective teaching, but also undesirably influences the reliability of the examination, because they lead to the non-comparability of scores obtained on different permutations and combinations of questions selected for answering.

Tips for Framing Long Answer Questions: In view of the above stated potentials and shortfalls of long answer questions, there are some cautions, precautions and also directives that need to be observed in constructing them in a manner that they serve their unique purpose in examinations to the best possible extent. The long answer questions ought to:

- Present a definite problem or a proposition through a question.
- Clearly define the expected scope and length of the expected answer.
- Indicate, if a diagram has to be drawn or an example has to be given.
- Word the question so as to bring its purport within the effortless comprehension of the students.
- Explain what the students are expected to write as an answer, instead of writing cryptic directive words like, elaborate, enumerate, discuss, justify, review, interpret, etc. the meanings of which are not uniformly understood and lead to subjectivity in writing answers as also in evaluating them.

- The age group as a determinant of maturity level of the student should always be kept in mind.
- Allocate marks to different parts of questions and indicate these against the questions like (2 + 4 + 4) instead of just 10 in the question papers.
- Clearly indicate as part of directions whether marks will be deducted for lapses like spelling mistakes, or credit given for things like good handwriting.
- be followed by an outline of expected answer to each question, in the marking scheme, prepared at the same time as the framing of the question. Checking of the wording of the questions with the outline of the expected answers greatly helps in suitably modifying the language of the question so as to bring about its alignment with the expected answer and also in correcting so many mistakes which would otherwise go undetected.
- The evaluators ought to be provided with such a detailed marking scheme to study and follow. The problem becomes quite a serious one in external examinations where the number of scripts to be evaluated by an examiner are huge and there is also a crunch of time and above all inadequate supervision of the scoring process.

Some Examples of Long Answer Questions are given below:

1. *Subject* : Chemistry
   Topic : Diffusion of Gases
   Objective : Understanding

Explain the concept of diffusion of gases. Devise a suitable experiment to illustrate the phenomenon of diffusion. Draw a neat labelled diagram for the experiment suggested by you.

2. *Subject* : Biology
   Topic : Levels of Organisation of Life
   Objective : Application of Knowledge

On the basis of your knowledge of different levels of organisation of life, prepare a tree of biological organisation depicting the position of different plants and animals in relation to each other.

3. *Subject* : Mathematics
   Topic : Angles
   Objective : Application of knowledge

Two boats on the opposite sides of the bank of a river start moving on paths inclined at angles 40° and 30°, to their respective banks. If they meet at a place *P* in the river, find the angle between their paths at the point *P*. What effect will there be on the angle between their paths, if the first boat moves making an angle of 30° and the second making an angle of 40° to their respective banks?

4. *Subject* : English
Topic : Essay Writing
Objective : Written Expression

Write an essay to elaborate the following idea:

"Reading of books should aim at developing a taste for serious reading, which yields everlasting pleasure. This is a need of the mind exactly in the same manner as the body needs wholesome food. Mere reading of fiction does not satisfy such a need of the mind."

5. *Subject* : Economics
Topic : Transactions in Indian Economy
Objective : Understanding

Trace the changes that have taken place in the Indian Society, because of its transformation from a pre-dominantly agricultural to a near industrial one. Explain how it has affected the way of life of the people.

6. *Subject* : Civics
Topic : Man as a Social Being
Objective : Application of Knowledge

If you put away some individuals from their very birth, isolated from society, which faculties and attributes do you think will not develop in them which are necessary for social living?

7. *Subject* : Geography
Topic : Atmospheric Pressure
Objective : Application of Knowledge

Atmospheric pressure between 0° — 10° and 60° — 70° in both North and South latitudes is low. Explain the difference in the causes of the two lows that govern the phenomenon.

8. *Subject* : History
Topic : Indus Valley Civilisation
Objective : Application of Knowledge

Discuss any four aspects of Indus Valley Civilisation which have exerted a very powerful influence on the present day urban life of India.

Rules for Preparing Short Answer Type Questions

As has been mentioned earlier, Long Answer Type Questions are characterised by shortfalls in respect of objectivity and reliability, while they can best test abilities like organisation, analysis and synthesis. On the other extreme of the scale are the objective type questions which protect objectivity perfectly, but are not able to test certain other abilities effectively. Short Answer Type Questions on the other hand are a valuable via-media between the two.

Suggestions about the possible length of different forms of questions have already been broadly spelt out while discussing different forms of questions. However, a distinction has but to be made, about the concept of a *short answer question* and *a short note question.* Answers to a short answer question have but to be brief because of the constraints of specifically indicated dimensions in their very wording. A short note question more often than not gives themes like 'democracy' (for writing short notes on) on which even books can be written. Usually, there are no indications about the facets of the big theme to be covered by Short Note Questions.

A short answer question can test a variety of objectives, even expression, in a limited manner. Examples of short answer questions given below will further clarify the concept of Short Answer Questions:

Subject : Chemistry
Topic : Properties of Hydrogen Gas
Objective: Application of Knowledge

A balloon filled with Hydrogen goes up when left free. But if the Hydrogen filled in balloon is kept for a few hours, it does not go up. Explain the reason.

Subject : Economic Planning
Topic : Central Bank
Objective: Application of Knowledge

Which measure can be most effectively used by a Central Bank to control a situation where bank credit is likely to be utilised for speculative hoarding of essential commodities?

Subject : Biology
Topic : Tissues
Objective: Understanding

On the basis of your knowledge of tissues explain why it is painful when salt comes into contact with a wound on the body?

Subject : Chemistry
Topic : Electrons
Objective: Understanding

Which of the electrons are most loosely held in atoms?

Subject : Geometry
Topic : Angles
Objective: Application of Knowledge

In the following figure: *AB* and *CD* are parallel lines which are intersected by another straight line *PQ* which meets *AB* at *R* and *CD* at *S*. What is the relationship between angles *PRB* and *CSQ*?

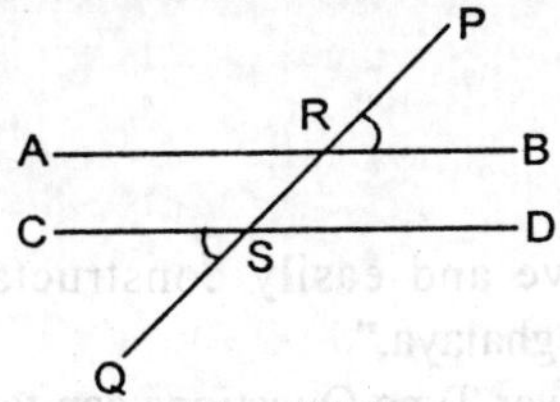

Fig. 44.3

Subject : Hindi
Topic : Usage
Objective : Expression
'ना' और 'मत' का भेद बतलाने वाले दो-दो वाक्य बनाइए।

Subject : Political Science
Topic : Powers of the Members of Parliament
Objective : Application of Knowledge
What courses are open to Members of Parliament for exercising a check on the Government?

Subject : Geography
Topic : Denudation ,
Objective : Understanding
Give one example from desert areas to clarify that the term 'Denudation' includes both erosion and weathering.

Subject : Chemistry
Topic : Temperature and Volume of Gas
Objective : Application of Knowledge
Draw a graph to show the mode of change of volume with temperature in the range of 200°C to 300°C, on the basis of the following data obtained for a certain quantity of a given gas:

Temperature	°C	100	100	200
Volume	ml	5.1	10.9	13.9

On the basis of the drawn graph find the volume of gas at 150°.

As we see, the Short Answer Questions require precise and to the point answers and hence, prompt students to develop and demonstrate the ability of selecting and organising relevant facts from their store of knowledge in a pin pointed manner, within the short time available for answering then.

Rules for Preparing Very Short Answer Type Questions

Very short answer type questions as mentioned earlier require an answer in *a word, a phrase or at the most a sentence.* Thus, they have all the qualities of a multiple choice question, except the time and skill required in framing them. They serve almost the same purpose as a multiple choice question. Instead of asking "Which among the following is the capital of Meghalaya?"

A. Aizawl
B. Guwahati
C. Kohima
D. Shillong

An equally effective and easily constructable question could be "Name the Capital of Meghalaya."

The Very Short Answer Type Questions can test the same objectives as are possible to be tested through multiple choice questions.

The following examples of very short answer questions will help further clarify the concept:

1. *Subject* : Biology
   Topic : *Cells*
   Objective : Understanding

Give an example of a particle which multiplies in a living cell (Virus)

2. *Subject* : Arithmetic
   Topic : Percentage
   Objective : Application of Knowledge

30% of X is 60. Find X and verify the result.

3. *Subject* : Hindi
   Topic : Elements of Language
   Objective : Expression

निम्नलिखित शब्दों का लिंग परिवर्तन कीजिए।

वर, गुणवान

4. *Subject* : Political Science
   Topic : Rights
   Objective : Understanding

Give one example each of the 'Civil' and 'Political' rights of a citizen.

Rules for Preparing Multiple Choice Type Questions

These questions are now used extensively and almost exclusively in Selection Tests and Admission Tests. In School and University level external examinations, they are usually used along with other forms of questions. Sometimes, there is also an independent part/ section of the question paper devoted to these questions. In some places, this section though administered simultaneously is collected earlier after a tight time limit. In some other places it is administered separately.

The responses to Multiple Choice Questions are amenable to statistical analysis through established procedures and formulae. The responses on answer sheets can also be machine scored for giving accurate results quickly.

Parts of a Multiple Choice Question

A multiple choice question has three parts:

1. Stem
2. Alternatives or distractors
3. The Key

Stem: The *Stem* is the first part of the multiple choice question which sets the problem. A stem could basically assume two forms:

- Completion form
- Question form

In the *completion type stem,* each of the distractors makes a complete sentence with the stem. The alternatives have to conform to the same language form, particularly in regard to verb and tense *e.g.*

The place which receives the highest rainfall in India is:

A. Cherapunji
B. Dharamshala
C. Manali
D. Darjeeling

In the *question form of stem* for the same question with alternatives remaining the same, it will be:

Which place in India receives the highest rainfall?

A. Cherapunji
B. Dharamshala
C. Manali
D. Darjeeling

A question type of stem is most commonly used, because the alternatives are easy to frame and to a great extent the question framers get emancipated from linguistic constraints as in the case of completion form of stems.

Alternatives/Distractors: These are the statements or words, or phrases which follow the stem. They ideally have a number of rules to follow. Some of the important ones are:

1. The distractors should all be homogeneous i.e. if they are names of states they should all be the names of states and no name of a capital of a state should then be a part of them.
2. The alternatives should all be of almost the same physical length.
3. All alternatives should be plausible answers, though only one of them should be correct.
4. All alternatives should be in the same language form and tense.
5. No alternative should give a clue regarding the correct answer.
6. The alternatives should be four or five in number. Four is now the accepted norm.

Key: This is the third and the last part of multiple choice test item. There should be only one fully correct alternative in a multiple choice type of a question and its serial number (A or B or C or D) should present the correct alternatives the serial number of which (A, B, C, D) is called the key. When there are a number of questions the key (correct answer) should remain distributed among A, B, C, and D. The placement of the correct answer (alternative) should not be in the same position but randomly distributed.

SOME SAMPLE MULTIPLE CHOICE QUESTIONS

Subject : Botany
Topic : Fungus
Objective : Application of Knowledge

A fungus will grow best when a piece of bread is:

• A. soaked in water and covered
B. kept in the refrigerator
C. buried in the soil
D. kept under water

Subject : Physiology
Topic : Muscles
Objective : Understanding

Which of the following organs of the human body is not operated by muscles?

A. Heart
B. Urinary Bladder
C. Stomach
• D. Spleen

Subject : Chemistry
Topic : Composition of Air
Objective : Application of Knowledge

The table given below indicates the change in the composition of AIR after a particular process was carried out in it, through an experiment:

Gas	*Composition before the Experiment*	*Composition after the Experiment*
Oxygen	20.5%	16.5%
Nitrogen	78.5%	78.5%
Carbon dioxide	0.94%	4.04%
Water Vapour	Average	More than before

The above data leads to the conclusion that the process carried out was one of:

A. Carbon Assimilation
B. Condensation
C. Slow combustion
• D. Evaporation

Subject : Geography
Topic : Soils
Objective : Application of Knowledge

The sub-soil is less fertile than the top soil because of the absence of:

A. Abundant water
B. Heat from the sun
C. Air between its particles
• D. Organic matter

Subject : Physics
Topic : Electrostatics
Objective : Application of Knowledge

If a glass-rod and a brass-rod are first rubbed with a piece of silk one after the other then touched by a finger and subsequently carried near a suspended uncharged pith ball, the pith ball will be:

A. attracted towards both the rods.
B. repelled from both the rods.
C. attracted towards the glass-rod and be neutral to the brass-rod.
• D. attracted towards the brass-rod and be neutral to the glass-rod.

Subject : Mathematics
Topic : Binomial Theorem
Objective : Understanding

In the expansion of $(1 + x)^{20}$ which of the following terms will have equal coefficients?

• A. 2nd and 20th
B. 5th and 18th
C. 6th and 18th
D. 10th and 11th

Subject : Political Science
Topic : National Integration
Objective : Understanding

Education in regard to which of the following areas is considered as most vital for forging National Integration?

A. Self-reliant technological progress
• B. Common cultural heritage
C. History of freedom movement
D. Non-alignment as a state policy

Rules for Preparing Objective Type Questions other than the Multiple Choice Ones

The other commonly used objective type questions other than the Multiple Choice ones are:

1. True/False Type

2. The Fill-in-the-blank Type
3. The Matching Type

As has been mentioned earlier in passing, the above three forms of objective type questions are not usually used in external examinations.

Without going into the technicalities it appears adequate to mention that the traditional form in which these three forms of questions normally assume, do have some shortcomings because of which they are not used in examination situations as compared to the advantages of using multiple choice questions.

The main shortcoming of *True/False Questions* is that responding to them involves a 50% chance of guessing which is enormous to be overlooked.

The *Fill-in-the-blank questions* often display the tendency of lifting of sentences from books read by the students with some crucial words culled out for creating gaps to be filled in. The filling-in of the gaps, thus, often involves nothing more than *'recall'* and even sometimes prompts making guesses for finding appropriate words.

The *matching questions* often have the same number of items to be matched on both the sides. In such a situation they suffer from the *process of elimination.* When an item is matched, one item less has to be matched in the next exercise and so on. There is no matching required to be done in respect of the last one when it already stands matched with the only remaining one. Another common shortcoming of matching questions is that quite often the items in the two columns are not homogeneous or of the same category. Whenever and wherever used one side of the items may have say three more alternations than the other side as well and items on both the sides homogeneous.

The valuable instructional uses of these three forms of objective type questions also deserve to be briefly touched upon. *The True/False questions* have a valuable use in the nursery classes where we are not interested in knowing the extent or degree of knowledge acquired but whether a student knows something correctly or not:. The questions have, however, to be developed with care, to ensure that the knowledge required for answering them is not peripheral but something which is likely to be useful to students in progressing further in educational pursuits.

The *fill-in-the-blank* type of questions too serve a useful purpose, where a student has to discover an appropriate word or a phrase or a statement for filling in the gap in a meaningful manner. These questions could be used very well up to Class II in examination situations.

The *matching questions* require that the items in the two columns are homogeneous, that in one of the columns there may be at least *three items more* than the other ones to be matched. All these additional items, however, should be plausible but not matchable with any of those items on the other side. Well constructed matching questions could be asked upto any stage.

It may be specifically mentioned *that all these three forms of questions possess great potential for being used as effective devices of teaching at all levels of education.* This potential, however, remains greatly unexplored in the current schemes of teaching and learning. A question of any of these three types could be put to the class and answers solicited. Then there could be a debate as to why a particular answer is correct or even more appropriate than the other. Such an interaction can lead to better internalisation of learning than any form of teaching or any other form of learning. This approach could be called as *use of the test material in teaching* and deserves to be explored and fully exploited.

Thus, the importance of objective type questions of types other than the multiple choice ones too cannot be underestimated.

It is hoped that the above considerations about the construction of different forms of questions will be able to offer valuable insight to teachers in preparing and using them.

45

Using Questions for Teaching

Introduction

Teaching and testing are two basic components of every instructional programme. They are dovetailed to the instructional objectives which provide directions for both. *Teaching is the criterion behaviour against which testing is validated.* Testing on the other hand also validates the whole teaching-learning process by providing relevant evidences about the degree of its effectiveness in realising the objectives. Thus, teaching and testing not only motivate students' learning, but can also be used as a means to effective instruction, through a regular feed-back mechanism.

Questions are mainly used for testing the achievement of pupils. At the same time it is not unusual to find students solving the question papers of previous years before the examination. As the questions in traditional public examinations used to generally test rote learning, students memorised answers to commonly expected questions in order to pass the examinations. In this chapter an attempt is made to highlight the *role of questions in classroom instruction.* Examples from some selected subjects of the curriculum have been taken to indicate the objective, specification, topic, problem, previous knowledge assumed, teachers' activities, pupils' activities and additional tasks. The teacher should ensure that he prepares his students adequately for this type of questions by suitably adapting his teaching. The test items presented in regard to different subjects will give them an indication of how he may shift emphasis in teaching-learning procedures from rote memorisation to real internalisation as displayed through comprehension and expression.

Every teacher should keep in view specific instructional objectives while teaching and testing, which should go hand in hand. Test items are normally used for determining the attainment levels of students. While using any such item in the classroom, the teacher himself should be very clear about the objective on which it is based, and also about the kind of expected learning outcomes. This will make him look back to the knowledge already imparted and also to fill in the gaps in learning. In the light of these gaps he can reinforce his teaching for improved learning on the part of students.

Use of question is one of the means the teacher can profitably use in classroom situations. However, it must be borne in mind that testing is no substitute for teaching.

Some Examples

Some examples in different subjects on this unfamiliar theme were developed by the then Examination Reform Unit of the NCERT in 1977. A few of these have been summarised and are being presented here.

ENGLISH

Topic

The Happy Prince: (Author: Oscar Wilde)

Question

If God had asked His Angel to bring only one most precious thing from the city instead of two, what would he have brought? Give reasons. Your answer should be limited to about 100 words.

Objective

- The student reads the story entitled 'The Happy Prince' with comprehension.
- The student writes answers to questions based on the text correctly and effectively.

Specific Learning Outcomes

In respect of the above story:

- ◆ *Comprehension*

  The Pupil

  - locates important events, facts and ideas.
  - reads between the lines.
  - identifies relationship between objects and events.
  - critically examines and evaluates events, actions, ideas, and feelings in the light of their outcomes.

- ◆ *Expression*

  The Pupil

  - uses appropriate vocabulary and structures.
  - culls and presents only relevant ideas and facts in logical order.
  - avoids unnecessary repetition.
  - organises ideas, facts, etc. appropriately into paragraphs and other forms of presentation.
  - displays imagination in writing.

Previous Knowledge

For being able to answer the above question, it is assumed that the students are:

- thoroughly acquainted with the story 'The Happy Prince'.
- acquainted with various events that occur in the story.
- able to appreciate the values of love, sacrifice, and service.
- able to organise their ideas and thoughts in a logical order.

Teaching-Learning Activities

- The students will be asked to read the story 'The Happy Prince' silently in the class.
- They will then be asked the above questions.
- They will be guided to identify significant events in the story.
- The likely reasons for bringing the two possible objects by the angel will be discussed in the class.
- The students will debate on the significance of the two possible alternative decisions on the part of the Angels.
- The students will critically examine and evaluate both the possibilities and reach their own conclusions.
- The teacher will guide them in substantiating their respective points with examples from the story.
- The teacher will help the students in expressing their ideas effectively.
- The teacher will help them to organise and arrange details in a logical sequence and coherent presentation so that the answer becomes effective.
- The students will then write the answers to the above question.

Follow-up Activities

The teacher may plan to undertake one or more of the following activities:

- The teacher, while correcting the answers, should note their mistakes and discuss them in the class.
- He may ask the students to write an imaginary incident in which the little swallow again helps the 'Happy Prince' in his service to humanity, in the event of the lives of both of them restored to them.

PHYSICS

Topic

Relative Density-Law of Floating Bodies

Question

A cork weighing 10 grams can just sink into water when a load of 40 grams is placed over it. What will be the relative density of the cork?

Objective

The students apply their knowledge of law of floating bodies, in the new situation.

Specific Learning Outcomes

The pupil:

- analyses the situation to identify the principle underlying in the given problems.
- makes some hypothesis regarding laws of floating bodies, etc.
- establishes relationship between mass of displaced water and the cork with the load placed on it.
- predicts the effect of increase or decrease in load placed on the cork.

Previous Knowledge

- Definition of density and relative density.
- Archimedes' principle.
- Density of water is 1 gram/c.c.
- Mass = Volume × Density.

Teaching-Learning Activities

- The teacher presents the problem listed above after teaching Archimedes' principle, laws of floating bodies, etc.
- The students try to understand the problem, analyse it and try to know what is given and what is required.
- The teacher helps the students to analyse the problem further and formulates the following hypotheses:
  (i) The weight of the floating body is equal to the upward thrust of the liquid.
  (ii) The volume of the displaced water is equal to that of the body inside water.
  (iii) The upward thrust is equal to the weight of water displaced.
- On the basis of the above hypotheses, the students find that the mass of water displaced is equal to the total mass of the cork and the load placed on it i.e. (10 + 40) gms. = 50 gms. Hence, the volume of the displaced water = 50 c.c. which is, therefore, the volume of the cork. The students finally find that the relative density of the cork = 10/50 gm/cc. = 0.2 gm/c.c.
- The teacher asks the students as to what will happen, if more load is placed on the cork.
- The students find that since the mass of the body is greater than that of the displaced water, the body cannot float, but will sink completely.
- The teacher asks a further question of the students as to what will happen, if a weight less than 40 gms. is placed on the cork.

- The students argue that in the above case the weight of the body (cork) being less than that of the displaced water, the body will float and some portion of the body will be above water.
- The teacher advises the students to remember that Archimedes' principle cannot be applied if the liquid is not in equilibrium.

Follow-up Activities

The pupils:

- arrange the experiment to get the results checked and comment on arrangements made by other friends.
- prepare similar question taking other factors as unknown: volume, mass etc.
- comment on questions prepared by friends. For example, if the problem is to find the relative density of the load put over the cork, then it cannot be solved.
- prepare similar questions taking a liquid other than water and then realise that the one additional data viz. the density of the liquid is needed to solve the problem.
- try to solve similar type of more complicated problems like a situation when the cork is immersed in a mixture of two liquids whose densities are known.

BIOLOGY

Content Unit

Levels of Organisation: (Concept of cell tissue organ and system)

The illustration given here deals with the concept of cell, tissue, organ and system. The question that follows is only one example of only one type which can be made use of in teaching as described below. The purpose is to emphasise and explore the possibility of using a question as a device of teaching. It is only through the discussion of relationships in each alternative that students arrive at the correct answer and learn about the concepts involved.

Questions

The relationship between cell and tissue is almost similar to the relationship between:

A. ptyaline and starch.
B. liver and the gall bladder.
C. carbohydrate and fat.
D. ectoderm and endoderm.
E. organ and the system

Objective

The student comprehends the concepts of cell, tissue, organ and system with respect to human physiology.

Specific Learning Outcomes

The pupil

- recalls different levels of organisation of life and recognises the structure of cell and of different tissues and organs of digestive system.
- identifies relationship among cell, tissue, organ and the system.
- compares different units of life.
- cites examples of tissues, organs and the system.
- observes and interprets correctly the given diagram or a slide showing transverse section of some organs.
- draws inferences about the given or observed situations involving different types of relationship.

Previous Knowledge

Students are already familiar with the following:

- The cell as the basic unit of all living organisms.
- Elementary idea of tissue.
- Elementary idea of the digestive system.
- Proximal constituents of food.
- Structure of multicellular animals like coelenterates.

Teaching-Learning Activities

- The teacher poses the above problem in the class.
- He explains the relationship involved in the cell and tissue for further clarification. He helps the students to recall that cell is the basic unit of life and the tissue is composed of a group of such cells. Therefore, cell is a component of the tissue which is a larger unit of life.
- Pupils study the problem, recall the structure and function of cells and tissues. They also try to identify the relationship between the two concepts and may give different answers to the problem stated.
- The teacher analyses the responses; takes note of the various categories of answers and discusses each choice with the students to enable them to establish relationship in each case. He educes with the help of students that in alternative 'A' the relationship is that of an enzyme and the substance digested; in 'B' it is that of a production and a storage unit; in 'C' it is that of two constituent units or components of a common substance (food) while in 'D' the relationship is spatial, i.e., external and internal positions of an organ.
- Pupils make comparisons of the relationship between cell and tissue with each of the relationship observed in each of the cases A, B, C and D and recognise that none of these relationships is similar to the one between cell and tissue.

- Pupils are especially asked to study the choice 'E' which may be the plausible answer in this case. They examine the functional relationship between organ and system.
- Pupils find out the different organs that go to make up a system just as cells go to make up a tissue. Thus, they establish that the relationship between a cell and tissue is the same as between organs and the system thereby arriving at the correct choice.
- Teacher then asks pupils to interpret the relationship between tissues and the organ on the basis of relationship established by them between organ and system.
- Pupils interpret the overall relationship among cell, tissue, organ and system.
- Teacher then shows to the class different charts of animal and plant organs showing different tissues and cells comprising the tissues, for students to observe and identify the various levels of organisation.

Activities in the practical class (Dissection)

Teacher guides the students to open the viscera of the frog and helps them to:

- observe the various organs found inside the body of the frog.
- recognise some organs which form one system e.g. digestive system and see which organs combine together to form that system (digestive system in this case).
- examine the microprepared slide of the T.S. of one organ made up of various tissue (e.g. stomach).
- interpret the internal structure of the stomach and infer relationship between tissues and organs.
- In the prepared slide of T.S. of stomach, the students examine one layer under the high power microscope and find out similar type of cells in the layer and draw inference that a group of similar cells form a tissue and tissues form the organ.

Follow-up Activities

- Pupils are asked to examine simple or isolated cells of an animal like Amoeba or a plant like Chlamydomonas.
- Pupils would examine a group of cells forming simple tissue, say in Hydra.
- Pupils may be asked to examine different tissues in an organ in any microprepared slide, say T.S. of intestine and report their observations regarding the relationship between the two.
- Teacher suggests to his pupils to prepare a chart depicting a particular system of an animal as also the organs, tissues and cells separately indicating relationship among them.
- Students are asked to discover and record other similar relationship that they might observe or locate from different sources.

MATHEMATICS

Topic

Polygon

Question

The quadrilateral obtained by joining the middle points of the adjacent sides of any quadrilateral is a:

A. square.
B. rhombus.
C. rectangle.
D. parallelogram.

Objective

The student applies his knowledge of the relationship between the straight line joining the middle points of any two sides of a triangle to the third side to find the solution of the problem.

Specific Learning Outcomes

The pupil

- identifies relationship between the line joining the middle points of any two sides of a triangle to the third side of it.
- compares different types of polygons.
- draws the inference that the required figure is a parallelogram.

Previous Knowledge

- Terms and concepts: Triangle, quadrilateral, square, rectangle, rhombus, parallelogram.
- Relationship; (a) The line joining the middle points of any two sides of a triangle is parallel to the third side and is equal to half of it. (b) A parallelogram is a quadrilateral having opposite sides parallel.

Teaching-Learning Activities

- The teacher presents the problem after teaching the theorem regarding the relationship between the straight line joining the middle points of any two sides of a triangle to its third side.
- The students try to comprehend the problem, analyse it and understand what are given and what is required.
- Pupils recall appropriate relationship and processes given above.
- The teacher ascertains through questions whether the students have a clear concept about a parallelogram and know the relationship between the opposite sides. The teacher explains the concept of parallelogram, in case he finds that it is not clear to the students. He helps them to understand *that a rhombus is a special parallelogram*

whose all four sides are equal, a square is a special type of rhombus whose one angle is a right angle and a rectangle is a special parallelogram whose one angle is a right angle.

- The students are asked to draw the figure according to the problem and measure the length of the opposite sides of the quadrilateral obtained by joining the mid-points of the adjacent sides of the quadrilateral.
- The students find that the opposite sides are equal and parallel and conclude that the figure is a parallelogram, and that the choice 'D' may be the correct answer. The possibility of the alternatives A, B and C being stated by the students as the correct answer is, however, not ruled out.
- By actual measurement of all the sides of the quadrilateral so formed, the students find that all are not equal and thus it cannot always be a rhombus or a square because all the four sides may not always be equal.
- By the measurement of one of the angles of the same quadrilateral, the students also find that it is not always a right angle. Hence, they conclude that the aforesaid figure is not always likely to be a rectangle.
- Students arrive at the conclusion that only 'D' is the correct answer.
- After the students have verified through a practical exercise that 'D' is the only correct answer, the teacher then asks the students to give an analytic proof of the proposition. He ascertains through questions what is given in the problem and what is to be proved. He also asks them about the method for proving it.
- Students give different answers to the problem stated.
- The teacher then tries to help him in arriving at the conclusion that this can be achieved only by joining the diagonals of the given quadrilateral.
- The students find that each pair of opposite sides of the inner quadrilateral is parallel to each diagonal of the given quadrilateral and is equal to half its length. They come to the conclusion that opposite sides of the given quadrilateral are equal and parallel.
- They find out that the two diagonals of any quadrilateral need not always be equal. Hence, all the sides of the quadrilateral obtained by joining the mid-points of the given quadrilateral need not be equal. This eliminates the possibility of answers A and C.
- The students find that the diagonals of any quadrilateral need not always intersect at right angles. Hence, the sides of the quadrilateral under discussion also need not always be at right angles. This eliminates the possibility of answers A and B.
- They finally arrive at the conclusion that the obtained figure is a parallelogram and thus D is the only correct answer.

Follow-up Work

- Students are asked to prove analytically similar problems based on the above concept.
- They are asked to draw similar figures taking square, rectangle, rhombus, trapezium instead of any quadrilateral.
- They are asked to find out the nature of the quadrilateral so that the figure obtained by joining the mid-points of the adjacent sides turn out to be a square, or a rectangle, or a rhombus.
- They are required to find whether the obtained figure can be none of the four alternatives suggested in the problem.

GEOGRAPHY

Content Unit

Geography of India: Climate (Monsoons).

Question

Compare and contrast the summer and winter monsoons in India with respect to their causes, direction of winds, duration and areas of occurrence.

Objective

The pupil exhibits an understanding of the role of the monsoons.

Specific Learning Outcomes

The pupil

- discriminates between such terms as summer and winter monsoons. South-west and North-east monsoons. Advancing and retreating monsoons, bursting of monsoons etc.
- interprets climatic data presented in different forms.
- analyses the effect of the northward shifting of the thermal zone in the summer season and its retreat in the winter season.
- compares the effect of the shifting thermal equator on the surface weather and conditions in the upper atmosphere.
- establishes relationship between temperature and pressure conditions in the atmosphere in summer and winter.
- establishes relationship between distribution of rainfall and various factors which affect their regional distribution.
- draws inferences about the sources of air-masses and direction of winds.
- selects relevant facts to explain the similarities and dissimilarities in weather and climatic conditions in different parts of India.
- predicts weather conditions in different parts of the country during different seasons (winter, summer and monsoon seasons).

Previous Knowledge

It is presumed that the pupils already know the following:

- The latitudinal and longitudinal position of India.
- Major relief regions of India.
- Seasons.
- Distribution of summer and winter temperatures and its relationship with pressure systems prevailing in these regions.
- Relationship between pressure systems and wind systems.
- Ferrels law.
- Cyclones-tropical and temperate.
- Seasonal and annual distribution of rainfall.

Teaching-Learning Activities

- Teacher illustrates with a relief map, rainfall map and temperature map of India, the temperature and pressure conditions of India in the different months, and the shifting of the centres of low pressure pockets.
- Pupils observe the facts and explain the changes in wind direction in relation to the occurrence of the monsoons.
- Teacher poses the problems of the vagaries of rainfall distribution in the country in all seasons and explains the relationship between intensity of low pressure and 'bursting of monsoons' and the march of the monsoon winds in the country.
- Pupils identify on maps, regions of heaviest rainfall in the different months and explain the real difference in occurrence of rains from June to September on the west coast and October to March on the east coast.
- The teacher highlights the phenomena of 'reversal' or 'retreat' of monsoon conditions and its relationship to distribution of temperature and pressure conditions. Thus, the classification of monsoon winds as summer and winter, wet and dry or North-east and South-west is explained.
- Pupils identify from a world climatic regions map the other areas which experience monsoons and the causes of such an occurrence. They differentiate the Indian monsoon from the Malayan monsoon and the Japanese and North Australian monsoons.
- Pupils identify from temperature and rainfall data of a few places in India, the regions of which they are representative.
- Teacher organises a discussion on the effect of monsoons on growing seasons in different parts of India and the problems created by monsoons, of flooding and erosion and steps to counteract such destruction. Similar discussions on the role of monsoon in respect of

(i) irrigation facilities (ii) forestry (iii) crop production, (iv) distribution of population, etc. could also be arranged.

Follow-up Activities

Practical work

- Preparation of maps of India showing seasonal distribution of rainfall, temperature, pressure wind direction, particularly during the spans June to September and March to October.
- Preparation of maps of the Indian Ocean showing distribution of pressure and direction of winds in different periods especially January, March, May, June, September and November.

Discussions and Group Work

- Effect of seasonal variation in rainfall on crop production.
- Problem of famine following failure of rainfall in different parts of India and steps taken to counteract this.
- Relationship of forests and rainfall.

The above illustration is just one of the many approaches in which a question could be tackled and used as a basis for teaching. The other activities which have potentials for using a good question as instructional material are: (i) self-study or assignment (ii) group study project (iii) classroom discussions on topical news, etc.

46

Setting Balanced Question Papers and End of Topic Tests

There are various *techniques* of testing like Written Examinations, Oral Examinations, Practical Examinations, Observation. Each of these techniques uses different tools of 'testing'. For example, we use observation schedules, check-lists, inventories, rating scales and question papers as *tools* of evaluation in different techniques as per need. Among these the question papers and tests are the most commonly used of the tools.

While tests and question papers are the basic tools of evaluation in written examinations, they are also used for other techniques.

As public/external examinations are the most common types of examinations used and since they are pre-dominantly written examinations, question papers have become the most important of the tools of testing.

The traditional form of question papers used to suffer from a variety of flaws which have been attempted to be overcome as a part of the Movement of Examination Reform Programme of the NCERT where in the author played a crucial note. These reforms, however, have been, by and large, limited to the school stage and the universities do still by-and-large use the traditional form of examinations in a substantial measure. In some places these school level reforms have also influenced university education.

Examination Reform at the school stage has been influenced by the latest developments in the science of evaluation which have revolutionised education in respect of its concept, content and process. Earlier it was thought that anybody who knows a subject can teach it, anybody who can teach can also test. These notions no more hold ground with the evolution of the Science of Pedagogy and the Science of Evaluation. In fact, both pedagogy and evaluation have germs of science and art.

Without getting way-laid into the wider realms of pedagogy and evaluation let us revert to the central theme of Setting Balanced Question Papers.

Shortcomings of Traditional Question Papers and their Remediation

Some of the main shortcomings that had come to infest traditional written examinations particularly because of the pattern of question papers were:

- Over-emphasis on memorisation
- Subjectivity
- Poor Content Coverage and
- Some administrative shortfalls

Let us now take up these one by one and analyse the nature of the shortfall its implications on teaching and testing and the measures for overcoming them.

Over-Emphasis on Memorisation

The questions contained in the traditional question papers were mainly focussed on content where the examinees were supposed to *memorise and reproduce.*

Since we tended to *teach what was tested rather than testing what we taught*, the development of higher abilities like understanding, application analysis, synthesis, critical thinking, evaluation were almost completely overlooked. Education so imparted, turned children into parrots and mechanical beings rather than creative individuals not just in examinations but also often in their future lives. While this served the needs of the foreign rulers for developing lower and middle level workforce, for running a colonial administration, they have turned out to be utterly inadequate for the emerging demands of independent India.

It has been because of this that the *ability* dimension has been forcefully added to the *content* facet in testing. In addition to the sub-division of the content (topics and sub-topics), objectives (abilities/competencies) too have been identified in respect of each subject and these further sub-divided into specifications. For example, the objective of comprehension/understanding has been divided into its constituent components like discrimination, classification, comparison and contrast, identification of relationships, giving examples, detecting and correcting errors, etc. These ability sub-divisions have thus now become integral and focal components of testing devices (questions) besides content. The phenomenon has encouraged schools to try to develop the higher mental abilities also, besides memorisation—recognition, recall and reproduction, which in the good old days used to be almost the sole ability tested because of the main focus on the memorisation of content.

Furthermore, in the traditional scheme of things the focus was pre-dominantly on the mental abilities. The reformed system also attempts to cover the *total personality consisting of the abilities of the head (cognitive abilities), of the heart (affective abilities) and those of the hands (psycho-motor abilities)*. Taxonomies of these objectives too now stand developed as discussed earlier in the chapter on objectives. Evaluation of different cognitive, affective and psycho-motor abilities is being taken up as a part of Comprehensive and Continuous School-based Evaluation.

Testing in written examinations through question papers, however, mainly covers the cognitive area and only partly the psycho-motor and the affective areas of personality. In developing balanced question papers, objectives desired to be tested in the concerned subject are listed and weightages allocated to each of them (in terms of marks) on the basis of the relevance of a particular objective in the subject in question. For example, in subjects like Geography and Biology a substantial chunk of marks would be devoted to 'skills', in subjects like Physics and Chemistry to Application of Knowledge, in History to Knowledge and so on.

The next step is to construct questions equivalent to the allocated weightages to content and objectives. In this process the choice of the form of question will be an important criteria, for example, for testing the ability of expression, a long answer/essay type question and not an objective type question has to be chosen to be constructed. Furthermore, each form of question has to follow some rules which have already been discussed separately in the chapter on preparing questions of different forms.

All these measures help overcome the over-emphasis on memorisation by systematically including questions testing higher abilities in the question papers in due proportion.

The steps will also help improve the validity of the question papers.

Subjectivity

Traditionally subjectively too has been a great shortcoming of the written examinations. It operates mainly at three levels. *Subjectivity of the question paper setter* used to operate in a wild manner particularly because the question paper setters enjoyed complete unrestricted freedom to pick up or drop any item from the syllabus for setting question papers and nobody could question their authority. The questions were basically factual and the directive words like 'elucidate', 'illustrate', 'elaborate' were indiscriminately used. Invariably there was a short note question giving themes like 'Democracy' on which books could be written.

This unlimited freedom stands checked now because the paper setter is now given a 'Design' (Format appended) of the question paper to be set and clear instructions given about the language of the questions, their unambiguous/ specific wording indicating the precise scope and length of the expected answer. The paper setter is also now required to develop a marking scheme indicating the parts of the expected answer and the marks to be allocated to each part. This curbs the paper setter's vagaries and helps him correct many mistakes in the questions on their own.

While the format of the design is appended to the chapter, it is pertinent to mention its main parts which are:

- Weightage to objectives
- Weightage to major areas of content

- Weightage to different forms of questions
- Scheme of sections
- Pattern of options

In addition to this the paper setter is also required to prepare a '*Blueprint*' (Format enclosed) for setting the question papers. This indicates the precise placement of each question in respect of objective and topic attempted to be tested by it, the form in which it is to be framed, and the marks it carries. This makes him check the comparability/compatibility of the design with the blueprint, and of the blueprint with the questions, and of the questions with the marking scheme. The question paper setter besides preparing the blueprint, the questions, the marking scheme is also required to prepare a question-wise analysis (format appended) which is yet another check for him to conform to the paradigms of each question he has prepared. This table incorporates the following details about each question or part thereof:

1. Objective and specification tested
2. Content Area (topic & sub-topic) covered/tested
3. Form of the question
4. Marks carried by the question
5. Estimated difficulty level (easy/average/difficult)
6. Estimated time for answering

Subjectivity of the Examinee

This too is a common phenomenon and occurs mainly because of the vague wording of the questions where the student himself has to interpret about what he has to write. In response to the questions in the traditional question papers anything and everything could be written. Students, therefore, *chose to write all that they knew about that topic rather than answering the question as such.*

With restrictions on the language of the questions which has now to be precise and pinpointed, exactly spelling out the scope and length of the expected answer, the examinee now precisely knows what is expected of him to write and what the parts of the answer have to be, how long the answer has to be and what marks each part of the answer would carry. In the new question papers the marks carried by different questions are not given as say 10 in all, but the marks to parts of the expected answer as well like (2 + 4 + 4).

Subjectivity of the Examiner

This too has been a common phenomenon and one which stands scientifically proved. The technical term 'Standard Error of Measurement' owes its origin to it.

Edwin Harper's study 'Hundred Marking Ten' in 1967 done at Allahabad proved that marking variations operate within a range of 5% and 8% and in more than 50% of the cases, they are likely to be more than 5%.

The NCERT study of 1998 where 20 examiners evaluated the same

10 History answer scripts of Class XII of CBSE, did not have any different story to tell. The scripts and the examiners were both randomly selected. The examiners evaluated these photo-copied scripts when they were actually evaluating the actual answer scripts of the same subject, of the same examination, using the same marking scheme, which they were expected to follow in evalualting these photocopied scripts.

The marks awarded out of 100 by the most lenient and the most strict of the *twenty examiners* to the same ten scripts were as under:

Script No. / *Examiner*	*1*	*2*	*3*	*4*	*5*	*6*	*7*	*8*	*9*	*10*	*Mean*
Marks Awarded by the Most Lenient Examiner	50	66	23	35	37	74	54	53	39	37	46.8
Marks Awarded by the Most Strict Examiner	21	28	02	10	14	43	23	19	05	07	17.2
Difference Between the Two	29	38	31	25	23	31	31	34	34	30	29.6

The position could only be worse twenty years back. Though things have no doubt improved with double checking a lot still needs to be done.

A concrete measure taken by the Council for the Indian School Certificate Examination (CISCE) is that though a marking scheme already stands developed by the paper setter, each Deputy Head Examiner is required to evaluate 20 or so scripts. This is followed by a discussion in the course of the *Coordination Meetings*, only after which the marking scheme to be used is finalised. Another suggestion could be for the Boards and universities to make it compulsory for all affiliated institutions to depute teachers for purposes of evaluation for continuation of their affiliation to the Board. This is because the good institutions do not send their teachers for evaluation. The non-availability of examiners in adequate numbers also forces the Boards and universities to give more scripts for evaluation to each examiner than what should ordinarily be given for doing justice.

There should also be a provision for appointing some additional hands at the evaluation centres, who may only check that the totals are correct, that all parts of answers have been evaluated, that marks to all parts of answers have been individually awarded and that the marks have been correctly posted on the cover page of the script and also on the marksheet. They should also check that the member of supplementary sheets indicated are all there. The Deputy Head Examiners in-charge of evaluation centres should also actually check the sample of scripts they are supposed to check and not just initial them as a formality. He and the checker should ensure that the marking scheme is being followed for evaluation in letter and spirit so that the errors of measurement can be minimised.

With the above measures the objectivity will become possible to be ensured to a large extent.

Inadequate Content Coverage

When no 'Designs' and 'Blueprints' were used the situation was alarming. Comparatively it is better but a lot still needs to be done. It is *poor content coverage that leads to selective study and selective teaching.* The provision of options further aggravates the problem. Suppose there are 20 topics in the syllabus, 16 are covered by the question paper and a student can attempt full 100 marks questions, if he attempts questions on 12 topics and he can pass, if he gives correct answers to questions on say 5 topics. In this case:

20 Topics	imply	100%	Full coverage of content
16 Topics in the question paper	imply	80%	Apparent coverage of content
12 Topics which can yield full marks	imply	60%	Actual coverage of content
5 Topics for passing the examination	imply	20%	Real coverage for passing

In this commonly witnessed situation a student can easily omit 40% of the syllabus and yet aspire to get the highest possible marks. One needs to study just 20% of the course content to pass. Is the situation not shocking?

This is not all about options which do lead to selective study and selective teaching. They also make examinations a farce by making scores incomparable.

The traditional question papers normally used to have about 8 questions and the instructions used to be "All questions carry equal marks attempt any five". These *overall options* meant that any question could be substituted for any other. The presumptions that the situation made were that:

- if an examinee knew one topic it was taken that he knew any other.
- all questions tested the same ability and same content.
- all questions needed the same answering time.
- all questions were pitched at the same estimated level of difficulty.

all of which could not stand any of the above tests.

In addition, in such a situation, different students attempted different sets of questions – in effect, different question papers. If A got 40 marks, B got 50 and the C got 60, it *could not be said* that C is first, B is second, and A is third because all the three of them have not been subjected to the same tests. The situation is similar to the one when a student X does 1.83 m. long jump, Y does 1.22 m. high jump and Z 2.44 m. high pole vault, where one cannot say who is first, who is second and who is third.

Options could, therefore, be only provided, if the questions given as options:

- cover/test the same content/topic
- test the same objective/ability
- are of the same form
- are pitched at the same estimated level of difficulty
- take the same approximate time for answering
- carry the same marks

Satisfying all these conditions at the same time is not just difficult but near impossible for ensuring equivalence among options.

There are *overall options* like all questions carry equal marks, attempt any five, *internal option* within questions like write short notes on any three of the given five and *alternate options* of this or this type.

A rule of thumb in this regard if options have to be offered is:

Objective Type Very Short Answer Type Short Answer Type	No options
Long Answer Type	Alternate internal equivalent options

It, therefore, appears necessary that major areas of content may be identified and each given an appropriate weightage (marks) out of the total marks for the question paper for preparing questions on these weightages which could be determined on the basis of :

- the importance of the particular area in the subject
- the difficulty level of the area
- the time needed for covering the theme in teaching and learning

These weightages would stand indicated in the 'Design' prepared by the examining agency and should be appropriately reflected in the grid of the 'Blueprint' prepared by the question paper setters. Questions could then be framed on that basis. This is a technical exercise and cannot be done by anyone and everyone without training in the concept and techniques of evaluation with particular reference to setting of question papers, which should be arranged to be organised and become essential eligibility criteria for being appointed as question paper setters.

Administrative Inadequacies

Question paper setters, have but to be trained in the Concept and Techniques of Evaluation with particular reference to the Technology of Setting Balanced Question Papers, to execute the technical job assigned to them.

Detailed instructions should also be prepared and issued to the question paper setters, besides of course the design.

Three question papers based on the same design should be prepared at the same time. This should be a team task with the team of three consisting of *a content expert,* a *pedagogue and a practising teacher*. All the three should be given the same design for preparing their own blueprints and question papers on them. The three of them should then come together to discuss and finalise the three question papers, their respective marking schemes and question-wise analysis of their papers. The content expert would be able to check the accuracy of content of the questions, the pedagogue the technique of framing questions and the practising teacher the appropriateness of standard of the questions. The three sets of such question papers and related material be then packed and sealed separately. One of these may be picked up for the annual examination, the other for the supplementary examination and the third may be kept for a possible emergency. The three papers based on the same design will be parallel at the level of the design and hence substitutable.

Another administrative measure relates to the situation where a significant portion of the question paper/test may be consisting of objective type and very short answer type questions with some questions of the other forms as well. In this situation if the section with objective type and very short answer type questions remains with the examinees' for longer than necessary there could be a likelihood that in such instances they may try to check their answers with their neighbours. It is, therefore, desirable that the question paper be divided into two sections—one with objective type and very short answer type questions and the other section may have short answer and long answer questions. Both the sections may be administered together but the one with objective type and very short answer type questions be collected earlier at the end of the prescribed tight time limit.

Adequate publicity for carrying the public opinion along about this strategy will also be necessary for a general acquaintance about the merits of the proposal.

Steps of the Action Plan

In respect of each question paper, the following action points related to different sequential steps will need to be taken:

1. Preparation of a design of the question paper to be prepared by the examining agency/institutions.
2. Preparation of a blueprint based on the design to be prepared by the question paper setter. Format to be supplied by the examining agency alongwith instructions.
3. Transfer of blueprint details on to the *item sheets* (*see* format) with one question on each answer sheet with the details about objectives, specifications, topic, sub-topic, form, marks expected, answering time and estimated difficulty level in respect of each question filled in. The marking scheme with expected outline answers and marks to different parts of the expected answer written on the backside of the item sheet. This should be done at the same time as the setting of each question. Adequate number of item sheets to be provided by the examining agency alongwith instructions.
4. Papers for writing the consolidated question paper and consolidated marking scheme to be also provided to the paper setter.
5. Format/Proforma for the preparation of question-wise analysis be also supplied to the paper setter alongwith the instructions. These formats are given below for ready reference:

FORMAT OF A DESIGN QUESTION PAPER/TEST

Subject : ....
Unit/paper : ....
Class : ....
Time : ....
Marks : ....

Weightage to Objectives:

Objective	K/KE	U/CO	A/EX	S/AP	Total
Percentage of marks	....	....	....	....	....
Marks	....	....	....	....	....

Weightage to Forms of Questions:

Forms of Questions	E/LA	SA	VSA	O	Total
No. of Questions	....	....	....	....	....
Marks Allotted	....	....	....	....	....
Estimated Time	....	....	....	....	....

Weightage to Major Content Areas:

Units/Sub-Units	Marks
1.	....
2.	....
3.	....
4.	....
5.	....
6.	....
7.	....
8.	....

Scheme of Sections : ....
....

Pattern of options : ....
....

Estimated difficulty level:
Difficult : .... % marks.
Average : .... % marks.
Easy : .... % marks.

Abbreviations : K (Knowledge), U (Understanding), A (Application), S (Skill)
KE (Knowledge of Elements of Language), CO (Comprehension), EX (Expression), APP (Appreciation)
E (Essay or Long Answer Type), SA (Short Answer Type), VSA (Very Short Answer Type), O (Objective Type – Multiple Choice)

FORMAT OF A BLUEPRINT

SUBJECT: ____________________ CLASS: __________

UNIT/PAPER: ____________________ MAXIMUM MARKS: __________ TIME: __________

OBJECTIVE / FORM OF QUESTIONS / CONTENT UNITS/SUB-UNITS	ELEMENTS OF LANGUAGE KNOWLEDGE				COMPREHENSION UNDERSTANDING				EXPRESSION APPLICATION				APPRECIATION SKILL		TOTAL
	E	SA	VSA	O	E	SA	VSA	O	E	SA	VSA	O	E	SA	
SUB TOTAL															
TOTAL															

Notes: Figures within brackets to indicate the number of questions and figures outside the brackets to indicate marks

* Denotes that marks have been combined to form one question.

Summary:

Essay (E)	No.	Marks	Pattern of Options ....
Short Answer (SA)	No.	Marks	
Very Short Answer (VSA)	No.	Marks	Scheme of Sections ....
Objective (O)	No.	Marks	

ITEM SHEET FORMAT

Front Side of the Item Sheet

S.No. ....

Objective	....	Topic	....
Specification	....	Sub-Topic	....
Form	....	Expected Answering Time	....
Estimated Difficulty Level	....	Marks	....

Question : ....

....

....

....

....

....

....

Reverse Side of the Item Sheet

S.No. ....

SCORING KEY

QUESTION NO.	1	2	3	4					n
KEY									

MARKING SCHEME

EXPECTED OUTLINE ANSWER	MARKS TO EACH ASPECT	REMARKS

QUESTION-WISE ANALYSIS

S. No.	OBJECTIVE	SPECIFICATION	TOPIC	SUB-TOPIC	FORM	ESTIMATED DIFFICULTY LEVEL	MARKS	ESTIMATED ANSWERING TIME

47

Types of Tests and Test Characteristics

Achievement Tests

These tests are the most widely used ones in periodical, terminal and annual examinations. They attempt to test the prescribed subject matter for the concerned test and the envisaged abilities (objectives). They use one or more forms of test-items/questions. Achievement tests test a sample of the total content.

Diagnostic Tests

Diagnostic tests, basically are also achievement tests, but unlike achievement tests, they exhaustively test all facets of content, because only then they are able to precisely identify the aspects and facets which a particular student does not know and where s/he needs help for further improving his performance.

Psychological Tests

These tests started as tests for the mentally weak children. Subsequently the experts started working on mental brightness or intelligence. Intelligence was then treated as the sole single index of an individual's personality. Many Intelligence Tests were then developed. These were used for a variety of purposes. But it soon came to be realised that as intelligence has many facets, it is not justifiable to use it in an omnibus manner for judging an individual for everything. Then started a span when aptitude tests and aptitude test batteries were prepared and used for different trades and occupations. Tests based on Projective Techniques were then developed with the claim of discovering those facets of an individual's personality which normally remain under wraps.

Recruitment Tests

The preparation of Recruitment Tests should ideally be preceded by a *job analysis* which somehow is conspicuous by its absence from the actual scene to day. However, these tests by-and-large have the following components.

- General Awareness
- General Mental Ability
- Linguistic Ability
- Quantitative Aptitude
- Subject Knowledge

This test is in some cases on-line and in other cases the candidates respond on OMR sheets. Some recruiting agencies publish the KEY after the examination.

Some recruiters also have an interview of the candidates for the final selection.

Admission Tests

These are selection tests for admission to courses of higher academic or professional education. There is a lot of variation in the content and structure of these tests and these also keep on changing. The only permanent part of admission tests is a section on content knowledge.

Test Characteristics

To start with the following terminology needs to be understood.

Question Papers = Tests
Questions = Test Items.

Normally by test items we understand Multiple Choice Test Items. The formulae for determining test characteristics are available for Multiple Choice test items. In spite of this, the concepts related to test characteristics are surely applicable to other forms of questions as well, but only in spirit though not in the letter.

A brief enunciation of the test characteristics is attempted below:

- *Validity* (Accuracy) which implies that they are testing what they are expected to test, that is testing the desired content and desired mental abilities (objectives)
- *Reliability* (Dependability) which means that whether it is A or B or C, who assesses the performance or whether the performance is assessed in different settings or locations the scores by and large would be nearly the same.
- *Objectivity* (Justice) implying that planning, development, administration, scoring, etc. are all free from subjectivity and bias.
- *Practicability* (Feasibility) means that the environmental conditions, the standard, the available infrastructure for operational management are all appropriate for the test to sail through.

48

Some Ancilary Items

Teachers' Diary, Field Trips, Organisation of Exhibitions

Teachers' Diary

Original Expectation

In the 20th Century the concept of a Teachers' Diary used to be an elaborate document giving all the possible details of :

- teacher's expectations
- teacher's proposals for realising the expectations in terms of pupil growth and attainments
- the subject-matter he expected to cover
- the teaching strategies he desired to deploy
- the exercises he proposed to use for confirming that the students have learnt what they were expected to learn
- the outside text-books content which he wanted to incidentally introduce to the learners as enrichment material
- the aids to instruction which he proposed to use for better learning on the part of the students
- the testing exercises for evaluating the ability of the students to apply the knowledge gained in unfamiliar life situations.

Entries also included after the lesson had been taught about:

- The kind of difficulties he faced while teaching.
- The manner in which he proposes to overcome them in future.

Surprisingly, the aforesaid expectation of the educational administrators from the teachers were in *respect of each lesson of 40 to 45 minutes he taught for which a 24 Hour day was utterly inadequate.* This was even an uphill task when there were small classes and the correction load of the teachers was not that much.

Teacher's diary, thus, in course of time became a *compendium* of *repetitions* and a sham formality for the Heads of Institutions to blindly initial.

A Revised Format

Even though the impracticability of the aforesaid proposals was realized by academicians and administrators alike, their application was conveniently ignored.

It was only in the sixties with the establishment of NCERT and its influence that simplified versions of the format of the Teacher's diary were evolved by the states. These formats were simple and practicable even though repetition of some entries could not be avoided. By and large these formats included the following annual and term-wise entries and some skeleton entries about day to day teaching:

- Separate entries required to be made for each subject a teacher taught to a class.
- Objectives – enunciated subject/class-wise.
- A syllabus outline was worked out by the teacher from the prescribed curriculum.
- A time budget in terms of class periods required for covering each major area of content within the total time available.
- Proposed topic wise activities — assignments, surveys, projects experiments, field trips, seminars, panel discussions.

A lesson wise entry with date, class, subject indicating:

- The topic taught
- Activities incorporated (conventional and unconventional)
    - Assignments
    - Surveys
    - Projects
    - Field Trips, etc.
    - Consolidation Exercises

Organisation of Exhibitions

Introduction

Exhibitions too are important aids to teaching. Exhibitions involve the display of a variety of two or three-dimensional objects for communicating different ideas and pieces of information to the observer. An exhibition, therefore, has immense educational value.

As they are the pupils who participate in preparing the exhibits, setting them up and explaining them to the visitors, they not only learn new concepts but also consolidate their learning. Interesting exhibits also motivate pupils to explore further and obtain new information.

Basic Principles of Organising Exhibitions

- Have an overall theme. The exhibits should have an educational value, should always have a message to convey which may be possible to be immediately perceived without the need to read it. The message should be brief, crisp, clear and have an appeal. It should effectively convey the central idea and project the unity of the display.
- Locate the exhibit centrally at an easily accessible place.
- The settings of the display should not be crowded using bright colours and strong broad lines.
- Use movement, if possible.
- Follow artistic principles—proportion, balance, colour, shape, rhythm.
- Some exhibits have to be just seen, others understood. What has to be read should be placed at the appropriate eye distance.
- Label the exhibits properly. Labels should be possible to be read from a distance. Labels should be of uniform pattern and style.
- Display only latest up-to-date material, old, soiled and dust settled items should not be displayed.
- Give optimum dramatic effect—setting lighting etc.
- Have the exhibits of all children displayed. Parents will be interested in seeing the exhibits prepared by their children. Judicious use of colour and illumination help capture the attention of the viewers.
- Use the principles of advertising even in an educational exhibition as the objective of all advertisements is to sell ideas.
- Survey the place allocated and the material and accessories available. A map of the place be prepared and location of objects decided.
- Train students to explain exhibits. They should be level-headed, respectful and intelligent for giving pinpointed appealing answers to questions asked.
- Use a variety of display techniques for reaching ideas to many people to save time of the viewers, for appropriately targeting the viewers and to make them think.

Characteristics of Exhibits

- Exhibits should involve as many senses for appreciation as possible—visual, audio, tactile
- Colour imparts attraction to the exhibits and should be judiciously used particularly because colours also convey different attributes.

Yellow	–	prosperity
Red	–	danger
Brown	–	monotony
Green	–	production
Grey	–	submission

Orange – cheer
Black – sorrow

- Motion in exhibits is a great attraction but all cannot have that. Soft background, instrumental music adds interest to an exhibition.
- Provide for at least some opportunity to the viewers to touch, turn, press operate, open as that can sustain their interest in the exhibition.
- None can compel a person to look at an exhibit except the exhibit itself.

As mentioned earlier, harmony, balance, artistically designed setting are crucial for making an appeal.

Exhibitions need not always be an elaborate affair. There could even be exhibitions put up by different classes to share with the students of other classes. For example, for the conclusion of a project the class concerned may present the process and outcomes of the same.

Such events could also trigger a healthy competition among classes for sharing with others what they may have accomplished and which they may consider is worth sharing.

The classes or groups of students of representations of different houses could even produce a magazine periodically spurring creativity and innovation among students.

Educational Field Trips and Excursions

Introduction

Field Trips and Excursions enable on-the-spot study of different things/facets of the environment by putting the school on the wheels. Children are enabled to come face to face with realities. Field Trips and Excursions, offer such experiences which though necessary for learning cannot be brought into the classroom. They give meaning to classroom learning through personal observations and experience.

Purposes of Organising Field Trips

Field-trips and Excursions serve a variety of educationally fruitful purposes. They enable the pupils:

- a changeover from routine activities.
- to gain first hand experience about facts and phenomenon they study and investigate.
- to critically observe and scrutinise things for arriving at personally made conclusions which are never forgotten by them.
- to obtain clarifications about different concepts and processes.
- to launch on self-directed educational activities.
- to broaden and change attitudes in desirable directions.
- to discover areas of interest other than the existing ones.

Educational trips assume three main forms:

- *Field trips* are taken to places of the neighbourhood like a post office, a fire station, a construction site.
- *Excursions* to places where people live or work. They are outside the school but not very far from it. They may take a day or half a day. They may include visits to a bakery, a poultry farm, water purification plant, a nearby factory or a manufacturing unit like a sugar factory, a power generation plant, a museum, a zoo, a monument and so on.
- *Study Tours* are normally of longer durations and cover wider or distant areas. They may also involve long journeys.

Organisational Steps

There are some common essential steps for organising educational trips excursions/tours:

- *Identification of a trip*. This is done for different classes as per their curricular needs. The purpose of the trip is also simultaneously defined and impressed upon the pupils before commencement.
- *Planning* : Advance planning is a pre-requisite for a successful trip. This involves:
  - ➢ detailing of objectives of the trip in the context of its relationship with the curriculum.
  - ➢ listing of places to be visited and of details to be observed.
  - ➢ drawing-up an itinerary with dates and timings.
  - ➢ contacting the authorities for obtaining permission to visit the proposed sites.
  - ➢ obtaining the permission of the head of the school and the parents.
  - ➢ collecting necessary finances.
  - ➢ making arrangements for travel transport and accommodation.
  - ➢ delegation of responsibilities to the students during the trip.
  - ➢ collecting information about places to be visited in advance.
  - ➢ collecting necessary material/equipment, etc.
  - ➢ preparing a 'medical help kit'.
  - ➢ offering do's and don's to the students.
  - ➢ holding a stock-taking meeting every evening.
  - ➢ including sight seeing to make the trip interesting.
  - ➢ advising students to carry essential items.
  - ➢ asking students to carry note books for on the spot observations and cameras and learn to use mobile cameras.

Post-Trips Exercises

After the trip, on return to school some other often overlooked items of action are:

- writing thank you letters to all those who were helpful.
- reporting to other classes about the trip.

- writing poems, stories for the bulletin boards about the trip.
- convening PTA meeting, for acquainting parents about the highlights of the trip.

Field Trips and excursions could be used for several other useful purposes. Surveys of different kinds for collecting first hand information is one such potential use. In fact, when an individual himself collects informations and draws his own conclusions, this learning becomes abiding. Through the surveys they also acquires valuable insights about different things in the process of collecting, compiling analysing and interpreting information. No text book or any other enrichment material can offer, this kind of enlightenment. The student, thus, constructs his own set of tenets which yield him a sense of achievement.

49

Evaluation of Projects Programmes and Teaching Proficiency

Evaluation of the level of achievement and proficiency of learners does not set closed boundaries of the work of educational evaluators. The Educational Planners have to evaluate "Programmes"; Educational Administrators "projects" 'Teacher Educators the "Teaching Proficiency" and so on. In all these instances, more often than not, it becomes necessary to quantify qualitative information for purposes of taking financing and other decisions.

The concept of 'PREP INDEX', therefore, comes in as a handy, practicable and a scientific approach in this regards which possesses the potential of:

- being adaptable in different situations,
- warding off adhocism,
- ensuring proportionate weightage to all different areas/elements/ components,
- containing subjectivity.

Need

Educational evaluation is a process of estimating and appraising the degree and dimension of achievement and abilities possessed by an individual at a particular point of time.

Evaluation of educational practices is a process of estimating and appraising the proficiency of educationists in conducting educational programmes. In other words, it is a process of appraising the application of educational postulates into practice.

In some situations the outcomes of education are available only in qualitative terms and the outcomes of evaluation are expected in quantitative terms particularly for purposes of rating, grading or classification. To get over this problem an approach is being proposed and suggested here for quantifying qualitative outcomes of education.

Scope of Evaluation of Educational Practices

Educational practices and the activities can be broadly classified as under:

- Curricular activities related to the subjects of instruction, which are organised with a view to achieving the objectives of the cognitive domain.
- Activities related to the co-scholastic areas or those related to the other educational programmes and practices. The purpose of organising these activities is to ensure the coverage of those aspects of pupils' growth, which though important goals of the instructional programme, cannot be achieved through the teaching and learning of subjects alone. These could relate to the affective and the psycho-motor domains of human development.
- Activities related to diagnosis, prognosis, review, motivation, guidance, evaluation, etc. The very title of each of these activities itself explains the purpose and importance of their position in the curriculum.

Purpose of Evaluating Educational Practices

There may be several purposes or functions for which the evaluation of educational practices may be taken up. The area of *Teacher Proficiency* is being selected here to illustrate the proposed approach. Three *purposes of Teacher Education Programmes* are being stated here by way of an example:

- To discover the degree of competence developed by the teacher in initiating, organising and improving the educational practices and to diagnose the strengths and weakness of learners for further guidance.
- To make a suggestion about the likely educational practices which a particular teacher can best organise as a regular teacher.
- To certify the teacher competencies about the level of his proficiency acquired in initiating and organising a particular educational practice.

Methodology of Evaluating Educational Practices

Objectives

A good Teacher Appraisal Programme attempts to find out the degree of proficiency attained by the teachers in the various programmes and practices incorporated in the various programmes of the institution. It is, therefore, essential at the outset to identify the most prominent of teacher competencies to be subjected to evaluation. These are listed below:

- An understanding of the subject to be taught, the objectives of teaching it and the methods and techniques best suited for teaching it.
- Familiarity with the different philosophies of education and to acquire the ability of evolving a sound philosophy of his own.
- An understanding of the different aspects of pupils' development and behaviour and the factors related to them.
- An experimental attitude towards teaching and faith in the teaching profession.

- A motivation for one's professional growth.
- Acquisition of skills in planning and executing teaching-learning activities through observation, and actual teaching under observation/ supervision.
- Familiarisation with the salient features and problems of Indian education with reference to the different stages of general education, i.e., primary, secondary, university or professional education.
- Ability to organise activities related to both scholastic and co-scholastic areas as also other programmes and practices.
- Acquisition of the knowledge of evaluation procedures and the ability of developing and using tools for evaluating pupil behaviour continuously, comprehensively and for applying measures for improvement.

The above illustrative list can be further elaborated and some additions can surely be made to it.

Evidences

In order to evaluate teacher competencies it is necessary to collect evidences about the professional growth of the individual teacher in relation to the objectives. For this purpose a teacher will have to consider issues such as the following:

- What techniques and tools should be employed for evaluating different abilities in a given situation?
- What method should be used for obtaining evidences so that a variety of expected educational outcomes can be incorporated in the scheme of evaluation. This would also involve the sampling of situations?
- How much time should be spent on each task?

Taking the illustration further *to the specific area of classroom teaching*, it could be said that this area of evaluation comprises the following aspects for evaluation:

- Class management
- Pupils' co-operation
- Teacher's expression
- Teacher's subject-matter competence
- Activities incorporated in the instructional programme.
- Use of aids
- Evaluation.

These aspects of evaluation should be very clearly specified. Their enumeration should cover the entire gamut of the subject. They ought also help him in locating the most adequate tool for the assessment of each of the aspects. This would also imply the use of a variety of tools as the same tool may not prove to be effective for evaluating all the aspects of each area.

Developing Evaluative Criteria

For each aspect of evaluation detailed out, it will be necessary to develop evaluative criteria to make the assessment specific and accurate.

Taking the point still further, it could be said that if *subject-matter competence* of the teacher is taken as an aspect of evaluation, its evaluative criteria could be:

- Correctness
- Relevance and
- Richness

It will then be in respect of each of each of these evaluative criteria that the degree of proficiency of a teacher will be judged.

Collection of Evidences

After having developed the evaluative criteria for each area of evaluation, the next natural step will be the collection of evidences for evaluation on the basis of the identified criteria.

One of the most common techniques for the collection of evidences in the present situation will be *planned observation.* Other possible techniques could be interview, assessment of records of the process of execution and the outcome. In order to be able to collect usable evidences, it will also be necessary to select or develop appropriate tools.

Taking the illustration still further it could be said that if subject-matter competence is the aspect to be evaluated and if its correctness, relevance and richness are the criteria for evaluating it, the evidences could normally be collected from the following sources:

- Lesson plans for evaluating the degree and kind of preparation made by the teacher for teaching the particular lesson.
- Performance in actual teaching situations.

Evidences so obtained could be summarised in qualitative or quantitative terms. Qualitative evaluation based on the summarisation and interpretation of the evidences collected, is quite common. It can be obtained from the study of the lesson notes, the observation of lessons and the prepared teaching aids.

Evaluation in qualitative terms is not only possible but is also likely to prove of greater practical utility though it is not usually attempted probably because of the natural resistance to change. But in view of its scientific foundation, *a quantitative assessment of proficiency in educational practice based on qualitative evidences is likely to yield a more commonly acceptable measure.* It will also make comparisons possible and easier to make. Such a conversion of qualitative evidences into quantitative indices has, however, to be based on a scientific basis.

Summarisation of Data

Summarisation of data—So that the data collected could be used for educational ends, it is necessary that it may be appropriately summarised and interpreted.

Summarisation of data as already mentioned could either be in qualitative or quantitative terms. In qualitative terms it could focus on a particular individual aspect in respect of a specific ability. In quantitative terms, it could be summarised through a tool like a *rating scale* on which ratings could be awarded to different individuals for the degree of their accomplishment in a particular aspect of evaluation.

PREP Index and its Derivation

How a quantitative measure of a qualitative outcome could be obtained is illustrated below. The proposed tool is a Rating Scale. The following description further stretches the example of subject-matter competence of a teacher already enunciated earlier.

A nine-point rating scale with five points defined is devised for evaluating each of the aspects on the basis of the abilities assessed on identified evaluative criteria. The following is an illustration of such a scale developed for assessing *subject matter competence*:

8. – Fully correct, completely relevant and very rich
7.
6. – Rare evidences of incorrectness or irrelevance and richness
5.
4. – Usually correct and relevant and moderately rich
3.
2. – Several evidences of incorrectness and irrelevance and poor content
1.
0. – Mostly incorrect, irrelevant and very poor content

Such scales will need to be devised for all specified aspects of evaluation. The ratings on these scales could then be translated into a profile. Thus while evaluating a complete lesson, suppose it is found that particular teacher has been rated as follows on nine-point rating scale for in respect of different aspects;

Class Management	5
Pupil's Co-operation	3
Expression	4
Subject matter competence	7
Activities incorporated	5
Use of aids	3
Evaluation	4

These ratings could then be translated into a profile like the one given below :

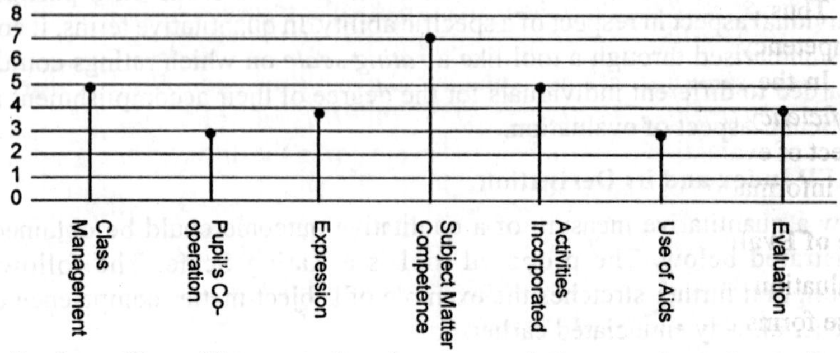

Such profiles will prove to be of very great help not only to the evaluator but also to the teacher himself for making his own self-evaluation. Giving profiles from time to time, will enable the teacher to judge for himself, his own strengths and weaknesses in specific aspects of evaluation and the progress that he may have made between one point of time and another in respect of each one of them individually.

The representation on these profiles could as well be quantified by the following method to arrive at the *Index of Proficiency in Educational Practice* (PREP Index)

Suppose there are 75 marks in all out of which teacher's teaching proficiency has to be evaluated and the different weightages to each of the aspects of evaluation are as given in the table as follows. Suppose also that on each of these aspects of evaluation the respective scores obtained out of eight (the points 0-8 on the scale), are also as indicated in the table, the PREP INDEX will be calculated as follows:

S. No.	*Aspects of Evaluation*	*Weightage to Aspects*	*Scores on the Rating Scales*	*Weighted Scores*
1.	Class Management	10	5	50
2.	Pupil Co-operation	5	3	15
3.	Expression	20	4	80
4.	Subject-matter Competence	10	7	70
5.	Activities incorporated	10	5	50
6.	Use of aids	10	3	30
7.	Evaluation	10	4	40
	Total	75	31	335

Total of weighted scores = 50+15+80+70+50+30+40 = 335

Maximum scores out of which the total weighted scores have been obtained = 8 × 75 (8 being the maximum point of scales and 75 the total weightage to all the aspects of the particular area of evaluation)

= 600

$$\text{Score} = 335/600$$
$$\text{PREP INDEX} = 335/600 \times 100 = 55.83$$

Thus, 55.83 is the Prep Index of the particular teacher in regard to teaching competency.

In the same manner as explained above, *'Prep Index' or the Index of Proficiency (PR) in Educational (E) Practice (P)* could be calculated for each aspect of evaluation and will help the evaluator in the different ways in which this information can be used.

Use of Evaluation Data

Evaluation data, as we know, could be either qualitative or quantitative. Both these forms of data can be used for a variety of purposes. These are:

Diagnosis

Educational practices are incorporated in institutional programmes with a view to achieving some well-defined educational objectives. The achievement of these objectives leads to learner growth in desirable directions, in organising the various school programmes and in conducting educational practices, to ensure pupil growth as enunciated through the objectives. The degree to which he is successful also needs to be evaluated. The primary purpose is to identify the strengths and weaknesses of a particular teacher so as to guide him in making better progress and in achieving higher successes.

Self-Evaluation and Guidance

Evaluation of educational practices, particularly in regard to the development of profiles and derivation of the *Prep Index*, in respect of each aspect of evaluation for a particular teacher, serves another very important purpose of self-evaluation and self-guidance. This also provides him motivation for achieving better success on subsequent occasions.

The evaluator also finds himself on a better footing in assessing the teacher on the basis of the evaluation data referred to above and not on any conjectures. As the evaluator would specifically know a particular teacher's hard sports, he can be more precise and more effective in giving him guidance.

Certification

Certification in regard to the degree of competence acquired by him in different areas of evaluation is also one of the most important functions of evaluation data. The derivation of the PREP INDEX will again prove to be of a more valid measure of proficiency than the arbitrary assessments based on vague perceptions, which are very often attempted. Certification on the basis of this data will not only be more valid and reliable but also more meaningful to the employer for being used for different purposes.

Prediction

The evaluation data could also be used for the purpose of prediction as to what a particular teacher is capable of accomplishing.

Conclusion

Evaluation of educational practices used to be mostly undertaken in the past in an arbitrary manner, endangering both the reliability and validity of the measurements. The development of a Methodology for Evaluating Educational Practices has, therefore, been a long felt need. The fore-going discussion is an attempt at 'developing' such a methodology which could be applied to all educational practices and even in other disciplines Evaluation done on the basis of such a methodology will, it is hoped, yield data which will be more authentic, specific and meaningful than the one arrived at through the usual arbitrary conclusions of a few individuals who may find it difficult to overcome their biases while making assessments.

This could as well be a valuable approach for assessing practice-teaching lessons in teacher's colleges. The format of the profile could be printed in a corner of each page of the criticism book and the faculty members observing the lesson could just *put in the dots* and the learner teacher may then calculate the Prep Index in respect of each observed lesson. This may be in addition to the written observations.

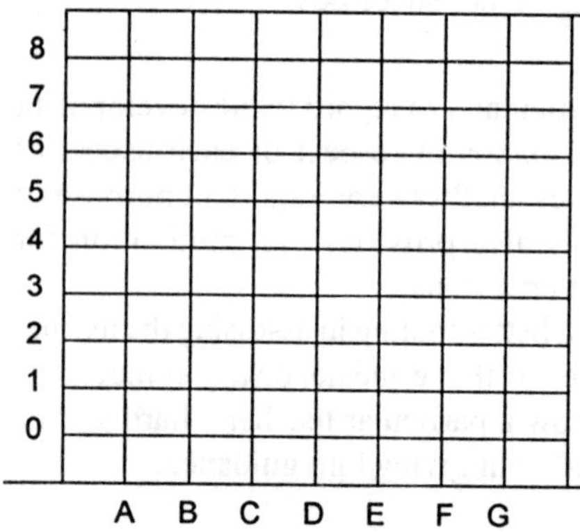

INDEX

A. Class Management
B. Pupil Co-operation
C. Teacher's Expression
D. Subject-Matter Competence
E. Activities Incorporated
F. Use of Aids Evaluation

PREP INDEXs

The final annual index could also then be calculated on this basis and become a valid source for making a conclusion, about the final grade of the learner teacher for the examination.

Adapted from the chapter contributed by Dr. R.H. Dave & Dr. H.S. Srivastava for "Evaluating Teacher Effectiveness" brought out by the ETS, Princeton (New Jersey), U.S.A.

Methodology of Evaluating Educational Practices—Graphical Presentation of Steps

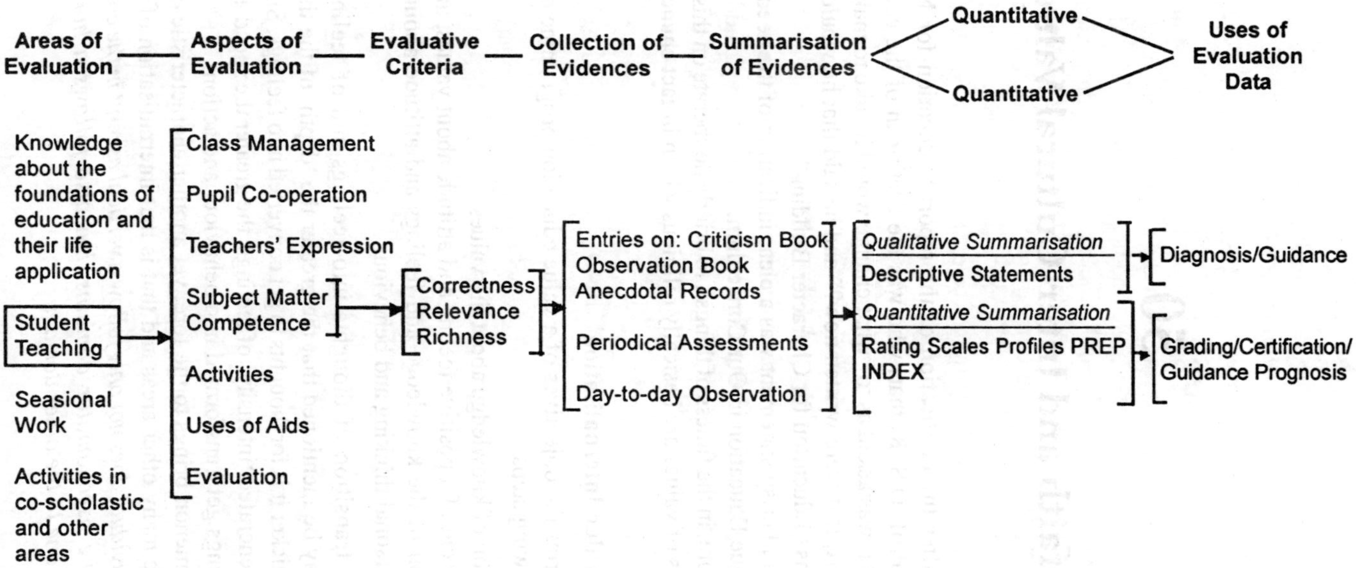

* Selected as illustration for explaining different steps of the methodology

Diagram 49.1

50

Inter-faith and Inter-Cultural Values

Twenty years after the publication of the report "Education for National Development" Prof. D.S. Kothari who was the Chairman of the committee that had drafted it was asked as to "what change would he like to make in the title of the report, if it were written now?" and he said that he would like to call this report as "Education for Character Building".

This brief and crisp statement was a clear indication of the need for the inclusion of Value Education in Our Curriculum.

It is, therefore, in the fitness of things', to briefly deliberate on this aspect.

The sources of values are basically religious which in fact enunciate the "ways of life".

Mechanics of Value Internalisation

In functional terms the objectives of a value education programme ought to follow the following steps :

- acquisation of knowledge about the values,
- development of a positive feeling and attitude about values, and
- translation of the knowledge and feelings and attitude about values into personal thinking and behaviour.

About this transition of thoughts into feelings and of feelings into behaviour, it may be mentioned that the greater the 'depth' of the thoughts, the easier and quicker it is for thoughts to get converted into feelings. Similarly, the greater the generated 'intensity' of feelings, the greater the speed and ease with which feelings get transformed into behaviour and action.

This phenomenon brings to the fore, yet another characteristic of value education unlike many other areas and that is that internalisation of a value system in an *individual does not only follow a vertical ascent/ in the cognitive, affective and the psychomotor domains, but also follows a horizontal movement from one to the other domain.*

In the final analysis, the interalisation of ethical values establishes a compatibility between thought, speech and action.

As values and ethical concepts, cannot be communicated and absorbed through a blackboard demonstration or an OHP/video presentation, as is possible, in say Mathematics, we must identify some viable approaches for succeeding in our mission.

Deliberations of the Leaders of Schools of Indian Educational Thought

In April 1994, the Council for the Indian School Certificate Examinations, convened a Conference of the Leaders of Major Schools of Educational Thought in India where the author played a central role. Some extracts from the Conference Report are reproduced below:

The Conference

Appreciates

- that the world of today stands taken-over by materialism and selfishness, where sacrifice for others is considered as foolishness, patience as inertness, humility as cowardice, obedience as slavery, honesty as lack of foresight and respect for law as timidity.
- that standing firm and fast in adherence to values, amidst the debasing and de-stabilising buffets of pressures, threats and temptations, needs a powerfully charged emotional anchorage.

Realises

- that a valueless society is bound for doom.
- that children learn more from what they observe, than from what they read or what they are taught or told.
- that education is only one of the innumerable inputs of social reconstruction, that education will not be pardoned by posterity, if it does not rise to the occasion, for squarely meeting the challenges of the erosion of values in society.

Recommends

- that the ambience of educational institutions presents and upholds through personal example the ideals of values, that stories of rewards from adherence to values, may form an important part of the curriculum material specially for the formative years (6 + to 14+).

Aesthetic Sense

Aesthetic sense has been a serious casualty in modern education, a situation that needs to be urgently corrected. In this regard we all need to :

Appreciate

- that aesthetic appreciation leads the mind to newer explorations for discovering 'books in brooks' and 'sermons in stones'.

- that admiration of beauty sensitises individuals, evokes humane qualities and motivates people to explore nature and discover its resources and potentials,
- that the best examples of equality and equity are found in nature and the processes of our natural environment.

Realise

- that presently the activities organised in institutions for realising these are only limited to exposures and experiences related to dance, music and drama, with a focus on annual functions and in respect of art and painting on display at exhibitions.
- that these activities are pursued as routine, without attaining the basic goals related to the stimulation of sentiments and the development of finer elements of creativity, ingenuity, originality, etc., for the internalisation of the value of appreciation (gratefulness to the Creator) and cultivation of a sublime mind, that is sensitised to examine the moral and spiritual dimensions of life.

Recommend

- that the school setting, may be so structured, as to naturally and imperceptibly sensitise students to the inculcation of aesthetics.
- that the teachers may present suitable examples in aesthetics through their day-to-day behaviour.
- that the school programmes may provide adequate teaching-learning situations, for enabling students to instinctively catch and absorb aesthetic concepts and ideas and for displaying the same in their behaviour.
- that instructional material too may be so selected and/or evolved as to provide opportunities for aesthetic appreciation.
- that the transaction of curriculum be strewn with activities aimed at stirring the emotional make-up of students for adhering to values.

Reflection

In ancient education whatever was learnt was pondered upon, by the educand. This enlightened him through a process of internal mental churning of the ideas. The process which could be termed as "rumination" helped in better 'digestion' or internalisation and assimilation of the intake.

This is something which deserves to be revived as an important core component of education. In this regard we need to :

Appreciate

- that internalisation of learning experiences is an ability that yields immeasurable power to the mind.

- that cultivation of the ability to ponder over issues, for decision making, is a safe insurance for success.
- that motivation and aspiration are the precursors (parents) of 'concentration' and patience, and diligence its products, (off-springs)
- that acquisition of ideas is the first step towards acquiring abilities and skills, to enable their assimilation and use, for future good.
- that the gainful outcomes of intellectual pursuits based on thinking develop humbleness of the *mind* and ennoblement of the *spirit*.

Realise

- that introspection and reflection, which are the fundamental foundations of mental power, are not being sufficiently stressed by current educational programmes.
- that acquisition of macro-level information about facts and phenomena, has waylaid the natural process of scrutiny, analysis, reasoning and inference.
- that casual attitude to work has devoured the spirit of taking responsibilities seriously and with commitment.
- that the realisation of 'What' has blunted the edge of the quest of 'Why' and 'How', in the context of the immediate and distant goals.
- that extrovertness has become a more socially accepted indicator of potential, than thoughtful pensiveness.

Recommend

- that reflection and introspection be built into the process of curriculum transaction.
- that teacher education programmes may incorporate methodologies for making pupils think about issues.
- that the instructional materials may incorporate situations requiring students to ponder for arriving at their own independent inferences.

A Plan for the Treatment of Values

The main outcome of the seminars on Value Education in different parts of the country was the evolution of plan of action for working on each of the identified values.

It was decided that each of the 41 identified values be given the following treatment:

- An overview giving the definition and relevance of the particular value in life
- Objectives of internalising and externalising the concerned value
- A content analyses giving the various ramifications of the value and the basic principles and understandings underlying it.

- Methodological approaches spelling out the strategies and techniques of communication and possible internalisation exercises in respect of each value.
- Evaluation techniques and procedures for determining the degree of internalisation of values in terms of observable indicators.
- A Diagramatic representation highlighting the positive and the negative forms of the values like love and hatred.

An example of the value of Love is given below:

Value of Love

A Conceptual Statement

- Love begot man, who was in turn created to love, a gift that must be lavished generously on others.
- Hatred works actively for the destruction of its opponent, at the same time playing havoc with the health of man, for hatred is also self destructive — a psychological self-sabotage.
- True love is fearless and totally unselfish. It revers the object of its love and asks for nothing in return. It is sublime and rises above pain, jealousy or anything resulting in inefficacious action.

International Quest for Identification of Interfaith Values

In the context of the above background it appeared necessary that we got to a list of universally accepted values. Then realising that religions are the main sources of values; that religions are the roads converging to the same point and that religions basically focus on ways of life, it was decided to seek such information about values from this most powerful source. Letters were then written to the leaders of all major religions of the world requesting them to send a list of moral/ethical values, which an individual religiously following their respective religions ought to posses and demonstrate. The living leaders of different religions faiths and of their different factions of the following and some other religious responded to these letters:

Buddhism	Judaism
Christianity	Shintoism
Confucianism	Sikhism
Hinduism	Taoism
Islam	Zorastrianism
Jainism	

The list of expected personal attributes among followers of different religious faiths received, added upto the terrifying number of more than 1200 personal attributes. There was, of course, quite a lot of overlap. It was then decided to telescope these personality attributes in a bid to get to a managable number eg. love the family, love of the neighbour, love of the community, love of the country, love for God, love for people of the world, were all brought within the fold of "Love".

These telescoped values alongwith their ramifications were referred to all those to whom the first letter was written, irrespective of the fact whether they had responded to the first letter or not. Surprisingly even some of those who had not responded to the first letter, responded to this second one. A couple of them even wrote back saying that they are replying to the letter because they have got convinced about the ernestness of the endeavour. Some of the replies to the second letter suggested some modifications in our telescoping exercise and these were incorporated.

In this second letter yet another tall request was made for sending us the meanings and implications of the identified values. This letter, therefore, took more time, than the first one to be responded to and in some cases needed many many reminders. However, replies were received from a large number of them. When we made a tally of the responses received, we were ourselves surprised about having got a response (to the combined figure of dispatches of the two letters) from about 80% of those to whom the first letter was written. Perseverance worked, but the process turned out to be more time consuming than what we had planned and provided for.

A Classification of Values

Thus a concrete list of 41 ethical values accepted by almost all the religions of the work became available. The next problem that confronted us was about the classification of these values. A number of classifications were tried like social, economic, political cultural, etc. or like ME and ME, ME and YOU, ME and SOCIETY, ME and GOD. After examining the pros and cons of these classifications the following classification was finally accepted:

Personal Values
Neighbourly Values
Community Values

The genesis of the values under each of the three categories and their respective lists are given below:

Personal Values : Personal Values refer to those which are practised by an individual alone, *irrespective of his social* relationships e.g. *Excellence.* Propelled by his own motivation, the individual determines his standards of achievement and can attain these targets, without assistance from any other person. Sixteen such personal values found a place in the list:

1. Cleanliness
2. Dignity of Labour
3. Diligence
4. Punctuality-Regularity
5. Honesty
6. Nature appreciation

7. Victory in suffering
8. Fortitude
9. Courage
10. Maturity
11. Self-reliance
12. Ambition
13. Excellence
14. Hope
15. Research
16. Evaluation

Neighbourly Values: Unlike personal values, the practice of neighbourly values necessitates the interaction of two or more persons, e.g. Patience. Though one can practise patience with oneself, essentially the value is best actualised in exercises of calmness and tranquillity with another or with others. The eleven values put together in this category were :

1. Dutifulness
2. Patience
3. Courtesy
4. Thrift
5. Magnanimity
6. Sportsmanliness
7. Loyalty
8. Gratitude
9. Tolerance
10. Freedom
11. Determination

Community Values : Community Values entail the complexities of wider interactions between groups of people, e.g. Brotherhood. Brotherhood could be practised, individually with one's immediate neighbours; however, the essence of the internalisation of the value, presupposes a positive brotherly attitude towards one's community, society, nation and the world at large expressed in the concrete, commencing with smaller groups and fanning out to embrace wider ones. Fourteen such community values found a place in this category, viz.

1. Love
2. Dialogue
3. Brotherhood
4. Forgiveness
5. Repentence
6. Sharing
7. Service
8. Team-spirit
9. Responsibility
10. Accountability
11. Sympathy
12. Hospitality
13. Justice
14. Non-violence

Facets of Love and some of their behavioural manifestations

Love of God

- Love appreciates all the blessings it receives.

Love of Self

- Aspiring to fulfill personal potentials is a display of true love of self.

Love of the Family

- Family love blossoms in a climate of sharing and co-operation.
- Love is prompt in making any type of sacrifice.

- Family re-unions cement the bonds of family love.

Love for the School

- Love reaches out to the needy.
- Duty performed with dedication reflects love.
- Love glories in the achievements of the school.

Love for Society

- Happy relationships flower in the warmth of love.
- Love has the power of forgiveness.
- Loves bounty is not measured, it overflows.

Love of the Nation

- A patriot is proud of his nationality
- The fulfillment of duties flows from a sense of responsibility.
- A citizen exults in the achievements of the nation.
- Love of the nation embraces the heritage of its culture.

Love of the People of the World

- Love widens its horizons to participate in international activities.

Love Related Sentiments

What leads to love ?	*What leads to hatred?*
Understanding	Non-acceptance
Appreciation	Illogically
Acceptance	Prejudice
Concern	Unconcern
Caring	Jealousy
Sharing	Injustice
Sentiments evoked in the 'lover'	*Sentiments evoked in the 'hater'*
Happiness — Joy	Bitterness
Security	Vengeance
Fulfilment	Self-destruction
Enrichment	Tension
Togetherness	Frustrations
Growth	Isolationism
Sentiments evoked in the 'lover'	*Sentiments evoked in the 'hater'*
Happiness	Hurt feelings
Security	Hatred / Fear
Trust — Love	Contempt
Growth	Mistrust
Gratitude	Insecurity
Affiliation	Indifference

References

Adams, G.K., *Measurement and Evaluation in Psychology and Education*, Holt, Rinehart and Winston, New York, 1965.

Ahmann, J.S. and Block, M.D., *Measuring and Evaluating Educational Achievement*, Alyn and Bach Inc., Boston, 1975.

Association of Indian Universities, Scaling Techniques, New Deli, AIU (1985).

Berliner, D.C. (1987). 'Ways of thinking about students and classrooms by more and less experienced teachers'. In J. Calderhead (ed.) *Exploring Teachers' Thinking*, London: Cassell.

Biggs, J. (1987). 'Student approaches to learning and studying', *British Journal of Educational Psychology,* 63, 1-19.

Blood, D.F. and W.C. Budd, *Educational Measurement and Evaluation*, N. York, Harper and Row, 1972.

Bloom, B.S., Hastings J.T. and Madaus G.F., *Handbook of Formative and Summative Evaluation of Learner Learning*, New York: Mc Garw Hill (1971).

Bose, P.K. and Choudhury S.B., Scaling Procedures in Scholastic and Vocational Tests, *Sankhya* (1955) 15. 197.

Brown, S. and McIntyre, D. (1993). *Making Sense of Teaching,* Buckingham: Open University Press.

Charles, E. Skinner, *Essentials of Educational Psychology*, Asia Publishing House, Bombay, 1960 (Passage to Learning).

Clandinin, J. (1986). *Classroom Practice: Teachers' Images in Action,* London: Falmer Press.

Cooper, P. (1993c). 'Learning from the pupil perspective', *British Journal of Special Education,* 20, 4.

Cooper, P. and McIntyre, D. (1995). 'The importance of power sharing in classrooms'. In M. Hughes (ed.) *Teaching and Learning in Changing Times,* Oxford: Blackwell.

Cronbach, I.J., Designing Evaluation of Educational and Social Programmes, San Francisco: Jossey-Bass (1982).

Dale, Edgar, *Audio Visual Methods in Teaching*, Dryden Press, Holt Rinehart and Winston Inc., New York, 1969. (Conventional methods of Teaching).

Elbaz, F. (1981). 'Teachers' practical knowledge, report of a case study', *Curriculum Inquiry,* 11(1), 73-7.

Ghosh, B. and Others, *Handbook for Primary School Teachers of Social Studies*, National Council of Educational Research and Training, New Delhi, 1966 (Methods of Teaching, Social Studies).

Gronlund, N.E., *Measurement and Evaluation in Teaching*, Macmillan, New York, 1981.

Kaplan, R.M. and D.P. Saccuzzo, *Psychological Testing*, Brooks Cole Publishing Co., California, 1993.

National Curriculum Frameworks, National Council of Educational Research and Training, New Delhi (1965, 1988, 2000 and 2005).

NCERT and Board of Secondary Education Rajasthan, Ajmer, Scheme and Manual of Instructions on Comprehensive Internal Assessment (1966).

NCERT and Directorate of School Education, Madras, Scheme of Comprehensive Internal Assessment and Manual of Instructions, Madras (1973).

NCERT Guidelines on Scaling and Grading, New Delhi (1988).

NCERT Research in Educational Evaluation, New Delhi (1961).

Patton, Michael Quim, *Qualitative Evaluation and Research Methods*, Sage Publications India Pvt. Ltd., New Delhi.

Pritam, Singh, *Criterion Referenced Testing*, NCERT, New Delhi (1982).

Pritam, Singh, *Evaluating Learners in Elementary Schools*, NCERT, New Delhi (1982).

Rastogi, K.G. and Others, *Preparation and Evaluation of Textbooks in Mother Tongue*, National Council of Educational Research and Training, New Delhi, 1970 (Methods of Teaching Mother Tongue).

Robert, L. Ebel (Ed.), Encyclopaedia of Educational Research, The MacMillan, London, (1969) (Curriculum the Rationale of Teaching).

Robert, W. Richey, *Planning for Teaching*. McGraw Hill Book Co. Inc., New York, 1958 (Objective-based Teaching).

Saha, S.N. and Others, *Preparation and Evaluation of Textbooks in English*, National Council of Educational Research and Training, New Delhi, 1970 (Methods of Teaching English/Second Language).

Saiyidain, K.G. and Others, *The Committee on Improvement of Art Education in Our Schools,* National Council of Education Research and Training, New Delhi, 1967 (Methods of Teaching Art).

Schofield, H., *Assessment and Testing: An Introduction*, George Allen and Unwin Ltd., London, 1972.

Shavelson, R., Webb, N. and Burstein, L. (1986). 'Measurement of teaching'. In M. Wittrock (ed.) *Handbook of Research on Teaching*, London: Macmillan.

Simpson, M. (1989). *A Study of Differentiation and Learning in Schools*, Aberdeen: Northern College.

Skinner, B.F., *The Science of Learning and the Art of Teaching*, D. Van Nostraned Company, New York, 1962 (Methods of Teaching and Programmed Learning).

Sources Tapped for Ideas and Extracts

Srivastava, H.S., *Challenges in Education Evaluation*, Vikas Publishing House, New Delhi (1999).

Srivastava, H.S., *Comprehensive Evaluation in Schools*, NCERT, New Delhi (1989).

Srivastava, H.S., *Curriculum and Instructional Designing*, Shipra Publications, New Delhi (2017).

Srivastava, H.S., *Curriculum and Methods of Teaching*, Shipra Publications, New Delhi (2006).

Srivastava, H.S., *Examination Manual*, S. Chand & Co., New Delhi (2001).

Srivastava, H.S., *Manual for Schools*, S. Chand & Co., New Delhi, (2002).

Srivastava, H.S. and Others, *National Study of Scholastic Achievement*, NCERT, New Delhi (1997).

Srivastava, H.S., Khandelwal, B.P. and Sharma, D.V., *Comprehensive School-Based Evaluation*, S. Chand and Co., New Delhi (1997).

Srivastava, H.S. and Shourie, J.P., *Instructional Objectives of School Subjects*, NCERT, New Delhi (1989).

Srivastava, H.S., *Manual for Schools*, S. Chand & Co., New Delhi (Fourth Revised Edition (2013).

Srivastava, H.S., Singh, Pritam and Anand, V.S., *Reforming Examinations: Some Emergent Issue*, National Council of Educational Research and Training (NCERT), New Delhi (1978).

Taylor, H.J. and Taluanga L.N., *Scaling Tables*, Guwahati: Examination Research Unit, Guwahati University (1963).

Thorndike, Robert, L. & Kagen, Elizabeth, P., *Measurement and Evaluation in Psychology Western,* Eastern United, New Delhi, 1979.

Wittrock, M.C. (1986). 'Students thought processes'. In M.C. Wittrock (ed.) *Handoook of Research on Teaching*, 3rd edn., London: Macmillan.

Wittrock, M.C. (ed.) *Handbook of Research on Teaching*, 3rd edn., London: Macmillan.

Woods, P. (1990). *The Happiest Days? How Pupils Cope with School*, London: Falmer Press.